Rosa Luxemberg,
Women's Liberation, and
Marx's Philosophy of Revolution

Rosa Luxemburg, Women's Liberation, and Marx's Philosophy of Revolution

SECOND EDITION

Raya Dunayevskaya

Foreword by Adrienne Rich

University of Illinois Press
Urbana and Chicago

First University of Illinois Press edition, 1991

© 1981 by Raya Dunayevskaya

"Marxist-Humanism's Challenge to All Post-Marx Marxists" and "New Thoughts on *Rosa Luxemburg, Women's Liberation, and Marx's Philosophy of Revolution*" © 1991 by the Raya Dunayevskaya Memorial Fund

Foreword © 1991 by Adrienne Rich

Editorial emendations © 1991 by the Board of Trustees of the University of Illinois

Originally published in 1981 in the United States by Humanities Press and in the United Kingdom by Harvester Press

Manufactured in the United States of America

1 2 3 4 5 C P 5 4 3 2 1

This book is printed on acid-free paper.

Library of Congress Cataloging-in-Publication Data

Dunayevskaya, Raya.
   Rosa Luxemburg, women's liberation, and Marx's philosophy of revolution / Raya Dunayevskaya.—2nd ed.
      p.   cm.
   Includes bibliographical references and index.
   ISBN 0-252-01838-9 (cloth : alk. paper).   ISBN 0-252-06189-6 (pbk. : alk. paper)
   1. Luxemburg, Rosa, 1871–1919.   2. Marx, Karl, 1818–1883.   3. Women and socialism.   4. Revolution and socialism.   I. Title.
HX273.8.L88D86   1991
335.43'092—dc20   90-21458
                                                                                CIP

I'm telling you that as soon as I can stick my nose out again I will hunt and harry your society of frogs with trumpet blasts, whip crackings, and bloodhounds—like Penthesilea I wanted to say, but by God, you people are no Achilles. Have you had enough of a New Year's greeting now? Then see to it that you stay human . . . *Being human means joyfully throwing your whole life "on the scales of destiny" when need be, but all the while rejoicing in every sunny day and every beautiful cloud. Ach, I know of no formula to write you for being human. . .*

Rosa Luxemburg, 1916

Everything depends upon the historical background in which it finds itself . . . If the Russian Revolution becomes the signal for a proletarian revolution in the West, so that both complement each other, the present Russian common ownership of land may serve as the starting point for a communist development.

Karl Marx, 1881, 1882

Contents

Acknowledgments

I thank the following for permission to quote from their publications:

George Braziller, Inc., New York, for quotations from Edith Thomas, *The Women Incendiaries*;

Cambridge University Press, New York, for quotations from Annette Jolin and Joseph O'Malley, *Karl Marx's Critique of Hegel's Philosophy of Right*;

Campus Verlag, Frankfurt, for quotations from *The Ethnological Notebooks of Karl Marx*, transcribed and edited by Lawrence Krader, published by Van Gorcum, Assen;

Grove Press, Inc., New York, for quotations from *Rosa Luxemburg: Selected Political Writings*, edited by Robert Looker;

Harper & Row, New York, for quotations from Maximilien Rubel and Margaret Manale, *Marx Without Myth*;

International Publishers, New York, for quotations from *Karl Marx-Frederick Engels, Collected Works*; Karl Marx, *Pre-Capitalist Economic Formations*, translated by Jack Cohen, edited by Eric Hobsbawm; Frederick Engels, *The Origin of the Family, Private Property, and the State*;

Charles H. Kerr Publishing Co., 600 W. Jackson, Chicago, for quotations from Karl Marx, *Capital*, vol. 1 translated by Samuel Moore and Edward Aveling, vol. 2 and 3 translated by Untermann; and *A Contribution to the Critique of Political Economy*, translated by N.I. Stone; Frederick Engels, *Herr Eugen Dühring's Revolution in Science* (Anti-Dühring);

Monthly Review Press, New York, for quotations from Rosa Luxemburg, *The Accumulation of Capital*; and *The Accumulation of Capital—an Anti-Critique*, edited by Kenneth J. Tarbuck and Rudolph Wichmann; *The National Question: Selected Writings by Rosa Luxemburg*, edited by Horace B. Davis; *Selected Political Writings of Rosa Luxemburg*, edited by Dick Howard;

New Left Books, London, for quotations from Herbert Marcuse, *Studies in Critical Philosophy*;

Oxford University Press, Oxford, for quotations from Peter Nettl, *Rosa Luxemburg*;

The Pennsylvania State University Press, University Park, Penna., for quotations from *Black Women in 19th Century American Life*, edited by Bert James Loewenberg and Ruth Bogin;

Pluto Press, Ltd., London, for quotations from Mikhail Lifshitz, *The Philosophy of Art of Karl Marx*; and Roman Rosdolsky, *The Making of Marx's 'Capital'*;

Random House, Inc., New York, for quotations from Leon Trotsky, *1905*, translated by Anya Bostock;

Simon and Schuster, Inc., New York, for quotations from Leon Trotsky, *The History of the Russian Revolution*, translated by Max Eastman;

Westview Press, Boulder, Colorado, for quotations from *The Letters of Rosa Luxemburg*, edited by Stephen Bronner.

"Marxist-Humanism's Challenge to All Post-Marx Marxists" and "New Thoughts on *Rosa Luxemburg, Women's Liberation, and Marx's Philosophy of Revolution*" are printed here by arrangement with the Raya Dunayevskaya Memorial Fund, 59 E. Van Buren St., Chicago, Ill., 60605.

Foreword

Raya Dunayevskaya was a major thinker in the history of Marxism and of women's liberation—one of the longest continuously active woman revolutionaries of the twentieth century. In fierce intellectual and political independence, her life and work defied many mind-numbing labels that self-described conservatives, liberals, and radicals have applied to voices for political and social change. Born in 1910, between two revolutions, she said of her beginnings:

> I come from Russia 1917, and the ghettos of Chicago, where I first saw a Black person. The reason that I'm starting that way—it happens to be true—but the reason that I'm starting that way is that I was illiterate. You know, you're born in a border town—there's a revolution, there's a counter-revolution, there's anti-Semitism—you *know* nothing, but experience a lot. . . . That is, you don't know that you're a revolutionary, but you're opposed to everything.
>
> Now, how does it happen that an illiterate person, who certainly didn't know Lenin and Trotsky, who as a child had never seen a Black, had begun to develop all the revolutionary ideas to be called Marxist-Humanism in the 1950's? It isn't personal whatsoever! If you live when an idea is born, and a great revolution in the world is born—it doesn't make any difference *where* you are; *that becomes the next stage of development of humanity.* (Raya Dunayevskaya Archives, microfilm no. 5818, September 1978, published in *News and Letters*, July 25, 1987, p. 11)

Dunayevskaya was using her own early life to illustrate a core theme of her writing: the inseparability of experience and revolutionary thinking, the falseness of the opposition between "philosophy" and "actuality." Her readings of past history and contemporary politics were drenched in the conviction that while thinking and action are not the same, they must continually readdress and renew each other. For the spontaneous responses of a Russian Jewish girl, growing up

in a climate of revolution, brought at the age of twelve to the Jewish ghetto in
Chicago (in the twenties she "moved herself" to the black ghetto), to become the
on-going catalyst for a lifetime's commitment to human freedom, required a
structuring of her experience that Marx's (not Marx*ist*) theory was soon to pro-
vide her. She was to become not just literate, but learned in philosophy and history—and here again labels fail us, since for Dunayevskaya philosophy *was* the
making of history: the envisioning of "the day after," "the creation of a new
society" (*Women's Liberation and the Dialectics of Revolution,* p. 228). At
the same time, her political activities—first among black activists, then with the
West Virginia miners' strike of 1949–50, and so on into the Women's Liberation
Movement of the past two decades—set her on a lifelong path of both participating in and reflecting on mass movements.

The separation—willed or unaware—of intellectuals from the people they the-
orize about, the estrangement of self-styled vanguards and their "correct lines"
from actual people's needs and aspirations is hardly news. Dunayevskaya tried,
in the very structure of her life and writings, to show us a different method. What
does it look like when, as part of a movement, we try to think *along with* the human
forces newly pushing forth, in ever-changing forms and with ever-different faces?
How can we conceptualize a miners' strike, a poor people's march, a ghetto revolt,
a women's demonstration *both* as "spontaneous activity" *and* as the embodiment
of new ideas—not yet perhaps written down except in rain-blurred flyers—about
power, resources, control of the products of one's labor, the ability to live hu-
manly among other humans? How do we extract new kinds of "reason" or "idea"
from the activities of "new passions and new forces" (Marx's phrase) without
losing continuity with past struggles for freedom? How do we think clearly
in times of great turmoil, revolution, or counterrevolution without resorting to a
party line based only on past experience or on internecine graspings for power?
How do we create a philosophy of revolution which itself helps make revolution possible? The American Communist party was to lose its way among such
questions.

Dunayevskaya's way of grounding herself was to turn to Marx. Not, I should
emphasize, as a *turning backward* but as rescuing for the present a legacy she
saw as still unclaimed, having been diminished, distorted, and betrayed by post-
Marx Marxists and the emerging "Communist" states. But she didn't simply turn
to Marx, or to Hegel (whose work she saw as a living, still uncomprehended,
presence in Marx's own thought), as texts. Her work, including *Rosa Luxemburg,* is an explication of the fullness of Marx's thought *as she came to live it,* in
living through the liberation movements of her own era. She translated Marx,
interpreted Marx, fitted together fragments of Marx scattered in post-Marxist
schisms, refused to leave Marx enshrined as dead text, ill-read, or relegated to
"the dustbin of history."

It was Marx's humanism above all which she felt had never been adequately understood—in particular his recognition of what she called the black and women's dimensions, but more largely as he sought not merely the "overthrow" of capitalism but a vision of "revolution in permanence," a dynamically unfolding society in which the human individual could freely develop and express her or his creativity; not a static Communist utopia but an evolving human community.

I come out of a strain of feminism that saw itself as a leap forward out of Marxism, leaving the male Left behind, and for which a term like *Marxist-Humanism* would, in the late sixties and early seventies, have sounded like a funeral knell. A major problem (a problem not just of language but of organizing) was to break from a paradigm of class struggle that erased women's labor except in the paid workplace (often even there), and also from a "humanist" false universal deriving from the European Renaissance glorification of the male. Radical feminists were of necessity concerned with keeping the political focus on women because in every other focus—race, class, nation—women had gotten lost, put down, marginalized. In addition, we were fighting a dogma of class as the primary oppression, capitalism as the single source of all oppressions. We insisted that women were, if not a class, a caste; if not a caste, an oppressed group *as women—within* oppressed groups *and* within the middle and ruling classes.

And, as Dunayevskaya is quick to point out, "the Women's Liberation Movement that burst onto the historic scene in the mid-1960s was like nothing seen before in all its many appearances throughout history. Its most unique feature was that, surprisingly, not only did it come out of the left but it was *directed against it,* and not from the right, but *from within the left itself"* (*Rosa Luxemburg,* p. 99). It's clear how eagerly she welcomed this new force as it sent shock waves through radical group after radical group, starting with the Student Nonviolent Coordinating Committee in 1965. But although her own thinking was obviously incited and nourished by the contemporary Women's Liberation Movement, she had, as early as the forties, recognized "the woman dimension," and one of her earliest essays in *Women's Liberation and the Dialectics of Revolution* (1985) is an account of organizing by miners' wives in the 1949–50 anti-automation strikes in West Virginia. Dunayevskaya recognized women not just as revolutionary "Force" (contributing courage, support, strength) but also as "Reason"—as initiators, thinkers, strategists, creators of the new.

The first thing to strike a reader, ranging through Dunayevskaya's books, is the vitality, combativeness, relish, impatience of her voice. Hers is not the prose of a disembodied intellectual. She argues; she challenges; she urges on; she expostulates; her essays have the spontaneity of an extemporaneous speech (some of them are) or of a notebook—you can hear her thinking aloud. She has a prevailing sense of ideas as flesh and blood, of the individual thinker, limited by her or his individuality yet carrying on a conversation in the world. The thought of the philosopher is a product of what she or he has lived through.

Marxism and Freedom (1957) is a history of the process of Marx's thought, as it evolved out of eighteenth century philosophy and Hegel's dialectic through the mass political movements of the nineteenth century, as it became adapted and modified by Engels, Trotsky, and Lenin and finally, in Dunayevskaya's words, "totally perverted" by Stalin. She traced the shift from Marx's idea of a workers' state with no separation of manual and mental labor, to Lenin's failed attempt to create a "workers' state," to Stalin's creation of a corporate totalitarian state run by the Communist party—which she defines as counterrevolution. She saw, in the East German workers' strike of 1953 and the Hungarian Revolution of 1956, evidence of a continuing revolutionary spirit in Eastern Europe (which was to capture world attention in the upheavals of 1989). She ends the first edition of *Marxism and Freedom* with the Montgomery bus boycott as a spontaneous movement kept within the hands of the blacks.

In *Marxism and Freedom,* Dunayevskaya grapples, in the face of the Stalinist legacy, with the question: *What happens after?* What happens when the old oppression has been successfully resisted and overthrown? What turns revolutionary leaders into tyrants? Why did the Russian revolution turn backward on itself? How do we make the "continuing revolution," "the revolution in permanence" in which this cannot happen? She is passionate about "the movement from theory to practice and from practice to theory" as a living process and about the necessity for new voices speaking for their own freedom to be heard and listened to, if a movement is to keep on moving. She had the capacity, rare in people learned in Western philosophy and theory—including Marxists—to respect and learn from other kinds of thinking and other modes of expression: those of the Third World, of ordinary militant women, of working people who are perfectly aware that theirs is "alienated labor" and know how to say that without political indoctrination. Maybe Dunayevskaya would claim she originally learned this from Marx.

Marxism and Freedom has as its focus the "movement from practice to theory." Dunayevskaya writes of the shaping impact of American slavery and the Civil War on Marx's thought when he was writing *Capital;* she acknowledges the unfinished legacy of Reconstruction and recognizes the acute significance of the Montgomery bus boycott—the "Black dimension." Women's liberation is not yet a focus, although already in the fifties, long before *Marxism and Freedom* was written, Dunayevskaya was keenly attuned to women's leadership and presence both within and outside radical groups. In "The Miners' Wives" (1950) she notes that while the press depicted the women as bravely going along with the strike they were in fact activists, sometimes pushing the men. In a long-unpublished essay of 1953, she sharply criticizes the Socialist Workers party for failing to recognize that the women who had streamed by the millions into factories in the United States during World War II were "a concrete revolutionary force" searching for "a total reorganization of society." "By continuing her [sic] revolt daily at home, the women were giving a new dimension to politics" (*Women's Liberation and the Dialectics of Revolution,* p. 34). Perhaps it's not by mere oversight that this essay remained so long unpublished. In it Dunayevskaya makes clear that the equality of some women as leaders within the party did not extend to any real recognition of women as a major social force. Possibly her own consciousness of women, though keen, received only negative responses in the organization of which she was then a part. But her entire life was a demonstration of "Woman as Force and Reason," activist and thinker.

Philosophy and Revolution (1973) retraces some of the history of philosophy in *Marxism and Freedom*, moving on from there to discuss the Cuban revolution and the student and youth uprisings of the sixties, along with the emergence of the women's liberation movement. This work feels—until the last chapter—less dynamic and more laborious, more like a political philosophy textbook. But in both books, Dunayevskaya is on a very specific mission: to rescue Marx's Marxism from the theoretical and organizational systems attributed to him; to reclaim his ideas from what has been served up as Marxism in Eastern Europe, China, Cuba, and among Western intellectuals. She insists that you cannot sever Marx's economics from his humanism—humanism here meaning the self-emancipation of human beings necessarily from the capitalist mode of production, but not only from that. The failure of the Russian revolutions to continue as "revolution in permanence"—their disintegration into a system of forced labor camps and political prisons—was the shock that sent Dunayevskaya back to "the original form of the Humanism of Marx," translating his early humanist essays herself because "the official Moscow publication (1959) is marred by footnotes which flagrantly violate Marx's content and intent" (*Marxism and Freedom*, 2d ed., p. 17). "Marxism is a theory of liberation or it is nothing" (p. 22). But she refuses to "rebury" Marx as "humanist," shorn of his economics (p. 17).

Rosa Luxemburg (1982) is much more than a philosophical biography. But that it certainly is: a sympathetic yet critical account of Luxemburg as woman, thinker, organizer, revolutionist. A central chapter is devoted to Marx and Luxemburg as theorists of capital, dissecting Luxemburg's critique of Marx in her *Accumulation of Capital*. Dunayevskaya dissents at many points from Luxemburg's effort to fulfill, as she saw it, Marx's unfinished work. But beyond the economic debate Dunayevskaya asserts that Luxemburg, despite her eloquent writings on imperialism, never saw the potential for revolution in the colonized people of color in what is now called the Third World; and, despite the centrality of women to her antimilitarist work, never saw beyond the purely economic class struggle. Where Marx had seen "new forces and new passions spring up in the bosom of society" (*Rosa Luxemburg*, p. 150) as capitalism declined, Luxemburg saw only the "suffering masses" under imperialism (p. 47).

Luxemburg was "a reluctant feminist" (*Rosa Luxemburg*, p. 85) who was "galled in a most personal form" by the "Woman Question" but, "just as she had learned to live with an underlying anti-Semitism in the party, so she learned to live with . . . male chauvinism" (p. 27). (Does this have a familiar ring?) In particular, she lived with it in the figure of August Bebel, a self-proclaimed feminist who wrote of her "wretched female's squirts of poison," and Viktor Adler, who called her "the poisonous bitch . . . clever as a monkey" (p. 27). However, when she was arrested in 1915 it was on the eve of organizing an international women's antiwar conference with Clara Zetkin. Of their relationship Dunayevskaya says: "far from Luxemburg having no interest in the so-called 'Woman Question,' and far from Zetkin having no interest outside of that question, . . . both of them . . . were determined to build a women's liberation movement that concentrated not only on organizing women workers but on having them develop as leaders, as decision-makers, and as independent Marxist revolutionaries" (*Rosa Luxemburg*, p. 13). In fact, from 1902 on Luxemburg had been writing and speaking on the emancipation of women and on woman suffrage; in 1911 she wrote to her friend Luise Kautsky, "are you coming for the women's conference? Just imagine, I have become a feminist!" (*Rosa Luxemburg*, p. 95). She debated Bebel and Kautsky over the "Woman Question," and broke with Kautsky in 1911, yet, in her short and brutally ended life, feminism and proletarian revolution never became integrated. Dunayevskaya is critical of Luxemburg but also impatient with present-day feminists who want to write her off.

In Luxemburg, Dunayevskaya portrays a brilliant, brave, and independent woman, passionately internationalist and antiwar, a believer in the people's "spontaneity" in the cause of freedom; a woman who saw herself as Marx's philosophical heir, who refused the efforts of her lover and other men to discourage her from full participation in "making history" because she was a woman. But the biography does not stop here. The book opens into a structure generated, as Dunayevskaya tells us, by three events: the resurgence of the Women's Liberation Movement out of the Left; the publication for the first time of Marx's last writings, the *Ethnological Notebooks;* and the global national liberation movements of the seventies that demonstrated to her that Marxism continues to have meaning as a philosophy of revolution. Luxemburg's life and thought become a kind of jumping-off point into the present and future—what she saw and didn't see, her limitations as well as her understanding. We can learn from her mistakes, says Dunayevskaya, as she begins developing the themes she would pursue in *Women's Liberation and the Dialectics of Revolution.*

In this thirty-five-year collection of essays, interviews, letters, lectures you see Dunayevskaya going at her central ideas in many different ways. Agree or not with her analysis here, her interpretation there: these working papers are some of the most tingling, invigorating writing since the early days of Women's Liberation when writing and organizing most often went hand in hand. In her irresistible depiction of women in movement, across the world and through history, Dunayevskaya really does hold to an international perspective. She chides and criticizes Simone de Beauvoir, Sheila Rowbotham, Gerda Lerner; she praises *Wuthering Heights, A Room of One's Own,* the "Three Marias" of the *New Por-*

tuguese Letters, the poetry of Gwendolyn Brooks and Audre Lorde; she says Natalia Trotsky went further than Trotsky; she chastises Engels for diluting and distorting Marx, and post-Marxists and feminists for accepting Engels's *Origins of the Family* as *Marx's* word on women and men. Her quarrel with the Western post-Marxists is that they've taken parts of Marx for the whole, and that what has been left out (especially the dimensions of women and the Third World) is crucial in our time. Her quarrel with the Women's Movement is that feminists have jettisoned Marx because he was a man, or have believed the post-Marxists without looking into Marx for themselves. She insists that Marx's philosophy, far from being a closed and autocratic system, is open-ended, so that "in each age, he becomes more alive than in the age before" (*Women's Liberation and the Dialectics of Revolution*, p. 174). That Marx was himself extraordinarily open to other voices than those of European males.

But why do we need Marx, anyway? Dunayevskaya believes he is the only philosopher of "total revolution"—the revolution that will touch and transform all human relationships, that is never-ending, revolution in permanence. Permanence not as a party-led state that has found all the answers, but as a society all of whose people participate in both government and production and in which the division between manual and mental labor will be ended. We need such a philosophy as grounding for organizing, since, as she says in *Rosa Luxemburg*, "Without a philosophy of revolution activism spends itself in mere anti-imperialism and anti-capitalism, without ever revealing what it is *for*." (p. 194).

Dunayevskaya bases her claims for Marx on her reading of his entire work, but attaches special importance to the *Ethnological Notebooks* (only transcribed and published in 1972) as showing that at the very end of his life, as in his early writings, he was concerned with humanism—not simply class struggle but with the values and structures of precapitalist, non-European societies and the relationship of the sexes in those societies. In these manuscripts, jotted between 1881 and 1882, Marx reviewed the anthropological-ethnological writings of Lewis Henry Morgan (Engels based his *Origins* on Marx's notes on Morgan), John Budd Phear, Henry Maine, and John Lubbock. And indeed, as I read the *Notebooks*, Marx seems to be on a search for how gender has been structured in precapitalist, tribal societies.

Marx didn't go along with the ethnologists in their definitions of the "savage" as measured against the "civilized." Capitalism doesn't mean progress; the civilized are also the damaged. He saw "civilization" as a divided condition—human subjectivity divided against itself by the division of labor, but also divided *from* nature. He was critical of Morgan for ignoring white genocide and ethnocide against the American Indians, of Phear's condescension toward Bengali culture, and of the ethnocentricity of the ethnographers in general.

But neither did Marx idealize egalitarian communal society; he saw that "the elements of oppression in general, and of woman in particular, arose from *within*

primitive communism, and not only related to change from 'matriarchy,' but began with the establishment of ranks—relationship of chief to mass—and the
economic interests that accompanied it" (*Rosa Luxemburg*, pp. 180–81). He
watched closely how the family evolved into an economic unit, within which
were the seeds of slavery and serfdom, how tribal conflict and conquest also led
toward slavery and the acquisition of property. But where Engels posited "the
world historic defeat of the female sex" (*The Origin of the Family, Private Property and the State*, New York: International Publishers, 1971, p. 50), Dunayevskaya notes that Marx saw the resistance of the women in every revolution,
not simply how they were disempowered by the development of patriarchy and
by European invasion and colonization. The *Ethnological Notebooks* are crucial
in Dunayevskaya's eyes because they show Marx at a point in his life where his
idea of revolution was becoming even more comprehensive: the colonialism that
evolved out of capitalism forced him to return to precolonial societies to study
human relations and "to see the possibility of new human relations, not as they
might come through a mere 'updating' of primitive communism's equality of the
sexes . . . but as Marx sensed they would burst forth from a new type of revolution" (*Women's Liberation and the Dialectics of Revolution*, p. 202).

Dunayevskaya vehemently opposes the notion that Marx's Marxism means
class struggle is primary or that racism and male supremacism will end when
capitalism falls. "What happens after?" she says, is the question we have to be
asking all along. And this, she sees in the Women's Liberation Movement, both
women of color and white women have insisted on asking.

And, indeed, what is finally so beautiful and compelling about the Marx she
shows us is his resistance to all static, stagnant ways of being, the deep apprehen-
sion of motion and transformation as principles of thought and of human process,
the mind-weaving dialectical shuttle aflight in the loom of human activity.

Raya Dunayevskaya caught fire from Marx, met it with her own fire, brought
to the events of her lifetime a revitalized, refocused Marxism. Her writings, with
all their passion, energy, wit, and learning, may read awkwardly at times because
she is really writing against the grain of how many readers have learned to think:
to separate disciplines and genres, theory from practice. She's trying to think,
and write, the revolution in the revolution. Anyone who has tried to do this, in
any medium, knows that the effect is not smooth or seamless.

Rosa Luxemburg may not fit the expectations of many readers schooled in left-
ist, feminist, or academic thought. It is, first of all, not a conventional biography
but rather the history and critique of a thinking woman's mind. It supplies no
anecdotes of Luxemburg's childhood, no dramatic version of her assassination. It
does, however, explore the question of how Luxemburg's sexual and political
relationship with Leo Jogiches expressed itself both in intimate letters and in her
theory. But Luxemburg's central relationships, in Dunayevskaya's eyes, were her
intellectual relationship with the work of Marx as she understood it and the rela-

tionship of her whole self to the revolution. Most biographers of women still fail to recognize that a woman's central relationship can be to her work, even as lovers come and go. And Dunayevskaya doesn't end the book with Luxemburg's death, because she doesn't see that death as an ending. She goes on to throw out lines of thinking for the future, lines that pass through Luxemburg's fiery figure but don't finish with the woman who "joyfully [threw her] whole life 'on the scales of destiny'" (*Rosa Luxemburg*, p. v).

"No one knows where the end of suffering will begin," writes the white, Jewish South African Nadine Gordimer about the 1976 Soweto schoolchildren's uprising in her novel, *Burger's Daughter*. In her 1982 essay "Living in the Interregnum," she muses about the sources of art and goes on, "It is from there, in the depths of being, that the most important intuition of revolutionary faith comes: the people know what to do, before the leaders" (Nadine Gordimer, *The Essential Gesture: Writing, Politics and Places*, New York: Alfred A. Knopf, 1988, p. 277). In a note, Gordimer adds: "This thought, deriving from Rosa Luxemburg, forms a significant motif in *Burger's Daughter*" (p. 338).

Dunayevskaya ends this book:

It isn't because we are any "smarter" that we can see so much more than other post-Marx Marxists. Rather, it is because of the maturity of our age. It is true that other post-Marx Marxists have rested on a truncated Marxism; it is equally true that no other generation could have seen the problematic of our age, much less solve our problems. *Only live human beings can recreate the revolutionary dialectic forever anew* [emphasis mine]. And these live human beings must do so in theory as well as in practice. It is not a question only of meeting the challenge from practice, but of being able to meet the challenge from the self-development of the Idea, and of deepening theory to the point where it reaches Marx's concept of the philosophy of "revolution in permanence." (*Rosa Luxemburg*, p. 195)

And this work is indeed going on. Chicana lesbian-feminist poet, activist, and theorist Gloria Anzaldúa writes, in 1990:

What does being a thinking subject, an intellectual, mean for women-of-color from working-class origins? . . . It means being concerned about the ways knowledges are invented. It means continually challenging institutionalized discourses. It means being suspicious of the dominant culture's interpretation of "our" experience, of the way they "read" us. . . .

. . . Theory produces effects that change people and the way they perceive the world. Thus we need *téorias* that will enable us to interpret what happens in the world, that will explain how and why we relate to certain people in specific ways, that will reflect what goes on between inner, outer and peripheral "I"s within a person and between the personal "I"s and the collective "we" of our ethnic communities. *Necesitamos téorias* that will rewrite history using race, class, gender and ethnicity as categories of analysis, theories that cross borders, that blur boundaries. . . . We need theories that point out ways to maneuver between our particular experiences and the necessity of forming our own categories and theoretical models for the patterns we uncover. . . . And we need to find practical applications for those theories. . . . We need to give up the notion that there is a "correct" way to write theory. (Gloria Anzaldúa, "Haciendo caras, una entrada," in Anzaldúa, ed., *Making Face, Making Soul: Haciendo Caras: Creative and Critical Perspectives by Women of Color*, San Francisco: Spinsters/Aunt Lute Books, 1990, pp. xxv–xxvi)

It's made so difficult, under the prevailing conditions of capital-shaped priorities, male supremacism, racism, militarism to envision that revolution without an end to which Dunayevskaya devoted her life. Most of us, even in our imaginations, settle for less. Living under these conditions, we can lose sight of the fact that *we* "live human beings" are where it all must begin—even to the point of denying the degree to which we are suffering (*Rosa Luxemburg*, p. 195). At certain moments, if we're lucky, we touch the experience, the flash, of "how it would feel to be free." Raya Dunayevskaya clearly never let go of her experiences of the fullness of being human, of "how it would feel"—and she wanted that experience to be the normal experience of every human being, everywhere.

                                                                                     Adrienne Rich

Introduction

Three very different types of events in the 1970s have prompted this work. One. The transcription of the last writings from Marx's pen, *The Ethnological Notebooks of Karl Marx*, created a new vantage point from which to view Marx's *oeuvres* as a totality. This cast so new an illumination, on both his first (1844) historic-philosophic concept of Man/Woman and his last (1881–82) analysis, as to undermine the long-held view of post-Marx Marxists that Frederick Engels's *The Origin of the Family, Private Property, and the State* was a "joint" work of Marx and Engels. What became as translucent, when out of the archives had come Marx's unpublished draft letters to Vera Zasulich, was Marx's concept of permanent revolution. This made clear, at one and the same time, how very deep must be the uprooting of class society and how broad the view of the forces of revolution. It led Marx to projecting nothing short of the possibility of a revolution occurring in a backward land like Russia ahead of one in the technologically advanced West.

Two. It cannot be altogether accidental that those writings came to light in the period of the emergence of an historic objective event—the transformation of Women's Liberation as an Idea whose time had come into a worldwide Movement. However, it is not only the objectivity of this event that has led this author to focus on Rosa Luxemburg. First and foremost, it was Luxemburg who raised so forcefully the question of spontaneity of the masses that it impinges on an urgent question of our day: what is the relationship of spontaneity to both consciousness and "the Party"? The total disregard of the feminist dimension of Rosa Luxemburg by Marxists and non-Marxists alike calls for the record to be straightened on that dimension in Luxemburg. Moreover, there is a need for today's Women's Liberation Movement to absorb Luxemburg's revolutionary dimension, not for history's sake but for their demands of the day, including that of autonomy.

Today's Women's Liberation Movement has introduced new and unique aspects, previously raised neither by non-Marxists nor Marxists. But the very fact that the task remains unfinished points to the need to study further Luxemburg's works both as feminist and as revolutionary. And that means grappling with Marx's works, not just as "writings" but as a philosophy of revolution. To do anything short of that impedes the development of the Women's Liberation Movement to its full potential as Reason as well as force.

Three. In this age when the myriad crises reached a global climax with the 1974–75 economic crisis, there is no doubt whatever that, far from being a question of the 1970s, it is a question of what Marx called "the law of motion of capitalist society" to its collapse, the rise of the Third World, and the imperative need for a totally new society on truly human foundations. Even matters such as the publication of newly discovered unpublished works and new English translations of old works—including a new translation of Marx's greatest theoretical work, *Capital*, restoring to it Marx's own "Hegelian" language in "economics"—point to the intense, continuous interest in Marxism. It far transcends any single decade's preoccupation, or any single revolutionary force's aspirations, be it Labor or Woman, Youth or the Black Dimension. It discloses a passion for revolution, as well as for a philosophy of revolution, that would assure its continuance also after the conquest of power.

It is because Marx discovered a whole new continent of thought and of revolution and because he so creatively held together in unison both concept and practice that grappling with Marx's Marxism has become a matter of global urgency. Whether one looks at the economic crises or their opposite— not only class struggles but the national liberation movements, even where they now are forced to function under the whip of counter-revolution—the fact is that new forms of revolt keep emerging. They have erupted in Portugal, and in China in "the year of great troubles under heaven," when nevertheless there was the spontaneous great mass outpouring even before Mao had said his last hurrah. They have erupted in Iran, and in benighted South Africa, where the Black Dimension is forever rising from the ashes. They have erupted from under Communist totalitarianism, as in Poland, and from under Latin American oligarchy propped up by United States imperialism, as in El Salvador and Nicaragua.

The greatest contradiction in all these crosscurrents stems from the very depth of the economic–political–social crises, which produce a great desire for shortcuts to freedom. Instead of grappling with the working out of a philosophy of liberation for our age, theoreticians look only for "root causes" of oppression. This is good, but hardly good enough. It narrows the whole relationship between causality and freedom; it impedes the dual rhythm of revolution that demands not only the overthrow of the old, but the creation of the new. In place of hewing out a road to total freedom, it gets hemmed in by one form or another of economic determinism. This is why it is necessary not to be diverted from a return to the totality of *Marx's* Marxism, which never separated philosophy of revolution from actual revolution: each by itself is one-sided.

What Marx developed in his discovery of a new continent of thought is that Mind is free and, when tightly related to the creativity of the masses in motion, shows itself to be self-determined and ready for fusion in freedom. Indeed, before he openly broke from bourgeois society, Marx in 1841, though still a

"Prometheus Bound" in academia, posed the problematic of the day: the relationship of philosophy to reality.

As against the familiarly-held view that Marx developed from providing a philosophic critique to an economic basis for his theory of revolution, Marx developed Historical Materialism as a theory of permanent revolution, not merely by standing Hegel "right side up" and "taking over" the Hegelian dialectic, but by going back to *history's* root of the Hegelian dialectic—the problem which determined *Hegel's* dialectic, i.e., the dual rhythm of the French Revolution. It is the negation of the negation which Marx singled out as *the* creative force and Reason of dialectic methodology. It is that which Feuerbach failed to grasp, and Hegel himself had covered with a "mystic veil." In saving the Hegelian dialectic from what Marx called Hegel's "dehumanization" of the Idea, as if its self-determination were mere thought rather than human beings thinking and acting, Marx dug deep into revolution, permanent revolution. Marx's unyielding concentration on revolution, on revolutionary *praxis*—revolutionary ruthless critique of all that exists—reveals that dialectical philosophy was the basis of the *totality* of Marx's work, not only in philosophy but in practice, and in both politics and economics. This being so, the transformation of reality remains the warp and woof of the Marxian dialectic. This dialectical principle will show itself, I hope, to be the unifying force for all three parts of the book, that is to say, not only of Part Three—"Karl Marx: From Critic of Hegel to Author of *Capital* and Theorist of 'Revolution in Permanence'"—but also Parts One and Two—"Rosa Luxemburg as Theoretician, as Activist, as Internationalist," and "The Women's Liberation Movement as Revolutionary Force and Reason."

Gathering together the threads of the three parts of this work was made relatively easy by gathering the threads of Marx's development because there we become witness, at one and the same time, to "how" Marx transformed Hegel's revolution in philosophy into a philosophy of revolution, and to how sensitively Marx had his ears attuned to the voices from below, so that what he had named his philosophy—"a new Humanism"—was continuously developing. Just as the young Marx, in first turning to what he called "Economics," had discovered the proletariat as the Subject who would be the "gravedigger of capitalism" and the leader of proletarian revolution, so, at the end of his life, Marx made still newer discoveries as he turned to new, empirical anthropological studies like Morgan's *Ancient Society* as well as to the imperial incursions into the Orient and the carving up of Africa.

That seems to have been the first point so misunderstood by post-Marx Marxists, beginning with Frederick Engels, who, without having known all of the massive *Ethnological Notebooks* Marx had left behind, undertook to write his own version of Morgan's work—his *Origin of the Family*—as a "bequest" of Marx. When Ryazanov discovered these notebooks, he rushed—before he ever had a chance to decipher them, to characterize them as "inexcusable pedantry."

If an Engels, who was a close collaborator of Marx and without whom we would not have had volumes 2 and 3 of *Capital,* could nevertheless so suddenly have become overconfident about his own prowess of interpreting Marx as to assume he was speaking for Marx; if an archivist-scholar like Ryazanov could, at a time when he was actually publishing those magnificent early essays of Marx (the 1844 Economic-Philosophic Manuscripts), spend a good deal of his first report on the Archives of Marx in asking for twenty to thirty people to help him sort these manuscripts out, and yet pass judgement before he dug into them—it says a great deal about literary heirs but nothing whatsoever about so great an historic phenomenon as *Marx's* Marxism.

Isn't it time to challenge all of the post-Marx Marxists, when even those who have achieved great revolutions (and none was greater than the 1917 Russian Revolution) did not, in thought, measure up to Marx? Isn't it time to dig into what Marx, who had discovered a whole new continent of thought, had to say for himself? (Chapter 12 concentrates especially on the last writings of Marx, in which this author found a trail to the 1980s.)[§]

From the study of primitive communism Marx made still newer discoveries, including, at one and the same time, a substantiation of his early Man/Woman concept and of the way he had, in his summation of the Paris Commune, singled out as its greatest achievement "its own working existence." As will be clear from Marx's letters to Zasulich, in the very period during which he was working on the *Ethnological Notebooks*, he viewed the peasants not only as a "second edition" of the Peasant Wars to assure the success of the proletarian victory, but also as possibly instrumental in still newer revolutions. As Marx dug into the history of the remains of the Russian peasant commune, he did not think it out of the question that, if a union with Western technologically advanced society was possible, a revolution could actually come first in backward Russia. This was in 1882!

No wonder that our age too feels the impact of the problematic Marx grappled with in his day: the new revolutionary forces that do not easily arise and are not easily imagined, which were so profoundly posed in Marx's new continent of thought and of revolution. Whether or not our age rises to the historic task of transforming reality, of one thing there is no doubt: Marx had hewed out a road, not only for Luxemburg's generation, but for ours.

May 5, 1981   Raya Dunayevskaya
Detroit, Michigan

[§] See "New Thoughts on *Rosa Luxemburg, Women's Liberation, and Marx's Philosophy of Revolution,*" pp. xxxiii–xxxiv. The preceding two paragraphs were added by Raya Dunayevskaya after the first edition of the book was published in November 1982.—Ed.

Marxist-Humanism's Challenge
to All Post-Marx Marxists

Editor's Note: This text, written in 1981, forms part of Raya Dunayevskaya's summation of what she called her "trilogy of revolution"—*Marxism and Freedom: From 1776 until Today* (1957), *Philosophy and Revolution: From Hegel to Sartre and from Marx to Mao* (1973), *Rosa Luxemburg, Women's Liberation, and Marx's Philosophy of Revolution* (1982). In this summation, Dunayevskaya projected both her critique of Marxism since the death of Karl Marx and her view of Marxist-Humanism's historic continuity with the Hegelian-Marxian dialectic as Hegel and Marx had articulated it. This writing was edited by the author from a presentation she had given to Marxist-Humanist colleagues in September 1981 as the manuscript of the book was being readied for the publisher. The full text excerpted here is on deposit in the Raya Dunayevskaya Collection at Wayne State University Archives of Labor and Urban Affairs, pp. 7118–26.

I. PHILOSOPHIC CONFRONTATION WITH POST–MARX MARXISTS ON THE GROUND OF THE MID-1950s MOVEMENT FROM PRACTICE

Although what we have been talking about all day and will continue to talk about is "organizational responsibility for Marxist-Humanism," I will discard that expression. The reason is this: unless you understand the historic link of continuity, there is no point in saying "Take organizational responsibility for Marxist-Humanism." So I want to challenge what you understand as Marx's Humanism and its relationship to Marx*ist* Humanism.

When I said I was opposed to all post-Marx Marxists beginning with Engels, I

xxvi   Marxist-Humanism's Challenge

didn't mean only the gap between Marx's *Ethnological Notebooks* and Engels's reductionism in *Origin of the Family, Private Property and the State*. I am challenging Engels also on nearly all of his interpretations of the dialectic, not because he betrayed; he didn't. He did the best he possibly could. That's the trouble. The best he could wasn't good enough.

You have to begin seeing what it means to be a great genius, a "thought-diver" like Marx. And if you don't grasp the uniqueness of that, loving Marx won't help. All you would then do, as Engels did, would be to popularize him. Anyone who thinks he understands when it is made bite-size doesn't understand what it means to appreciate and work out and re-create the dialectic at every single stage. Sure, six people will get up who will understand you and not understand Marx—and praise you as the "projector." That doesn't mean Engels had any right to think he was really projecting Marx's whole continent of thought—Marx's Historical Materialism, Marx's Humanism, Marx's "economics," much less his philosophy.

How many people think there is nothing greater than Mehring's biography of Marx? It stinks. And not only because he was a Lassallean, which was bad enough, but because, as an intellectual, he thought he could do better in projecting what Marx "really meant." Do you realize that the German Social-Democracy didn't even ask Engels—he was still alive, and much superior to *them,* including Mehring who was the one writing the history—for his views of the history of socialist ideas and organizations, a history he had lived through with Marx and with all tendencies who truly made history?

Ryazanov, who was known as the greatest Marx scholar, an archivist and analyst of Marxism, had discovered a great store of writings by Marx which had never been published. He introduced them in a scholarly and historic fashion, and that's how we came to know the young Marx. That didn't hold true for the last writings of Marx, which, though he hadn't deciphered nor had a chance to read, he had the gall to characterize as "inexcusable pedantry." This characterization was directed mainly to what we now know as [Marx's] *Ethnological Notebooks.* As all the rest of the post-Marx Marxists, he was happy enough with Engels's *Origin of the Family,* which was supposed to have summarized Marx's ninety-eight pages of notes on Morgan's *Ancient Society.*

This attitude to Marx's archives, even among the best of "Marx scholars," who rush to publish their own views instead of publishing Marx's unpublished works, is one of the major reasons it has taken us one hundred years to find out all that Marx had worked out. Worse yet, we have been left with the impression that Marx was so ill that he did nothing in the last years of his life. The trip to Algiers at the end of his life was described as if it were only a matter of his health, whereas in fact he studied Africa there and "fell in love" with the Arabs. He had written to his daughters, as we have seen, that, nevertheless, [the Arabs] would all go to the Devil if they didn't have a revolution.

Catching the historic link to Marx is not only a matter of finally seeing all his writings, but of grasping, at one and the same time, that something had to happen *both* in the movement from practice *and* in the movement from theory. I want to depart for a moment from Marx's day to our age, specifically the years 1950 to 1953. It was after the General Strike of the miners in 1949–50 that I felt we had reached a new stage both in Marxism and in proletarian consciousness. I therefore insisted that a worker be present when I gave my next report on what we then called "Marxism and State-Capitalism" and what became [my book] *Marxism and Freedom*. (Until then, the discussion had been limited to myself, C. L. R. James, and Grace Lee.) Clearly, something was stirring in the world; I felt it very strongly after the death of Stalin, which had lifted a heavy incubus from my brain. Before the actual outbreak of the June 17, 1953 revolt in East Germany— the first ever from under totalitarianism—I turned to the study of the Absolute Idea, splitting that category into two, i.e., saying that there was not only a unity of theory and practice, but that there was a *movement from practice,* and not only one from theory.

[Later,] I went to check what Marx had written on Hegel's *Philosophy of Mind*. I found that where I began [in my letter of May 20, 1953] with paragraph #385, Marx had left off precisely at paragraph #384—saying he would return. But he never got to finish.

What makes somebody, a century after the event, without knowing where Marx had left off, start focusing on the very next paragraph? I don't know. I do know that there are certain creative moments in history when the objective movement and the subjective movement so coincide that the self-determination of ideas and the self-determination of masses readying for revolt explode. Something is in the air, and you catch it. That is, you catch it if you have a clear head and if you have good ears to hear *what is upsurging from below.* All this happened May 12 and May 20, 1953, six weeks before the actual revolution on June 17 in East Berlin.

That is something very different from just being the first one to translate Marx's 1844 Humanist Essays and Lenin's 1914 Philosophic Notebooks and publish them [in *Marxism and Freedom*] as the basis for what we as Marxist-Humanists were doing on the American roots of Marxism, beginning with the Abolitionists and climaxing in the 1949–50 General Strike of the miners. That is to say, you translate *because* you have already been on the road to working out all these relations in your own country and your own time. Under those circumstances you cannot possibly look at masses in motion and not feel stirred to the marrow of your bones. That is what happened on June 17, 1953, as the German workers destroyed the statue of Stalin and raised the slogan: "Bread and Freedom!" That is what led to the transformation of "Marxism and State-Capitalism," which became *Marxism and Freedom* by 1957. By then we had become not just a State-Capitalist Tendency, but a Marxist-Humanist group, News and Letters Committees.

II. FROM ABSOLUTE IDEA AS MOVEMENT *FROM PRACTICE* AS WELL AS FROM THEORY TO THE ABSOLUTE IDEA AS NEW BEGINNING (1968–73)

It was different by 1973 and *Philosophy and Revolution*. Why was it different? Because this time it did not come only from the fact that East Europe had arisen against Russian totalitarianism (and there had been a revolt from within the slave labor camps of Vorkuta). This time it came from the revolts against Western imperialism as well. This time it was the youth the world over, as well as the Black revolution. Unfortunately, all the youth thought was needed was more and more activity, dismissing theoretical debates as "factional struggles" and considering that theory was so easy it could be picked up "en route." These were not just "factional struggles" but *historic-philosophic* tendencies in a very new form that at one and the same time caught the historic link to Marx and had an original contribution to record. That theory was needed, that there could be no revolution without a philosophy of revolution, was shown by the fact that De Gaulle, without firing a single shot, succeeded in aborting the great 1968 revolt in France. Something had to be done. The youth in revolt had not betrayed; they thought they were very original in rejecting "factional struggles" and insisting, instead, on more and more activity. But they didn't achieve what they were after. So this time we had to find the link *from theory* and not only from practice.

Before (1957), we stressed the movement from practice, the split in the Absolute Idea. Now (1973) we were saying Absolute Idea *as new beginning,* as totality which is just a beginning for a movement forward. *Philosophy and Revolution,* then, with its first Part, "Why Hegel? Why Now?" dug into Hegel *as Hegel, as well as into Marx who re-created that dialectic, and as Lenin rediscovered it in 1914 at the outbreak of World War I.* All this was measured against the rise of both a whole new Third World and a whole new generation of revolutionaries.

III. 1981: *ROSA LUXEMBURG, WOMEN'S LIBERATION, AND MARX'S PHILOSOPHY OF REVOLUTION*

The point this time is that in the work on Rosa Luxemburg, which is also on Women's Liberation, which is also on Marx's work as a totality, which is also on Lenin, and which is also on Trotsky, I not only take up revolutionaries, but great revolutionaries who were also theoreticians. Nobody was greater than Lenin in Russia in 1917 or greater than Luxemburg both in 1905 and 1919; how could they possibly be inadequate for our day? The point nevertheless is that before we spoke about the theoretic void left by Lenin's death, which had never been filled; now we are speaking about the fact that even Lenin, who had made the great philosophic breakthrough, had remained ambivalent.

He had philosophically reorganized himself in relationship to Materialism and

Idealism, on the nature of the revolution that would not stop at the democratic stage but go all the way to the proletarian and elemental and international revolution. He also was for self-determination of nations as the actual bacillus for proletarian revolution. But, but, but . . . he did stop short of reorganizing himself on the Party, though he had introduced many modifications [under the impact of] 1905 and 1917. He was especially great when he threatened to resign from the leadership and "go to the sailors," if the Party did not put the question of the conquest of power on the agenda. And he didn't stop criticizing the new bureaucracy. But when it came to breaking with the Party then, far from "going to the sailors," he was thinking that the Bolshevik layer was so thin that it was them he must trust fully. We certainly could not accept that. We, who have suffered thirty years of Stalinism, the transformation of the workers' state into its total opposite, a state-capitalist society, and have witnessed *new revolts from below,* will not accept any vanguardism-to-lead; they have done nothing but mis-lead.

In a word, if Lenin had accomplished as great a reorganization of himself on the Party Question as he had done on the Self-Determination of Nations, we might have had some ground for today, but we don't. And when it comes to the Woman Question, I don't believe he ever thought of reorganizing himself. There we have to start totally anew.

As for Trotsky, it is not only that question of vanguard-party-to-lead on which he accepted Lenin's 1903 position; it is also that his theory of permanent revolution, which sounds as though it is Marx's, is not—*is not*. Let's stop here a minute. First of all, we must remember that Trotsky did not name his analysis of 1905 as a theory of permanent revolution. It was a Menshevik who so named it; and Trotsky was glad to accept the name, *without any reference to Marx's theory whatsoever.* He was great, and way ahead of his time, in pointing out that the revolution would not stop at its democratic bourgeois stage; that once unleashed the proletariat would go all the way. On the other hand, he did not recognize the peasantry as a revolutionary force, nor pay attention to the fact that they were the overwhelming majority in Russia. On that one, Lenin was right and Trotsky was wrong—that is to say, Lenin was right that you cannot consider that a revolution can be successful when it disregards 90 percent of its population. Lenin agreed that the proletariat must be a "leader" but insisted it had to be a "revolutionary democratic dictatorship of the proletariat and the peasantry." Otherwise, Lenin maintained, it meant "skipping" stages of revolution, playing down its forces. Marx, it is true, spoke of "rural idiocy," but he never forgot that "a second edition of the Peasants' War" was needed to have the proletarian revolution succeed.

Allow me to divert back to Marx's time. Marx first used the expression "permanent revolution" back in 1843 in an essay on the Jewish Question, that is, on the civil rights of a minority, insisting that civil rights were insufficient and that there had to be totally new human relations. The next time he spoke of it was during an actual revolution, 1848. Once that was defeated, Marx, instead of bowing to the defeat, insisted on the need for a "revolution in permanence." His point was that, first, one must remember the highest point achieved by the revolution. It was proletarian independence: "Never again must we go with the bourgeoisie." Secondly, the revolution, to be successful, must have the peasantry with it. Thirdly, indeed above all, Marx was always looking for ever-new live forces to create a new dialectic, not just philosophically, but a new dialectic of revolution. In a word, when he used the expression, "revolution in permanence," in the Address to the Communist League in 1850, he was talking about continuous revolution *in transition to a class-less society.*

Two decades later, Marx continued to work out *his* theory of revolution in permanence, this time in the form of actually predicting the revolution coming first in a backward country, rather than a technologically advanced country. In his 1881 letter to Vera Zasulich, praising primitive communism in Morgan's *Ancient Society,* he neither failed to mention that Morgan's report was government-sponsored, nor stopped at the primitive stage. It is true that the Iroquois women had more power than women under capitalism and collective property of the tribes could lead to a higher state. But Marx wasn't just recording facts; he was interested in what the facts signified. Marx had lived through the Paris Commune, and a decade later there was nothing on the horizon of that nature, and he was questioning whether a new dialectic of revolution could start within Russia and the Peasant Communes that still existed there. So non-determinist was he, and so open to all new beginnings, that he now held that his "Historical Tendency of the Accumulation of Capital" was not to be made into a universal. It was a generalization of what had happened in Western Europe, but Russia had the best chance in the world to avoid the monstrosity of Western capitalism.

He was not predicting as a prophet. He was analyzing dialectically the law of motion of capitalist society to its collapse, the live forces of revolution who were re-creating the dialectic of revolution in new circumstances. And precisely because his vision was of a new form of society, a class-less society, he didn't stop at any historic stage as the ultimate.

I began by saying that unless Marxist-Humanists fully grasped the historic continuity to Marx's Humanism *and* worked out the trail to the 1980s on the basis of those new moments in Marx's last decade, the expression, "taking organizational responsibility for Marxist-Humanism," would have no meaning. In a word, my "rejection" of that expression meant that the prerequisite for it was, at one and the same time, catching the historic *continuity* as well as working it out for our age. What I was stressing in Chapter XII of the book was the new openings in what Melville had called "abrupt intermergings" and what we called the "new moments" in Marx's last decade, be it in the *Ethnological Notebooks,* both as they concerned Asiatic mode of production and the role of women among the Iroquois and the Irish, and for that matter, what Marx had written of the Paris Commune, or the projection of a revolution in Russia ahead of one in the West.

The imperative need to fill the philosophic void in post-Marx Marxism is most clearly seen in Leon Trotsky's reduction of the ground for the Fourth International to a matter of leadership, or, as he put it: "The crisis of the world is the crisis of leadership," as if substitution of good leaders, like Trotsky, instead of bad leaders, like Stalin, would change the course of the world. Instead, as we know, the Fourth International became the stillbirth it is. Had he considered, instead, that it was his historic responsibility to fill the philosophic void, he *might* have found the trail to lead us back to Marx and forward to the transformation of society.

The philosophic concept of leadership became correctly, with us, the projection of Marx's Humanism. That is to say, philosophy of revolution rather than the vanguardist party. It becomes all the more imperative that we project all the new moments in Marx that we did discover. And that is not limited to the new in organizational form—committee-form against the "party-to-lead"—*that didn't separate theory from practice.*

We have all too often stopped at the committee-form of organization rather than the inseparability of that from philosophy. And it is the philosophy that is new, unique, our special historic contribution that enabled us to find historic continuity, the link to Marx's Humanism. It is this which is totally new, *not* the committee-form of organization, as crucial as that is.

As I put it at the end of the new book: "What is needed is a new unifying principle, on Marx's ground of humanism, that truly alters both human thought and human experience. Marx's *Ethnological Notebooks* are a historic happening that proves [one hundred years after he wrote them] that Marx's legacy is no mere heirloom, but a live body of ideas and perspectives that is in need of concretization. Every moment of Marx's development, as well as the totality of his works, spells out the need for 'revolution in permanence.' This is the absolute challenge to our age."

September 5, 1981

New Thoughts on *Rosa Luxemburg,*
Women's Liberation, and
Marx's Philosophy of Revolution

Editor's Note: This text was written by Raya Dunayevskaya in August 1983 as a letter describing each of the passages she wished to add to *Rosa Luxemburg, Women's Liberation, and Marx's Philosophy of Revolution* after the book had been set in type and could no longer be changed. Several of these passages had their origins in questions raised by audiences during Dunayevskaya's two-month-long national lecture tour for the Marx centenary in the spring of 1983. The full text of the letter excerpted here is on deposit in the Raya Dunayevskaya Collection at Wayne State University Archives of Labor and Urban Affairs, pp. 15370–74. The precise locations suggested by Dunayevskaya for placement of these passages have been indicated by section marks in the body of this 1991 edition of the book.

I would like to explain all the paragraphs that [would be] added [to the latest theoretical work, *Rosa Luxemburg, Women's Liberation, and Marx's Philosophy of Revolution*], after its publication, in the following context:

(1) That it is no accident that it is the Marx centenary which prompted the new publication of our other two fundamental works, *Marxism and Freedom* and *Philosophy and Revolution,* and

(2) That this led us to call the theoretical foundations of Marxist-Humanism, as a totality, a "trilogy of revolution."

Here, then, are the paragraphs as they [would be] added to each section:

In the Introduction, just before the final paragraphs, I saw a need not to have the reader wait for the final chapter to know that we are challenging post-Marx Marxists. With that in mind, the added paragraph makes clear at once that the very first point misunderstood by post-Marx Marxists, beginning with Frederick Engels, was Marx's work in the last decade regarding what we now call the Third World, and what Marx called, in the *Grundrisse,* "the Asiatic mode of production," as well as commenting on it as he read Morgan's *Ancient Society.* In the new paragraph, we also ask: Isn't the Marx centenary high time to challenge the post-Marx Marxists on their understanding of Marx's last writings? And we point to the fact that we do just that in the last chapter.

(The new paragraph [would be] added on pp. xxiii–xxiv, just before the paragraph which begins: "From the study of primitive communism . . .")

* * *

Chapter III of Part One jams up the different views of Luxemburg and Marx on "Accumulation of Capital" in order to show that the new events which Luxemburg called "reality," which she contrasted to Marx's "theory," could have been so contrasted because she failed to fully work out dialectic methodology—which would have revealed a single dialectic in both objective and subjective worlds. To that end, the whole subject of methodology was expanded to reveal the difference between how Absolute appeared in the phenomenal world (and the phenomenon she had in mind was imperialism) and how Absolute was worked out in *Philosophy of Mind,* where it cannot possibly be separated from Subject, i.e., revolutionary force as Reason. As the added paragraph puts it: "Therein is the nub of the Great Divide between *Phenomenology* and *Philosophy*—and because it is no abstraction, but a live Subject, *it unites rather than divides theory and reality.*"

(The new paragraphs [would be] added on p. 45, immediately after the paragraph that ends with the italicized sentence: "This, indeed, is the nub of Luxemburg's error.")

Methodology being the dialectic movement both in the *Phenomenology of Mind* and in the *Philosophy of Mind,* let us look deeper into their difference. While it is true that in the *Phenomenology* we speak not just of appearance, much less of mere show, but of a *philosophy* of appearance, it is not true that the methodology, as we follow the movement of the dialectic in *Philosophy of Mind,* is either the philosophy of phenomena or even of essence. Rather, the dialectic in the Notion is that the Absolute there opens so many new doors in both the objective and subjective spheres as to reveal totality itself as new beginning.

Thus, as against the phenomenology of imperialism being merely a reflection of new surfacings of oppression, new appearances surface as so profound a philosophy of revolution as to disclose that what inheres in it is a living Subject that will resolve the great contradiction of its absolute opposites, imperialism and national oppression. It is this which Marxist-Humanists call the new revolutionary forces as Reason. Therein is the nub of the Great Divide between *Phenomenology* and *Philosophy*—and because it is no abstraction, but a live Subject, *it unites rather than divides theory and reality.*

* * *

In Part Two on the Women's Liberation Movement, especially the section on the "Unfinished Task," the point I chose to elaborate was, once again, the conception of Women's Liberation not just as force but as Reason. The new here, however, was that the "proof" came from history itself—February 23, 1917. This was for purposes of showing that the women were the ones who *initiated* that revolution. Even now I am not sure that we totally understand that that, in turn, depends on women *practicing* the immediate problems inseparable from the philosophic context. This is why I have two final suggestions: (1) Do, please, consider the paper worked out for the anthropology conference, "Marx's 'New Humanism' and the Dialectics of Women's Liberation in Primitive and Modern Societies," as well as the talk I gave at the Third World Women's Conference, as integral to the expansion of Part Two.[§]

(2) The second and key suggestion is the imperativeness of a study of Part Three without which there can be no total comprehension not just of Part Three, in and for itself, but of the fact that it is that Part that informs the whole work. *It is Marx's Marxism as a totality after it has gone through combat with the greatest revolutionaries of the post-Marx period—Lenin and Luxemburg, without whom we could not have reached the new stage we have achieved.*

(The paragraph [would be] added on p. 109, immediately after the paragraph which ends: ". . . or by using them only as helpmates.")

> Quite the contrary. History proves a very different truth, whether we look at February 1917, where the women were the ones who *initiated* the revolution; whether we turn further back to the Persian Revolution of 1906–11, where the women created the very first women's soviet; or whether we look to our own age in the 1970s in Portugal, where Isabel do Carmo raised the totally new concept of *apartidarismo*. It is precisely because women's liberationists are both revolutionary force *and* Reason that they are crucial. If we are to achieve success in the new revolutions, we have to see that the uprooting of the old is total from the start.

(And to the end of the next, the penultimate paragraph, one sentence [would be] added, after the sentence ending: ". . . which do not separate practice from theory.")

[§] Both documents were published in Dunayevskaya's *Women's Liberation and the Dialectics of Revolution* (1985).—Ed.

Which is what Luxemburg meant when she defined "being human" as "joyfully throwing your life on the scales of destiny."

* * *

[The following passage was proposed by Dunayevskaya in September 1983 for addition to and substitution for two paragraphs on p. 180. It is inserted here where it would have appeared in the sequence of passages added to the text.—Ed.]

The whole question of the transition period, and the differences on it between Marx and Engels, is taken up on p. 180; that is, what happens during the transition from one stage to another, both as it relates to Women's Liberation and to the Asiatic Mode of Production, which Engels somehow omitted from his *Origin of the Family.* I had, indeed, considered that question crucial, as Marx always related it to new revolutionary upsurges:

> In the 1850s, for example, what inspired Marx to return to the study of pre-capitalist formations and gave him a new appreciation of ancient society and its craftsmen was the Taiping Revolution. It opened so many doors to "history and its process" that Marx now concluded that, *historically-materialistically* speaking, a new stage of production, far from being a mere change in *property-form,* be it "West" or "East," was such a change in *production-relations* that it disclosed, in embryo, the dialectics of actual revolution.
>
> What Marx, in the *Grundrisse,* had defined as "the absolute movement of becoming" had matured in the last decade of his life as new moments—a multilinear view of human development as well as *dialectic duality within each* formation. From within each formation evolved *both* the end of the old *and* the beginning of the new. Whether Marx was studying the communal or the despotic form of property, it was the human resistance of the Subject that revealed the direction of resolving the contradictions. Marx transformed what, to Hegel, was the synthesis of the "Self-Thinking Idea" and the "Self-Bringing-Forth of Liberty" as the emergence of a new society. The many paths to get there were left open.
>
> As against Marx's multilinear view which kept Marx from attempting any blueprint for future generations, Engels's unilinear view led him to mechanical positivism. By no accident whatever, such one-dimensionality kept him from seeing either the communal form under "Oriental despotism" or the duality in "primitive communism" in Morgan's *Ancient Society.* No wonder, although Engels had accepted Marx's view of the Asiatic mode of production as fundamental enough to constitute a fourth form of human development, he had left it out altogether from *his* analysis of primitive communism in the first book he wrote as a "bequest" of Marx—*Origin of the Family.* By then Engels had confined Marx's revolutionary dialectics and historical materialism to hardly more than Morgan's "materialism."

* * *

It is no accident that the paragraph that [would be] added to Chapter XII on the Black dimension is the one that at once became urgent to the National Tour [on the Marx centenary] itself—so much so that I read it out as if it actually were *in* the book, in my talks on the Black dimension. Nor is it an accident that Charles Denby [black autoworker and editor of *News and Letters*] suggested it be the center of the new introduction for *American Civilization on Trial.*[§] At the same time, by considering all that Marx had said in a single place rather than separately as they had been expressed in each specific decade, you could see the totality, so that it became inseparable from his concept of "revolution in permanence," including his very last work, the *Ethnological Notebooks.*

(The paragraph [would be] added on p. 194 immediately after the paragraph that ends: ". . . backward lands ahead of the advanced countries.")

With this dialectical circle of circles, Marx's reference in the *Ethnological Notebooks* to the Australian aborigine as "the intelligent black," brought to a conclusion the dialectic he had unchained when he first broke from bourgeois society in the 1840s and objected to the use of the word, "Negro," as if it were synonymous with the word, "slave." By the 1850s, in the *Grundrisse,* he extended that sensitivity to the whole pre-capitalist world. By the 1860s, the Black dimension became, at one and the same time, not only pivotal to the abolition of slavery and victory of the North in the Civil War, but also to the restructuring of *Capital* itself. In a word, the often-quoted sentence: "Labor cannot emancipate itself in the white skin where in the black skin it is branded," far from being rhetoric, was the actual reality *and* the perspective for overcoming that reality. Marx reached, at every historic turning point, for a concluding point, *not* as an end but as a new jumping off point, a new beginning, a new vision.

* * *

Finally, on p. 195 just before the final paragraph of the entire text, please add the following:

This is the further challenge to the form of organization which we have worked out as the committee-form rather than the "party-to-lead." But, though committee-form and "party-to-lead" are opposites, they are not absolute opposites. At the point when the theoretic-form reaches philosophy, the challenge demands that we synthesize not only the new relations of theory to practice, and all the forces of revolution, but philosophy's "suffering, patience and labor of the negative," i.e., experiencing absolute negativity. *Then and only then* will we succeed in a revolution that

---

[§]*American Civilization on Trial: Black Masses as Vanguard,* originally written in 1963, was republished in 1983, with a new Introduction by Raya Dunayevskaya.—Ed.

will achieve a class-less, non-racist, non-sexist, truly human, truly new society. That which Hegel judged to be the synthesis of the "Self-Thinking Idea" and the "Self-Bringing-Forth of Liberty," Marxist-Humanism holds, is what Marx had called the new society. The many paths to get there are not easy to work out.

With this final addition we have come to the question of Organization as likewise inseparable from the concept of "revolution in permanence."

August 26, 1983

PART ONE

Rosa Luxemburg as
Theoretician, as Activist, as
Internationalist

I

Two Turning Points in
Luxemburg's Life:
Before and After the
1905 Revolution

> *... the Russian Revolution is not just the last act in a series of bourgeois revolutions of the 19th century, but rather the forerunner of a new series of future proletarian revolutions in which the conscious proletariat and its vanguard, the Social-Democracy, are destined for the historic role of leader.*
> Speech of Rosa Luxemburg at the 1907 London Congress

ENTRANCE ON THE GERMAN SCENE

Rosa Luxemburg's very entrance, May 1898, into the German arena, center of the Second International, shook up the largest and most prestigious of world Marxist organizations—the German Social-Democratic Party (SPD). From the start, she became a subject of contention—contention that has not abated to this day.

No sooner had she arrived in Germany than she plunged to meet the greatest challenge ever to the theory of Marx, by no less a person than Eduard Bernstein, the literary executor of Marxism (so designated by Marx's closest collaborator, Frederick Engels). This first revision of Marxism, entitled *Evolutionary Socialism*, was answered by many orthodox leaders, but it was Luxemburg's *Reform or Revolution* (1899) that became the classic answer to revisionism. That a young woman of twenty-seven years, within a year of her arrival, could rise to such high stature tells a great deal more than just how dramatic her entrance was. It discloses the type of theoretician, the type of personality, the type of activist Luxemburg was.

It is true that, with Leo Jogiches, she already headed the small underground party in Poland; at age twenty-two she had already been made editor of its paper, *Workers' Cause*. But, in German eyes, that would not have counted for much alongside the achievements of the massive German party with its unchallenged international reputation. And surely, the quick acceptance of her as theoretician was not due to the fact that she had already shown Marxist-economist acuity in her doctoral dissertation on the Polish economy. Though her *The Industrial Development of Poland* was considered an important contribution—"for a Pole"—the German Social-Democratic Party had many economic theoreticians with reputations greater than hers.

Furthermore, the fact that she related this economic study to her intense opposition, as an internationalist, to self-determination for Poland—especially since it meant turning Marx's own position on Poland upside down—would hardly have won her the high praise she achieved within a single year. On the contrary: such overly bold self-confidence would only have led the German party hierarchy to keep her out of the leadership, as, indeed, was evident from the fact that they tried, at first, to limit her work to what was then called the "Woman Question." While this didn't mean that Luxemburg was oblivious to the "Woman Question"—though she tried to present herself that way (as do today's Women's Liberationists, and as did her old male colleagues)—she categorically refused to be pigeonholed.

Not only that. She did, indeed, feel herself to be "a land of boundless possibilities." As she wrote to Jogiches on 4 May 1899: "I feel, in a word, the need, as Heine would say, to 'say something great.' It is the form of writing that displeases me. I feel that within me there is maturing a completely new and original form which dispenses with the usual formulas and patterns and breaks them down . . . But how, what, where? I don't know yet, but I tell you that I feel with utter certainty that something is there, that something will be born."*

On the "Woman Question," too, she had something to report in her letter to Jogiches of 11 February 1902, about her organizational tour, which discloses that she was both theoretically and practically aware of the question: "I was formally interpolated on the women's question and on marriage. A splendid young weaver, Hoffman, is zealously studying this question. He has read Bebel, Lili Braun and *Gleichheit*, and is carrying on a bitter argument with the older village comrades who keep maintaining 'a woman's place is in the home' . . ."

She naturally sided with Hoffman and was pleased that her advice was accepted as "the voice of authority."

It was that theoretic "voice of authority"—not on the "Woman Question," but on revisionism—that made the party hierarchy recognize Rosa Luxemburg as one who would brook no limits to her range of interests. No matter what limitation would be attempted—be it the "Woman Question" or anti-

---

*Because the easiest way to find the correspondence of both Luxemburg and Marx in any language is by the date of the letters, I refer to dates, rather than to any single source, throughout the text.

Semitism (which, though never admitted, was not too far below the surface),[1] or concentration on *any* single issue—it was the totality of the revolutionary goal that characterized the totality that was Rosa Luxemburg.

She was uncompromising in her many-faceted involvements and made clear that they were as far-reaching as the whole new revolutionary continent of thought that Marx had discovered. She had every intention of *practicing it on an international scale*, beginning right there, and right then, at that world focal point of the Social-Democracy: Germany.

As she was to be throughout her life, Luxemburg was active enough that first year in Germany. And, whether or not it was her activity that energized the German Social-Democratic Party, it was, in her case, *intellect become will become act*. For that matter, it was not only the German Social-Democracy that her intellect challenged. Living in Germany also meant experiencing certain changes in herself insofar as her relationship with Jogiches was concerned. All one has to do to see the changes is to compare the letters she wrote from France in 1894 and those she wrote from Germany in 1898–99.

From Paris she wrote of love and sadness and complained that she could not share her impressions with her comrades, since "unfortunately, I don't love them and so I have no desire to do this. You are the one I love, and yet . . . but I just said all that. It's not true that now time is of the essence and work is most urgent. In a certain type of relationship you always find something to talk about, and a bit of time to write." From Berlin on 21 April 1899, she wrote: "Dziodziuchna, be a philosopher, do not get irritated by details . . . In general, more than once I wanted to write, that you are extending your methods, which are applicable only in our Polish–Russian shop of 7½ people, to a party of a million." And she followed that up with a postcard, 23 April, where she wrote: "Oh, Dziodzio, when will you stop baring your teeth and thundering . . . "

She may not have been fully aware of all that that signified. After all, there was not only deep love between them and deep comradeship, as well as shared leadership, but she held him in especially great esteem when it came to organization. Though he was nearly as young as she when they met in Zurich—four years separated them—he had already founded the first revolutionary circle in Vilna in 1885, had already been arrested twice, had already escaped from jail, and, at the very assembly point for army conscripts, had again escaped into exile. At the same time, as Clara Zetkin, who knew them both intimately, was later to express it, Jogiches "was one of those very masculine personalities—an extremely rare phenomenon these days—who can tolerate a great female personality . . . "[2] Nevertheless, it was a fact that Rosa Luxemburg was beginning to take issue with him in his very specific preserve—organization—where not only had she previously acknowledged his superiority, but where she, herself, had been quite indifferent to the whole topic.

As it happened, by no means accidentally, she had at once to plunge into the burning debate in Germany and in the whole International; in meeting the very first challenge to Marxism *from within Marxism* by the original revisionist, Eduard Bernstein, she established herself as the one who delivered the most telling blow, because it was so total. She battled Bernstein on all fronts, from analysis of Marx's economic laws of capitalism leading to collapse, through the political question of the conquest of power, to the proletariat's need for the dialectic.

As against Bernstein's nightmares about the fatal effect that would result from the proletariat's attempt to gain political power "prematurely," she maintained, in *Reform or Revolution*: "Since the proletariat is not in the position to seize political power in any other way than 'prematurely,' since the proletariat is absolutely obliged to seize power once or several times 'too early' before it can maintain itself in power for good, the objection to the 'premature' conquest of power is at bottom nothing more than a general opposition to the aspiration of the proletariat to possess itself of State power."[3]

And as against Bernstein's demand that "the dialectical scaffolding" be removed from Marx's theories, she wrote: "When he directs his keenest arrows against our dialectic system, he is really attacking the specific mode of thought employed by the conscious proletariat in its struggle for liberation. It is an attempt to shatter the intellectual arm with the aid of which the proletariat, though materially under the yoke of the bourgeoisie, is yet enabled to triumph over the bourgeoisie. For it is our dialectical system that . . . is already realizing a revolution in the domain of thought."[4]

Those first two years in Germany, where she had experienced so many changes, were also the years when she manifested that flash of genius on imperialism as *the* global shift in politics. Even before the word "imperialism" was coined by Hobson (to whom all *later* Marxists, from Hilferding to Lenin, expressed their indebtedness), Luxemburg posed the *world* significance of Japan's attack on China in 1895, which led to the intrusion of European powers into Asia and Africa. Indeed, an entire new epoch of capitalist development—the emergence of imperialism—had begun. As she wrote to Jogiches on 9 January 1899, she had meant to include this analysis in the *Reform or Revolution* pamphlet. On 13 March 1899, she wrote on this global shift in politics for the *Leipziger Volkszeitung*. She was to call attention to it, again, in the 1900 Congress. It became even more concrete, that is to say, directly related to the Social-Democratic party's silence on the "Morocco incident," and was to become, of course, an underlying cause for her break with Kautsky in 1910. And, we must emphasize once again, all of this happened long before anyone, including Lenin, had sensed any reformism in the unchallenged world leader of Marxism. It became, as well, the ground for her greatest theoretical work, *Accumulation of Capital.**

*See Chapter III, n. 1.

A FLASH OF GENIUS ON THE RISE OF IMPERIALISM AND THE FIRST RUSSIAN REVOLUTION

It is exciting to see that flash of genius at its very birth, in the letter to Jogiches on 9 January 1899:

> Around 1895, a basic change occurred: the Japanese war opened the Chinese doors and European politics, driven by capitalist and state interests, intruded into Asia. Constantinople moved into the background. Here the conflict between states, and with it the development of politics, had an extended field before it: the conquest and partition of all Asia became the goal which European politics pursued. An extremely quick dismemberment of China followed. At present, Persia and Afghanistan too have been attacked by Russia and England. From that, the European antagonisms in Africa have received new impulses; there, too, the struggle is breaking out with new force (Fashoda, Delegoa, Madagascar).
>
> It's clear that the dismemberment of Asia and Africa is the final limit beyond which European politics no longer has room to unfold. There follows then another such squeeze as has just occurred in the Eastern question, and the European powers will have no choice other than throwing themselves on one another, until the *period of the final crisis sets in within politics* . . . etc., etc.

By the beginning of the twentieth century the extension of capitalism into its imperialist phase opened a totally new epoch because there also emerged its total opposite—revolution. Beyond any doubt this new global dimension—the Russian Revolution of 1905, which was signalling a new world stage in the East as well—made the dialectic of history very real for Luxemburg. Far from the dialectic being either just an abstraction or a journalistic euphemism for attacking revisionism, it was now the very breath of new life. Soon the dialectic of revolution, as of history, came alive before her very eyes in the 1905 Revolution *in Poland*, which was then part of the Tsarist empire.

She wished to become one with the proletariat in *making history*. Jogiches, who was already in Poland making that history, and her German colleagues, however, were hardly encouraging her to return to Poland during such tumultuous times. The so-called "Woman Question" was no longer any sort of generalization, but galled her in a most personal form as she kept being told that the risks to her, as woman, were greater than to the male revolutionary emigrés, who were returning. Although she was delayed in leaving for Poland, this type of argument only assured her going.

She reached Poland on 30 December 1905 and at once plunged into a whirl-wind of activities. There was nothing she didn't attempt—from writing and editing to taking revolver in hand to force a printer to run off manifestoes, articles, leaflets, and pamphlets; from participating in strikes and demonstrations to making endless speeches at factory gates. Within three days, on 2 January 1906, she wrote to Kautsky: "*Mere general strike by itself* has ceased to play the role it once did . . . Now nothing but a general uprising on the streets can bring a decision . . . ''

It was awe-inspiring to see the familiar strikes of advanced German workers become a general political strike of "backward" Poles. No wonder that the whole concept of "backward" and "advanced" underwent a total transformation in the ongoing revolution. Luxemburg now saw the so-called "backward" Russian working class as the vanguard—not only of their own revolution, but of the world working-class movement. The leaflets and manifestoes made clear not only the class content of the revolution but the totality of the change that the revolution was initiating—from the General Political Strike as the new method of class struggle, to the Soviet as a new political form of organization; and from the call for, and actual practice of, the eight-hour day to the demand for "full emancipation of women."

She was to make a category of the General Political Strike both as road to revolution and as theory of revolution, as well as relationship of party to spontaneity of masses. As we shall see later, when we deal with the theory that resulted from the experience—*The Mass Strike, the Party and the Trade Unions*[5]—the actual events that gave rise to the so-called theory of spontaneity were happening before her very eyes. Moreover, not only the activities of the masses but the phenomenal organizational growth made a crucial impact on Luxemburg.

To witness a small underground party, which had no more than a few hundred members after a decade of work, grow nearly overnight into a mass party of thirty thousand was proof enough that it was neither conspiracy nor experience accumulated over slow years, much less the wisdom of the leaders, that "taught workers" either organization or class consciousness. It was the masses themselves, in motion, who brought about the end of Luxemburg's "German period." She began to "speak Russian"—Russian and Polish—rather than German.

With her participation in an ongoing revolution, Luxemburg's personal leap to freedom included also freedom from Jogiches, though she was not to become aware of that until the following year. Now there were endless activities, common principles, the momentum of an ongoing revolution. She was soon arrested and imprisoned. No sooner had she got out of prison than she proceeded to Kuokkala, Finland, where a group of Bolsheviks, including Lenin, were living in exile; and she joined them in intense discussions on the 1905 Revolution. It was in Kuokkala that she wrote one of her greatest pamphlets—the one on the mass strike, which she hoped to present to the German party so that they could see that it was not only a Russian event but could be "applied" in Germany.

When she returned to Germany and presented those ideas, she met with such great hostility that she wrote to Clara Zetkin on 20 March 1907:

The plain truth is that August [Bebel], and still more so the others, have completely pledged themselves to parliament and parliamentarianism, and whenever anything happens which transcends the limits of parliamentary action they are hopeless—no, worse than hopeless, because they then do their utmost to force the movement back into parliamentary channels, and they will furiously defame as "an enemy of the people" anyone who dares to venture beyond their own limits. I feel that those of the masses who are organized in the party are tired of parliamentarianism, and would welcome a new line in party tactics, but the party leaders and still more the upper stratum of opportunist editors, deputies, and trade union leaders are like an incubus. We must protest vigorously against this general stagnation, but it is quite clear that in doing so we shall find ourselves against the opportunists as well as the party leaders and August.

A Congress of all the tendencies in the Russian Marxist movement was to meet in London in April 1907,[6] and Rosa Luxemburg participated in a dual capacity—both as bearer of greetings from the German party and as Polish delegate.

An endless series of reports, analyses, disputes, and re-examinations continue to pour forth, very nearly ad infinitum, about the 1903 Second Congress, where the division between Menshevism and Bolshevism first appeared on the "Organizational Question." That avalanche notwithstanding, the 1907 Congress was pivotal because it centered about an actual revolution. It was that, *just that*, which became the Great Divide between Menshevism and Bolshevism, with *all* other tendencies needing to define themselves in relationship to it. As Luxemburg wrote to Emmanuel and Mathilde Wurm on 18 July 1906, while the revolution was still ongoing: "The revolution is magnificent. All else is bilge."

At the same time, it was that Congress which illuminates some of the major problems we face today. This is so in relationship not only to Rosa Luxemburg's life and thought, but to the very concept of the theory, the philosophy of revolution *in Marx.* Everyone at the Congress, no matter what their interpretation of that revolution was, focused on the 1848 German Revolution.[7] That intellectuals have paid so little attention to this Congress shows a great deal about how much more adept they are at rewriting history than at writing it.

Here we had a Congress where all tendencies came together to discuss a single topic which, though it seemed to be on the relationship to bourgeois parties was, in fact, on the nature of revolution. Here we had a Congress where everyone, everyone without exception, was present—be it a Plekhanov who was then a right-wing Menshevik and the only one who did not return to Russia during the revolution, or a Trotsky, who was the actual head of the first, and until 1917 the greatest, revolutionary Soviet, in St. Petersburg—as well as the one who drew a theory of Permanent Revolution out of the revolution of 1905;

be it a Lenin who was supposedly "all centralized organization," or a Luxemburg, who was "all spontaneity"; be it a Martov who was a left-wing Menshevik; or the Bund. Here was a Congress where all were talking about revolution—a very specific, ongoing revolution—and all were supposedly still grounded in the most unique philosophy, Marx's; where everything was fully recorded, so that it is very easy to prove or disprove almost any point of view. And yet, to this date, seventy-four years after the event, we are yet to have an English translation of the Minutes.* Why such total disregard for so revealing a Congress?

About all we have are participants' memoirs; and the authors of these are so busy emphasizing the "chaos" of the Congress that we get not a whiff of its significance.[8] Of course there was chaos; it began with the fight over the agenda precisely because the Mensheviks opposed Lenin's proposal that they put on the agenda the character of the present moment of revolution. And they were not alone. In supporting the Mensheviks, Trotsky, surprisingly enough, insisted that this Congress must be "business-like," must not go in for abstract theoretical resolutions: "What I want to say is that the Congress, from beginning to end, should be *political*, that it has to be a meeting of the representatives of revolutionary parties and not a discussion club . . . I need political directives and not philosophic discussions about the character of the present moment of our revolution . . . Give me a formula for action!"[9]

"Who would have thought that under such circumstances the proposal would be made to remove all questions of principles from the Congress agenda?" Lenin asked, as he offered his explanation: "What is this but sophistry? What is this but a helpless shift from adherence to principle, to lack of principle?"[10]

Later, Lenin expanded this to stress the relationship of theory to practice: "Our old disputes, our theoretical and tactical differences, always get transformed in the course of the revolution into direct practical disagreements. It's impossible to take any step in practical politics without bumping into these basic questions about the evaluation of the bourgeois revolution, about the relationship to the Cadets . . . Practice does not erase differences but enlivens them . . . "[11]

What Lenin had called "sophistry" does contain part of the answer to why the Fifth Congress has been so long disregarded, but it is not the whole answer, as is evident from the fact that, under the topic of relations of Marxists to bourgeois parties, the participants did, in fact, touch on the subject of the nature of the revolution. The full answer, rather, lies in the fact that most were not ready to stand up for the *theory* underlying their tactics; that is to say, the contradiction between theory and tactics was so glaring that evasiveness about the relationship of theory to practice ineluctably followed. The exceptions

*My translation of Luxemburg's first address to the Congress, given in Russian on 16 May 1907, appears as an appendix to this book.

were Luxemburg and Lenin. And even then it took Lenin a full decade, and the simultaneity of a world war and the collapse of the Second International headed by Karl Kautsky, before he would recognize Kautsky's affinity to the Mensheviks, and the right-wing Mensheviks at that.

THAT PIVOTAL YEAR: 1907

Luxemburg's personal break from Jogiches had come just before the London Congress, which both attended, and where they acted as one politically. That Luxemburg allowed none of the grave pressures—political and personal—to interfere with her very active participation and profound analysis of the burning question of the day, the Russian Revolution, was brilliantly clear from her three speeches to the Congress.[12]

In her very first speech, when she was merely supposed to be bringing greetings from the German party, Rosa Luxemburg, in fact, helped to determine the revolutionary character of the Congress, clearly separating herself from the Mensheviks. It is necessary here to reproduce at least the central point of that speech, which appears in full as an appendix:

> The Russian Social-Democracy is the first to whom has fallen the difficult but honorable task of applying the principles of Marx's teaching not in a period of quiet parliamentary course in the life of the state, but in a stormy revolutionary period. The only experience that scientific socialism had previously in practical politics during a revolutionary period was the activity of Marx himself in the 1848 revolution. The course itself of the 1848 revolution, however, cannot be a model for the present revolution in Russia. From it we can only learn how not to act in a revolution. Here was the schema of this revolution: the proletariat fights with its usual heroism but is unable to utilize its victories; the bourgeoisie drives the proletariat back in order to usurp the fruits of its struggle; finally, absolutism pushes the bourgeoisie aside in order to crush the proletariat as well as defeat the revolution . . .
>
> Marx supported the national struggles of 1848, holding that they were allies of the revolution. The politics of Marx consisted in this, that he pushed the bourgeoisie every moment to the limits of the revolutionary situation. Yes, Marx supported the bourgeoisie in the struggle against absolutism, but he supported it with whips and kicks . . .
>
> The Russian proletariat, in its actions, must show that between 1848 and 1907, in the more than half-century of capitalist development, and from the point of this development taken as a whole, we are not at the beginning but at the end of this development. It must show that the Russian Revolution is not just the last act in a series of bourgeois revolutions of the nineteenth century, but rather the forerunner of a new series of future proletarian revolutions in which the conscious proletariat and its vanguard, the Social-Democracy, are destined for the historic role of leader. (Applause.)

So sharply did Luxemburg express the class nature of the revolution, that what emerged was the relationship not only of the proletariat to the peasantry, but of the Russian Revolution to the international revolution. One could see, as well, the germ of future revolutions within the present revolution. What had been clear from the very start of Bloody Sunday when the Tsar's army fired on that first mass demonstration on 9 January 1905, was that Rosa Luxemburg was developing the question of continuous revolution.

And eight days before that mass demonstration, at the fall of Port Arthur to the Japanese in the Russo–Japanese war, Lenin had written: "Yes, the autocracy is weakened. The most skeptical of the skeptics are beginning to believe in the revolution. General belief in revolution is already the beginning of revolution ... The Russian proletariat will see to it that the serious revolutionary onset is sustained and extended."[13]

It is necessary to stress: revolution was in the air. Not only had both Mehring and Kautsky used the expression "permanent revolution" in the year 1905, but so had even the most right-wing of Mensheviks, Martynov. A good part of Trotsky's speech at the 1907 London Congress was devoted precisely to Martynov, contrasting the difference in his 1905 and 1907 positions. Lenin, of course, had seriously analyzed the *revolutionary* aspect of "the democratic revolution" going over "to the socialist revolution. We are for continuous revolution, and we shall not stop halfway" (14 September 1905). Ten days later he extended it even to Europe: "We shall make the Russian Revolution the prologue to the European socialist revolution."[14]

Nevertheless, it is true that it was Leon Trotsky alone who, at the conclusion of the 1905 Revolution, when he was in prison, created out of the 1905 events what later came to be known as a theory of Permanent Revolution. At the Congress, itself, however, that subject was not on the agenda. No whiff of it came from Trotsky, although Lenin, glad that Trotsky was voting for the Bolshevik resolution on the relationship to the bourgeois parties, said: "Quite apart from the question of 'uninterrupted revolution,' we have here solidarity on fundamental points in the question of the attitude toward bourgeois parties."

With much later hindsight, Trotsky referred to the affinity of Rosa Luxemburg's view to his on the question of Permanent Revolution in *My Life*: "On the question of the so-called Permanent Revolution, Rosa took the same stand as I did." At the Congress itself he said: "I can testify with pleasure that the point of view that Luxemburg developed in the name of the Polish delegation is very close to mine which I have defended and continue to defend. If between us, there is a difference, it's a difference of shade, and not of political direction. Our thought moves in one and the same materialistic analysis."[15]

But Luxemburg had not spoken on the question of Permanent Revolution, which was nowhere on the agenda. There is no doubt that, in speaking about the relationship of Marxists to the bourgeois parties, she was developing ideas of the dialectics of revolution and the role of the proletariat as vanguard. But it is more likely that what Trotsky suddenly found an affinity to, in Luxemburg's speech as Polish delegate, was her taking issue with Bolsheviks as well as Mensheviks. She had said: "True genuine Marxism is very far from a one-sided over-estimation of parliamentarianism as well as from a mechanistic view of revolution and over-estimation of the so-called armed uprising. On this point my Polish comrades and I differ from the views of the Bolshevik comrades."

However, she did not at all like the idea that the Mensheviks and other non-Bolsheviks suddenly applauded her; she decided to re-emphasize, in her concluding remarks, what she thought was the essence of her speech:[16]

> Truthfully speaking, the brouhaha into which my critics fell just because I tried seriously to illuminate the relationship of the proletariat to the bourgeoisie in our revolution seems odd to me. After all, there is no doubt that precisely this relationship, precisely the definition, above all, of the position of the proletariat in relationship to its social antipode, the bourgeoisie, constitutes the core of the dispute, is the crucial axis of proletarian politics around which the relationship to all other classes and groups, to the petty bourgeois, to the peasantry, and so forth, is crystallized. And once we conclude that the bourgeoisie in our revolution is not playing and cannot play the role of leader of the proletarian movement, then, in its very essence, it follows that their politics is counter-revolutionary, whereas we, in accordance with this, declare that the proletariat must look to itself, not as an assistant of bourgeois liberalism, but as vanguard to the revolutionary movement, which defines its politics independent of all other classes, deriving it exclusively from its own class tasks and interests . . .
>
> Plekhanov said: "For us Marxists the working peasant, as he appears in the contemporary commodity capitalist milieu, represents only one of the many petty, independent commodity producers, and, therefore, not without reason, we consider him to be part of the petty bourgeoisie." From this follows that the peasant, as petty bourgeois, is a reactionary social element of society, and he who considers him revolutionary, idolizes him and subordinates the independent politics of the proletariat to the influence of the petty bourgeoisie.
>
> Such an argument is, after all, only a classic example of the infamous metaphysical thinking according to the formula: "Yea, Yea; Nay, Nay; for whatsoever is more than these cometh of evil."[17] The bourgeoisie is a revolutionary class—and to say anything more than that cometh of evil. The peasantry is a reactionary class and to say anything more than that cometh of evil . . . [18]
>
> First of all, to try to make a mechanical transposition of the schema about the peasantry as a petty bourgeois reactionary layer onto the peasantry in a revolutionary period is, without doubt, a perversion of the historical dialectic. The role of the peasantry and the relationship of the proletariat to it is defined the same way as the role of the bourgeoisie, that is, not according to subjective desires and aims of those classes, but according to the objective situation. The Russian bourgeoisie is, despite its oral declamations and printed liberal programs, objectively a reactionary class, because its interests in the present social and historical situation compel a quick liquidation of the revolutionary movement by

concluding a rotten compromise with absolutism. As for the peasantry, despite
the confusion and contradictions in its demands, despite the fogginess in its
multi-colored aims—it is, in the present revolution, an objectively revolutionary
factor because it has placed the question of land seizure on the agenda of the
revolution, and because it thereby brings out the very question which is insoluble
within the framework of bourgeois society, and which therefore, by its very
nature, has to be solved outside of that framework.

It may be that just as the waves of revolution will recede, just as soon as the
land question finds, in the end, one or another solution in the spirit of bourgeois
private property, substantial layers of the Russian peasantry will again be
transformed into a clearly reactionary petty bourgeois party in the form of a
peasant union like the Bavarian Bauernbund. But so long as the revolution is
continuing, so long as the agrarian question is not solved, the peasant is not only a
political rock against absolutism but a social sphinx, and therefore constitutes an
independent ferment for revolution, giving it, together with the urban proletarian
movement, that wide expanse which relates to a spontaneous national movement.
From this flows the socialist utopian coloration of the peasant movement in
Russia, which is not at all the fruit of the artificial grafting and demagogy of the
Social Revolutionary Party, but that which accompanies all great peasant
uprisings of bourgeois society. It is enough to remember the Peasant Wars in
Germany and the name of Thomas Münzer.

Luxemburg also took issue with Plekhanov who had said: "Comrade Lieber
asked Comrade Rosa Luxemburg on which chair is she sitting. Naive question!
Comrade Rosa Luxemburg is not sitting on any chair. She, like Raphael's
Madonna, reclines on clouds . . . lost in day dreams . . . " But, in this case, it is
better to quote Lenin who had risen to his feet on that point, not for purposes of
defending Luxemburg, who needed no defense, but to stress what a miserable
evasion of the whole point of social revolution was Plekhanov's speech:
"Plekhanov spoke about Rosa Luxemburg, picturing her as a Madonna
reclining on clouds. What could be finer! Elegant, gallant and effective
polemics . . . But I would nevertheless like to ask Plekhanov about *the
substance* of the question? (Applause from the Center and the Bolsheviks.)
After all, it is a pretty bad thing to have to resort to a Madonna in order to avoid
analysing the point at issue. Madonna or not—what must our attitude be
towards 'a Duma with full powers'?"[19]

And, indeed, there was a great deal more involved than just the topic under
discussion, because what they were really discussing was: who were the
genuine forces of revolution—the proletariat and the peasantry or the
bourgeoisie? Lenin had already written about the "inborn creativeness" of the
masses, had called the Soviets "embryos of revolutionary power," and in
singling out the proletariat, considered it not only force but reason:

The point is that it is precisely the revolutionary periods that are distinguished
for their greater breadth, greater wealth, greater intelligence, greater and more
systematic activity, greater audacity and vividness of historical creativeness

compared with periods of philistine, Cadet, reformist progress . . . They shout about the disappearance of sense and reason, when the picking to pieces of parliamentary bills by all sorts of bureaucrats and liberal "penny-a-liners" gives way to a period of direct political activity by the "common people," who in their simple way directly and immediately destroy the organs of oppression of the people, seize power, appropriate for themselves what was considered to be the property of all sorts of plunderers of the people—in a word, precisely when the sense and reason of millions of downtrodden people is awakening, not only for reading books, but for action, for living human action, for historical creativeness.[20]

And for Rosa Luxemburg, too, it was not only "the proletariat supported by the peasantry" but, as we shall see from her 1906 pamphlet on the General Strike, she was already posing totally new questions of spontaneity and organization—and not only about this revolution, but about future revolutions. That, in fact, it was a question of wars and revolutions became ever clearer in that pivotal year of 1907, as they all prepared to go to the International Congress in Stuttgart in August.

At that Congress, what, not accidentally, became known as the "Luxemburg–Lenin Anti-War Amendment" (though it was not only Lenin but also Trotsky and Plekhanov who helped Luxemburg to formulate it) was meant to issue a warning to the bourgeoisie that, if they dared to start a war, the masses of Social-Democratic workers would oppose it. As Luxemburg put it in her speech to the International: "Our agitation in case of war is not only aimed at ending that war, but at *using* the war to hasten the *general collapse of class rule.*"[21]

In that same month of August 1907, just before the Stuttgart Congress met, Luxemburg was also involved in the International Socialist Women's Conference. There she reported on the work of the International Socialist Bureau; she was the only woman member of that august body. Urging the women to keep their center for the Socialist Women's Movement in Stuttgart, and stressing the importance of having a voice of their own, i.e., *Gleichheit*, she concluded: "I can only admire Comrade Zetkin that she has taken this burden of work upon herself."[22] In a word, far from Luxemburg having no interest in the so-called "Woman Question," and far from Zetkin having no interest outside of that question, the truth is that both of them—as well as Kollontai and Balabanoff and Roland-Holst—were determined to build a women's liberation movement that concentrated not only on organizing women workers but on having them develop as leaders, as decision-makers, and as independent Marxist revolutionaries.

* * *

Through that Fifth Congress of the RSDLP in London in 1907, when all tendencies were discussing the 1905 Revolution, 1907 let us witness the dress rehearsal for 1917. And just as that Russian Congress was followed by the

International Congress in Stuttgart where Luxemburg–Lenin attempted, with revolutionary antiwar politics, to prepare the proletariat to meet the challenge of the coming war, so what preceded the International Congress—the first International Socialist Women's Conference—proved that a new revolutionary force—women—had arisen which, in embryo, would become the genuine center of international antiwar activity at the very moment when the parent organization, the German Social-Democracy, would collapse once the imperialist war broke out. That pivotal year, 1907, was also the year when Rosa Luxemburg, a brilliant teacher of theory at the Party School, began "to apply" to a technologically advanced land what she had learned from the Russian Revolution, a development which was to lead to her break with Karl Kautsky in 1910. Therefore, it is imperative that we now turn to her Mass Strike pamphlet and grapple with that totally new phenomenon, the concrete relationship of spontaneity to organization.

NOTES

1. See her letter to Leo Jogiches, 1 May 1899, which makes reference to an anti-Semitic Polish jingle: "Hard up—what to do? / Go to the Jew. / Hard times are through? / Out the door, Jew!"

2. Paul Frölich, *Rosa Luxemburg: Her Life and Work* (New York: Monthly Review Press, 1972), p. 14.

3. Rosa Luxemburg, *Reform or Revolution*, trans. by Integer (New York: Three Arrows Press, 1937), p. 47.

4. Ibid, p. 50.

5. Luxemburg's pamphlet, *The Mass Strike*, is included in *Rosa Luxemburg Speaks*, Mary-Alice Waters, ed. (New York: Pathfinder Press, 1970), pp. 155-218.

6. The formal name of the Russian Marxist organization was Russian Social-Democratic Labor Party, abbreviated in Russian as RSDRP, in English as RSDLP.

7. We will later develop the fact that no one, nevertheless, drew the same conclusions as did Karl Marx in his 1850 Address to the Communist League following the defeat of the 1848 revolution. See chap. XI.

8. In *My Life* (New York: Pathfinder Press, 1970), p. 202, Trotsky writes: "It was a protracted, crowded, stormy and chaotic Congress." And in *Impressions of Lenin* (Ann Arbor: Univ. of Michigan Press, 1964), p. 17, Angelica Balabanoff stresses that "The discussion about the inversion of the agenda alone lasted over a week."

9. From "Minutes of the 1907 Fifth Congress of the RSDLP," in *Pyati Londonskii S'esd RSDRP, Aprel'-mai 1907 goda, Protokoly* (Marx-Engels Institute, Moscow: 1963), p. 49. (My translation.)

10. Lenin, *Collected Works*, 12: 439-40.

11. Ibid., p. 446. Lenin's concluding remarks at the May 14 session of the Fifth Congress.

12. In Luxemburg's first speech (which was to be the greetings from the German party) she presented her analysis of 1905. Her second speech was her summation following the discussion on her analysis. In her third speech, she spoke as Polish delegate.

13. Lenin, *Collected Works*, 8:54. Not to be forgotten is the demonstrative way the Russian and Polish Marxists displayed their internationalism. Thus, Lenin shook the hand of the Japanese Marxist leader, Sen Katayama, in the midst of the Russo-Japanese war, to demonstrate their total

opposition to their own governments. Rosa Luxemburg and other leaders of the International were included in a group photograph with Katayama.

See also Ivar Spector, *The First Russian Revolution: Its Impact on Asia* (New Jersey: Prentice-Hall, 1962). This study, which develops the impact of the 1905 Revolution on Iran, China and India, is also important for its Appendices, which reproduce the original "Petition of the Workers and Residents of St. Petersburg for Submission to Nicholas II on January 9, 1905," as well as the Soviet article on the twentieth anniversary of that Revolution by M. Pavlovitch. For the relationship of that revolution and its impact on the 1979 revolution in Iran, see my Political-Philosophic Letter, "Iran: Unfoldment of, and Contradictions in, Revolution" (Detroit: News & Letters, 1979).

14. Vol. 9 of Lenin's *Collected Works* contains all his writings on 1905 from June to November. See also Solomon Schwartz, *The Russian Revolution of 1905* (Chicago: Univ. of Chicago Press, 1967), especially his Introduction, pp. 1-28. See also my Afterword to chap. XI, pp. 165-73.

15. "Minutes of Fifth Congress," p. 397. (My translation.)

16. Excerpted from "Minutes of Fifth Congress," pp. 432-37. (My translation.)

17. Luxemburg is quoting from the Sermon on the Mount, *Matt., 5:37*.

18. Luxemburg is here being sarcastic about the way the "authoritative" Plekhanov had quoted the section of the *Communist Manifesto* in which Marx speaks of the bourgeoisie as being a revolutionary class in the overthrow of feudalism, as if that were applicable to the 1905 Russian Revolution.

19. Lenin, *Collected Works*, 12:471.

20. Lenin, *Selected Works* (New York: International Pub., 1943), 7:261. This 1906 pamphlet, *The Victory of the Cadets and the Tasks of the Workers' Party*, remained so integral to Lenin that he quoted large sections of it, after gaining power, in an article, "A Contribution to the Question of Dictatorship," published in 1920.

21. Luxemburg's speech and the Resolution are included in the Stuttgart Congress protocol. See Nettl, *Rosa Luxemburg*, 1:399-401.

22. See Rosa Luxemburg, *Gesammelte Werke*, vol. 2 (Berlin: Dietz Verlag, 1974), for her speech to the International Socialist Women's Conference held 17-19 August 1907, first published in *Vorwärts*, No. 192, 18 August 1907. See also Alexandra Kollontai, *Women Workers Struggle for Their Rights* (Bristol: Falling Wall Press, 1971), and Angelica Balabanoff, *My Life as a Rebel* (Bloomington: Indiana Univ. Press, 1973).

II

The Break with Kautsky, 1910–11: From Mass Strike Theory to Crisis Over Morocco—and Hushed-Up "Woman Question"

SPONTANEITY AND ORGANIZATION; SPONTANEITY AND CONSCIOUSNESS

Once spontaneity had taken the form of an outright revolution, Luxemburg's usual sensitivity to the phenomenon took on the dimension of a universal, *the* method of revolution. As she had written to Luise Kautsky early in 1906, soon after Luxemburg landed in Poland in December 1905: "The *mere general strike alone* has ceased to play the role it once had. Now nothing but a direct, general fight on the street can bring about the decision . . . "[1]

By mid-August, when Luxemburg was working on *The Mass Strike, the Party and the Trade Unions,*[2] it was clear that, far from the pamphlet's being restricted to the topics in the title, Luxemburg was, in fact, beginning to question not just the conservative trade union leadership, but the relation of Marxist leadership to spontaneity. She had always been highly responsive to proletarian acts of spontaneity. What was different this time was that the 1905 Revolution had disclosed a totally new relationship also to Marxist leadership. The most exciting new phenomenon was that the so-called backward Russian workers had proved themselves far in advance of those in the technologically advanced countries, particularly Germany. Moreover, the Russian Revolution was not just a national happening. In its impact on both East and West, it had displayed an elemental force and reason of *world* scope. Luxemburg at once began working out its application to Germany.

In a word, spontaneity did not mean just instinctive action as against conscious direction. Quite the contrary: spontaneity was a driving force, not only of revolution but of the vanguard leadership, keeping it left. As Luxemburg expressed it in her pamphlet: "The element of spontaneity, as we have seen, plays a great part in all Russian mass strikes without exception, be it as a driving force or as a restraining influence . . . In short, in the mass strikes in Russia, the element of spontaneity plays such a predominant part, not because the Russian proletariat are 'uneducated,' but because revolutions do not allow anyone to play the schoolmaster with them."

In working out the dialectic of the mass strike, Luxemburg moved from her characteristic search for "root cause" to a concentration, instead, on the interrelationship of cause and effect. History had shifted the question of the general strike from its anarchist nonpolitical "origins" to its genuine political nature. The 1905 Revolution actually revealed, Luxemburg maintained, "the historical liquidation of anarchism." Marxist leadership of the general strike signified the *unity* of economics and politics.

She traced the history of the strikes in Russia from 1896 to 1905 and concluded: "Throughout the whole of the spring of 1905 and into the middle of the summer there fermented throughout the whole of the immense empire an uninterrupted economic strike of almost the entire proletariat against capital . . . " Nor was it only a question of the general strike's embracing the entire proletariat. For the first time she was impressed even with what she disliked most—the lumpen proletariat. The revolution irradiated the genius of all people, and the revolutionary masses in motion "even knocked at the gates of the military barracks."

Luxemburg proceeded to show the effectiveness of the strikes: how the fight for an eight-hour day meant its immediate institution, even before the outbreak of the revolution in January 1905. The oil workers in Baku won the eight-hour day in December 1904; the printing workers in Samara in January 1905; the sugar workers in Kiev in May 1905. By the time of the October Days and the second general strike, the economic struggle formed "a broad background of the revolution from which, in ceaseless reciprocal action with the political agitation and the external events of the revolution, there ever arise, here and there, now isolated explosions and now great general actions of the proletariat . . . " Naturally, the question of the soldiers' revolts in Kronstadt, Libau, Vladivostok were singled out to show the breadth and depth of the revolution: *"Within a week the eight-hour day prevailed in every factory and workshop in Petersburg . . . "*

Once one recognizes that this was the essence of what Luxemburg considered to be the genius of revolution, then it is clear that—with her specific historic examples of how many mass strikes, what duration they ran, and how they were transformed from an economic to a general political strike leading in turn to "a general popular uprising"—she was actually developing a strategy of revolution. Moreover, she was developing it not only on the basis of Russia, a "backward" country, but also with eyes fixed on technologically advanced

Germany. Clearly, it was no longer a question just of experience, much less just a national experience, but a universal phenomenon that was so little separated from any national boundaries that it eliminated the difference between national and international as well as the difference between theory and practice.

In dwelling in detail on the mass strike in October, November, and December, Luxemburg not only emphasized how "the workers threw themselves with fiery zeal into the waves of political freedom," but stressed especially the fact that the proletariat's intellectual development was boundless: "The most precious, because lasting, thing in this rapid ebb and flow of the wave is its mental sediment: the intellectual, cultural growth of the proletariat." By the time Luxemburg came to the question of organization, of daily political meetings, of formation of clubs, she dealt with the question of trade unionism as something the new force of workers had "immediately taken in hand." What is especially striking about that new force "taking unions in hand" is that it was concerned not only with the organized but with the unorganized workers.

Put differently, Luxemburg was against the trade union leadership not only because they were conservative, but because they were concerned only with organized workers, whereas the unorganized workers, she showed, were every bit as revolutionary and important. And just as she included even the lumpen proletariat as likewise affected by the storm of revolution, so she drew into the totality and genius of spontaneity everyone from the lumpen proletariat to the artist as being in this great whirlwind of revolution. What, amazingly, was not singled out to the point of making it a universal was the soviet form of organization. However, the whole question of organization—be it the small Marxist organization that became a mass organization literally overnight, a mass organization, or totally new forms of organization like the soviets—had henceforth become inseparable from *mass* activity.

From 1906 until the break with Kautsky, 1910–11, Luxemburg kept singling out the general strike—the interrelationship of economic and political work that "formed a broad background of the revolution." Her historical tracing of strikes from 1896 to 1905, and her detailed examination of the actual 1905–06 Revolution, led her to the conclusion that the mass strike is: "*The method of motion of the proletarian mass*, the phenomenal form of the proletarian struggle in revolution . . . in a word: the economic struggle is the transmitter from one political center to another; the political struggle is the periodic fertilization of the soil for the economic struggle. Cause and effect here continually change places . . . Finally, the events in Russia show us that the mass strike is inseparable from the revolution."

Finally, Luxemburg approached the question of applying the lessons of the Russian Revolution to the German scene: "A year of revolution has therefore given the Russian proletariat that 'training' which 30 years of parliamentary and trade union struggles cannot artifically give to the German proletariat."

No doubt Luxemburg did not know then (1906) that her climactic ending—
that "the masses will be the active chorus and the leaders only the 'speaking
parts,' the interpreters of the will of the masses"—was actually laying the
ground, not only for her usual fights with the trade union leaders, but for a fight
with the established German Social-Democratic (that is, Marxist) leadership.
But, in fact, this was what happened in 1910. And since in that concrete period
and place we will best see both the ramifications of her 1906 general strike
thesis, as well as her sensitivity to the smell of opportunism in the highest levels
of "orthodox Marxism," it is necessary to delve deeper into 1910.

UNIFIED REVOLUTIONARY THEORY–PRACTICE VS "TWO STRATEGIES"

Luxemburg considered the interaction of economic strikes and political
demonstrations to be a pre-revolutionary situation. In 1910 she felt it
opportune to begin applying to Germany the lessons of the General Mass
Strike she had drawn from the Russian Revolution. Not only was it a year when
a new wave of strikes broke out in Germany, but on 4 February, when the
government published the draft of the so-called electoral "reform" bill, with its
three-class-tier voting limitations, there was mobilization of mass opposition.
Every single Sunday during the months of February and March there were
massive demonstrations for equal suffrage. At the same time, the waves of
strikes that had begun the year continued and expanded. Carl Schorske shows
that no less than 370,000 workers were involved in work stoppages that year.[3]

In mid-February, Luxemburg had written an analysis of the current
situation in relationship to the principle of the General Mass Strike. She
entitled it "What Next?"[4] and submitted it to the party paper, *Vorwärts*. It was
returned to her with a note saying that the "Executive" had instructed the
paper not to carry on agitation for the mass strike at present, when what was
most important was the electoral campaign. Luxemburg, on the contrary,
thought that it was precisely the present situation, both on the question of the
struggle for electoral reform and on the question of strikes, that made
discussion of the General Mass Strike relevant. She resubmitted the article,
this time to the theoretical organ *Neue Zeit*, of which, in name, she was deputy
editor. Where, heretofore, Luxemburg had considered the prestigious Party
School and her theoretical work in it to be so important that she allowed
nothing to divert her from it, this time her priority went to the need for agitation.
She took two months off from teaching at the Party School to go barnstorming
throughout Germany. Her talks both on suffrage and on work stoppages
naturally included the idea of a General Mass Strike. The opposition to
Luxemburg that had opened in the top echelons of the German Social-
Democracy (SPD) was revealed in some curious ways. Thus, while all the
papers in Frankfurt, for example, were reporting on Luxemburg's speeches
one way, *Vorwärts* struck out one sentence of the report, to wit: "The speaker

evoked the enthusiastic approval of the participants when she advocated propaganda for the mass strike." Luxemburg, meanwhile, was doing her reporting to Luise Kautsky. One letter dated 15 March 1910, described how many meetings she addressed, how large they were, and how enthusiastically she had been met by the last one, at which the audience had numbered fifteen hundred.

At the end of the two months' lecture tour, Luxemburg returned to Berlin. There she found a note from Karl Kautsky, as editor of *Neue Zeit*, that said her article was "important" and "very beautiful," but he suggested that the paragraph propagandizing for a republic be cut. Meanwhile, Kautsky was polemicizing against her views. She at once saw to it that her article was published in *Leipziger Volkszeitung*. As for the paragraph on the question of a republic, she had developed it into a separate article, and had that published as well—which did not mean that she would let Kautsky off the hook for not publishing her article, much less for starting a polemic against her views without even having published them.

Kautsky had opened up the floodgates of a dispute with Luxemburg that was to take up an inordinate amount of space of the most prestigious journal in the German Social-Democracy, which in this case meant *established* world Marxism. It presaged the birth of a new wave of opportunism, which soon led to the break with Kautsky. Luxemburg was out to expose that it was not just the trade union leaders and reformists who were opportunists. She was out to show that opportunism was eating at the very vitals of the Marxist leadership: the German Social-Democracy.

To this day, even those revolutionaries who, armed with hindsight, do see that the dispute between Luxemburg and Kautsky first exposed the abysmal opportunism at the top which ultimately led to nothing short of the party's betrayal, still act as if Luxemburg's prescient stand was "accidental." The truth is that Luxemburg sensed opportunism four years ahead of anyone else, Lenin included. The truth is that long before the party's outright betrayal at the outbreak of World War I, Luxemburg saw in the Social-Democracy's slavish parliamentarianism so great a diversion from the revolutionary road that she felt compelled not to let go of the "tactic" of general strike until all those who opposed it were shown to be opportunists. To try to deflate the dispute as if it were a mere "personal matter," and to say that it was simply that Luxemburg felt "insulted" at Kautsky's refusal to publish her article, is to blind oneself to just how historic, what a great determinant for world Marxist development, was Luxemburg's break with Kautsky.

Luxemburg's writings in that period demonstrate that, far from the "Luxemburg affair" causing the disturbance in the SPD, it was the objective situation, the actual strikes and the actual struggles for electoral reform, that caused the crisis. Her position rightly was: why let anyone, even if he were internationally recognized as the "greatest Marxist," gild the lily of parliamentarianism with "heaven-storming theory" when, in fact, that theory was nothing but a rationale for opportunist actions?

As was his wont in any debate, Kautsky was trotting out a brand new theory. The "strategy of attrition" ("*Ermattungsstrategie*") and "strategy of overthrow" ("*Niederwerfungsstrategie*"), culled from ancient Roman history, were now used with a great claim to erudition—but in a very different form than that used when those "two strategies" had first been introduced, in 1907 in Kautsky's *Social Revolution* and in 1909 in his *Road to Power*. Now (1910) in his "Theory and Practice" article, said Luxemburg, these same theories, which had been used in favor of the 1905 Revolution, had become "a frightfully fundamental revision" of the 1905 Resolution passed at the Jena Congress which recognized the general strike as the method of revolution—and not only for Russia.[5]

Luxemburg hit back with everything she could, entitling her article the same as Kautsky's. First she quoted from her own pamphlet on the mass strike:

So the mass strike shows itself to be no specifically Russian product, arising from absolutism, but a *universal form of proletarian class struggle resulting from the present stage of capitalist development and class relations.* From this standpoint, the three bourgeois revolutions—the great French revolution, the German March revolution, and the present Russian one—form an onrunning chain of development in which the prosperity and the end of the bourgeois century are reflected . . . The present revolution realizes, in the special circumstances of absolutist Russia, the universal results of international capitalist development; and in this *it seems less a final posterity of the old bourgeois revolutions than a forerunner of a new series of proletarian revolutions in the West.* Just because it has so inexcusably delayed its bourgeois revolution, the most backward land shows *ways and methods of extended class struggle for the proletariat of Germany and the most advanced capitalist lands.*[6]

Then she quoted Kautsky in 1910 portraying how "chaotic" the peasant uprisings of 1905 were and how "inapplicable" they were to Germany. She contrasted these 1910 statements to what he had written in 1907, holding that it was a reversal of the truth as to both facts and theory.

Kautsky, she continued, had written in his "Theory and Practice" article that he was re-establishing true Marxian dialectics "against the distortion of the dialectic totality through an over-emphasis on the limited and purely political aim." Luxemburg exposed Kautsky's claim as follows:

The picture of chaotic, "amorphous, primitive" strikes by the Russian workers . . . is a blooming fantasy . . . These strikes, from which as bold a creation as the famous St. Petersburg Council of Workers' Delegates was born for unified leadership of the entire movement in the giant empire—these Russian strikes and mass strikes were so far from being "amorphous and primitive" that in boldness, strength, class solidarity, tenacity, material gains, progressive aims and organizational results, they could safely be set alongside any "West European" union movement [pp. 18, 19].

In fact, Luxemburg insisted, the so-called two strategies of "attrition" and "overthrow" for which Kautsky was making that "crude contrast between revolutionary Russia and parliamentary Western Europe" was "nothing but a rationalization of Kautsky's refusal to favor a mass strike." Furthermore, she continued, spontaneity in the Russian mass strikes was not lacking in "a rational" strike leadership as Kautsky now claimed, but in fact, both as rational leadership and as spontaneous strikes, the General Mass Strike in Russia achieved more, concretely, for the Russian proletariat, than any "plan" of the SPD.

In her "Theory and Practice" article, she stressed that the so-called "two strategies," far from being "historically" justifiable, were a total deviation from the burning questions of the here and now—the 1910 strikes and demonstrations, as well as the preparations for the 1912 election. Not only was the real issue whether or not the SPD should, under the concrete circumstances of the day, agitate for a General Mass Strike, but with Kautsky the whole relationship of theory to practice was thereby made very nearly irreconcilable: "Heaven-storming theory—and 'attrition' in practice; most revolutionary perspectives in the clouds—and Reichstag mandates as sole perspective in reality . . . It seems that 'theory' does not merely 'stride forward' more slowly than 'practice': alas, from time to time it also goes tumbling backwards . . . Reichstag elections and mandates—that is Moses and the prophets!" (pp. 53, 52).

Finally, with her article, "Attrition or Collision?",[7] Luxemburg moved in, if not for the kill, certainly for the denouement of Kautsky's "history culling." Suppose, she wrote, that we could see some relevance for our day in those two strategies in ancient Rome; it would still remain a fact that the way Kautsky tells history, it is totally false. The great historian Mommsen has long since shown that the inventor of the theory of attrition, Fabius Cunctator, became "famous" for his "masterly inaction" theory since, far from winning any battles against Hannibal, he earned such infamy that the Romans decided not to suffer any longer from his generalship and had him replaced.

As she had already shown in both "Theory and Practice" and "Attrition or Collision?", this stretching into Roman history—which was supposedly more relevant to the 1910 dispute than were her articles on the General Mass Strike—was not only irrelevant but totally false. All it did was to lead Kautsky into glorifying German history as a "century of Prussian glory." As she pointed out in "Our Struggle for Power":

> And now let's take a look at the wars which Germany has fought in the meantime. The first was the "glorious" Chinese war, whose slogan ran: Prisoners will not be taken, etc. Then in 1904 came the even more glorious

Herero war. The Hereros are a Negro people who for centuries have clung to their native soil, and made it fertile with their sweat. Their "crime" lay in this: that they would not spinelessly surrender themselves to the rapacious robber barons of industry, to the white slave owners; that they defended their homeland against foreign invaders. In this war as well, German arms richly covered themselves with—renown. Herr von Trotha issued the well-known general order: every Negro found armed will be shot down—no quarter will be given. The men were shot; women and children by the hundreds were hunted into the burning desert, and the wreath of their parched bones bleaches in the murderous Omaheke—a glory garland of German arms![8]

"THE MOROCCO INCIDENT"

Ever since she had landed in Germany, back in 1898, and plunged into the debate against reformism, the question that kept cropping up was what we now call the "Third World." No matter what the year, no matter what the place, no matter whether it was a question of theory or of practice, with hawkeyed scrutiny she followed advanced capitalism's extension into imperialism. As we saw in the first chapter, Luxemburg had written to Jogiches in 1899 (in fact, it was published in the *Leipziger Volkszeitung* on 13 March 1899) that a new shift in global politics had been taking place ever since 1895, when Japan attacked China. Moreover, it wasn't only a question of Japan's imperialist intrusion. There was the German imperialist venture, the Anglo–Boer war, and the United States' intrusion into Latin America.

Now, in 1910, she found no less than a Kautsky lauding a "century of Prussian glory," as if it had not been personified by Wilhelm II's exhortation to the German soldiers in that "Hunn campaign"[9] to emulate their ancestors the Hunns and teach the Chinese a lesson in "frightfulness." The Chinese didn't forget; but they remembered it by exploding into an anti-imperialist popular uprising in northern China in 1899!

In 1900, at the very first Congress Luxemburg attended when she became a German citizen, she had already projected a need for anticolonial action. On 15 May 1902, she had an article in the *Leipziger Volkszeitung* on imperialist maneuvers worldwide, specifically in Martinique. In 1905, with the first "Morocco incident" she at once raised questions of antimilitarism and anti-imperialism.

As we see, her prescience of the pervasive opportunism in Karl Kautsky, when he was still considered the authoritative voice of Marxism, was by no means limited to the question of the General Mass Strike or that of suffrage, but was integral to her very concept of what is a proletarian revolution.

No doubt the SPD leadership thought they had brought her down to size when the congress that year rejected her resolution "that the fight for suffrage in Prussia can be waged to victory only through great determined mass action in which all means must be employed, including the political general strike if necessary."[10] But the 1910 battles with Kautsky and Bebel had no sooner ended than it once again became clear to her that the question of fighting opportunism was not only a matter of domestic policies, but of international policy.

On 1 July 1911 the German gunboat *Panther* sailed into Morocco. The first letters of the International Socialist Bureau that Luxemburg received as a member of the Bureau showed that the leadership was a great deal more concerned with the electoral battles in Germany than with Germany's imperialistic act in Morocco. Indeed, not only was no struggle against their government proposed at the moment, and not only was the news presented as if peace rather than war was in the air, but it was clear that the only thing that worried the SPD was that any opposition might harm the electoral victory they counted on for the 1912 elections.

Luxemburg published the "private" letter and her own analysis in the *Leipziger Volkszeitung* of 24 July 1911. When more letters and leaflets, each one more ambivalent than the one before, continued to flow her way, she wrote the sharpest of all critiques, "Our Morocco Leaflet," which appeared in the *Leipziger Volkszeitung* of 26 August 1911, after the executive manifesto had been published in *Vorwärts* of 9 August 1911. Luxemburg castigated the pusillanimity, not to mention belatedness, of the executive manifesto for any serious struggle against the war-mongering bourgeoisie. Instead of a serious Marxist analysis of a burning issue, she said, they were getting "Social-Democratic political twaddle." By now the question was more than "an international policy in general, and the Morocco affair in particular." What was imperative for German Marxists was an exposé as to how the "Morocco affair" was related to the "*internal* development of German militarism . . . and Germany's urge for world power." She concluded: "Let us add that in the whole of the leaflet there is not one word about the native inhabitants of the colonies, not a word about their rights, interests, and sufferings because of international policy. The leaflet repeatedly speaks of 'England's splendid colonial policy' without mentioning the periodic famine and spread of typhoid in India, extermination of the Australian aborigines, and the hippopotamus-hide lash on the backs of the Egyptian fellah."[11]

Whereupon, all the furies descended upon her for "breach of discipline," "disloyalty," and "indiscretion" for having published a letter meant only for the eyes of the ISB.

By the time the 1911 Congress opened in September the Executive Committee tried to reduce the question to what Luxemburg had done, and when she had done it, as if it were only a question of making public what had been sent to her in confidence. The name of the SPD was still so great, and the question of imperialism was still so far distant and unrelated to organizational growth, that the leadership succeeded in diverting attention from the political analysis to the question of "a breach of discipline."

TONE DEAFNESS TO MALE CHAUVINISM

In the process of the debate on the so-called "breach of discipline," male chauvinism had raised its ugly head, as we will shortly see. That it was not only male chauvinism's ugly head, but that of imperialism which the German Social-Democracy was not up to confronting, as Luxemburg rightly insisted, is seen clearest at the meeting of the International Socialist Bureau in Zurich, on 23 September 1911, the week after the Congress in Jena. There, with international representatives like Lenin present and voting, they withdrew their motion to censure Luxemburg, but managed, with the support of others, like Plekhanov, to contain the discussion over the Morocco crisis. Thus, when Lenin came to Luxemburg's defense, Zinoviev reported, "the thunder and lightning descended upon him as well. Vladimir Ilich appealed to Plekhanov . . . but . . . Com. Plekhanov replied that the ear should not grow beyond the forehead, that we (Russians) should keep silent; that when we had millions of members as the German Social-Democracy had, then we should also be considered. But for the time being we were merely 'poor relations.' After listening to Plekhanov, Vladimir Ilich slammed the door and left the meeting."[12]

The minutes of the SPD Congress in Jena[13] the week before tell the whole story: male chauvinism dominated the discussion on "the Morocco incident."

There was also some humor in the discussion, for, as Luxemburg put it: "When the party executive asserts something, I would never dare not to believe it, for as a faithful party member the old saying holds for me: *Credo quia absurdum*—I believe it precisely because it is absurd" (p. 204). And later she turned to Bebel, whom she accused of hearing only with his "right ear" (i.e., from the most conservative benches, where the Baden delegates sat): "In all my life, I have never seen a picture of such pathetic confusion. (Laughter. Bebel shouts: Now, now!) This is why I am not cross with you for your accusations. I forgive you and offer you the fatherly advice (Bebel: The motherly advice. Great amusement.): do better in the future" (p. 207).

Even when there were hisses for Luxemburg's attitude to Bebel, there was also great applause for her antimilitarist stand. Clearly, there was a deep antimilitarist and anticolonialist feeling in the German Social-Democracy. As Ledebour (who was no friend of Luxemburg's) put it, rising to her defense:

> As I prophesied, a trap was set for Rosa Luxemburg out of the publication of the letter, and they made use of the truly unjustified over-haste with which she criticized the leaflet. All that is being used to disguise the real heart of the matter. Com. Luxemburg has frequently come into conflict with me . . . we will come into conflict even more often . . . (but) the mass demonstrations against war and warmongers such as have taken place are not the achievement of Müller and the executive . . . but of Com. Luxemburg, through her critique [p. 212].

It wasn't for lack of awareness about the pervasive male chauvinism that Luxemburg acted tone deaf to it. But so determined was she that nothing should divert from the political issues in dispute that she allowed the leaders to hush up the matter, though it involved her own leadership. It had been her principle always to ignore any sign of male chauvinism, not even letting the word pass her lips. It isn't that she wasn't aware of its existence, but she held that since it was due to capitalism, it could be abolished only with the abolition of capitalism. Just as she had learned to live with an underlying anti-Semitism in the party,[14] so she learned to live with what in our era has been challenged by name—specifically, male chauvinism. She took no issue with it, though it was obvious that the polemics against her, now that she openly disagreed with the core of the orthodox leadership, had an extra-sharp edge which no male opponent had to suffer. Here, for example, is a sample of the letters that passed between Bebel and Adler:

> The poisonous bitch will yet do a lot of damage, all the more because she is as clever as a monkey (*blitzgescheit*) while on the other hand her sense of responsibility is totally lacking and her only motive is an almost perverse desire for self-justification . . . [Victor Adler to August Bebel, 5 August 1910].
> With all the wretched female's squirts of poison I wouldn't have the party without her [Bebel's reply to Adler, 16 August 1910].[15]

Male chauvinism was far from being just a creeping phenomenon in the *established* revolutionary socialist movement, nor was it confined to some rank-and-file members. In a well-documented thesis, "Clara Zetkin: A Left-wing Socialist and Feminist in Wilhelmian Germany,"[16] we see that, on the very same day that Bebel wrote the letter to Adler just quoted (16 August 1910), he wrote to Karl Kautsky: "It is an odd thing about women. If their partialities or passions or vanities come anywhere into question and are not given consideration, or, let alone, are injured, then even the most intelligent of them flies off the handle and becomes hostile to the point of absurdity. Love and hate lie side by side, a regulating reason does not exist."

Virulent male chauvinism permeated the whole party, including both August Bebel, the author of *Woman and Socialism*—who had created a myth about himself as a veritable feminist—and Karl Kautsky, the main theoretician of the whole International. Thus, after Luxemburg's break with Kautsky in 1911, when Zetkin also supported Luxemburg's position, and as they faced an approaching Party Congress in 1913, Kautsky warned Bebel: "the two females and their followers are planning an attack on all central positions." None of this changed the standing of that fundamental text of the socialist women's movement, *Woman and Socialism*, which had gone through innumerable editions.[17]

The myth very nearly continues to this day, and in any case, in the 1910–11 period, the authority of both the SPD in general and Bebel in particular on the

"Woman Question" was unchallenged anywhere in the world at the very time he was co-organizing the campaign against Luxemburg. It is high time to turn to this question now. This is not only because the hushed-up phenomenon of the "Woman Question" is totally unacceptable to women's liberationists today, but because it is only today that Marx's very different concept of women's liberation is first being grappled with. It is no accident that only in our own day—one hundred years after they were first written—have Marx's very last researches, *The Ethnological Notebooks of Karl Marx*, been published.[18]

It is therefore only now that we can see that not only had the "young Marx" in 1844 raised the Man/Woman relationship as a most important pivot in that new continent of thought he was discovering—a "New Humanism"—but that the mature Marx in the very last years of his life, 1880–83, was engaged in the latest research in ethnology as well as in answering the sharpest question raised on the concrete scene of Russia and on the concrete relationship between the "West" and the "East," that is, between the technologically advanced and the most backward countries. That this is also the most relevant question of our day is clear from both the emergence of the Third World and the new questions of world revolution.

The relationship of theory to revolution was a preoccupation of Luxemburg's long before the debate leading to the break with Kautsky. In 1908 at the Nuremberg Congress she identified opportunism with hostility to theory as she spoke on the need for the Party School to continue; in 1910 she related opportunism both to inaction and to lack of revolutionary theory; so, in 1911, there was no doubt whatever that Luxemburg considered theory the lifeblood of the movement in general and the leadership in particular, but she held that the established leadership was quite anemic on the question. She decided that the new crisis caused by the phenomenon of imperialism had to be probed further, much further.

In November 1911 she wrote to Konstantin Zetkin: "I want to find the *cause* of imperialism. I am following up the economic aspects of this concept . . . it will be a strictly scientific explanation of imperialism and its contradiction."

Her characteristic confidence in the masses and their spontaneity had, as we saw, so deepened with her experience in the 1905 Revolution that she considered leaders simply to be the ones who had "the speaking parts." Since "any mass action once unleashed, must move forward," the masses will also succeed in pushing the lackadaisical leadership forward. And what in the years 1910–11 did the leadership's role turn out to be? We are not given the answer. Only one thing is clear beyond the shadow of a doubt, and that is that Luxemburg's break with Kautsky and Bebel was irrevocable. However, there was no organizational break; the unity of the party remained to her unchangeable. But she kept her distance from the leaders, who practiced leadership as if they were government rulers, though they did not have state power.

NOTES

1. From letter to Luise Kautsky, 2 January 1906, in Luise Kautsky, ed., *Rosa Luxemburg: Letters to Karl and Luise Kautsky*, trans. Louis P. Lochner (New York: Robert McBride & Co., 1925).

2. *Massenstreik, Partei und Gewerkschaften* (1906), in Rosa Luxemburg, *Gesammelte Werke*, vol. 2 (Berlin: Dietz Verlag, 1974), pp. 90–170. The pamphlet was first translated into English by Patrick Lavin (Detroit: Marxist Educational Society, 1925). For those passages which were quoted by Rosa Luxemburg in her 1910 article, "Theory and Practice," I have used the translation of David Wolff (see n. 6 below).

3. Carl E. Schorske, *German Social Democracy 1905-1917* (Cambridge, Mass.: Harvard Univ. Press, 1955).

4. "Was Weiter?", in *Gesammelte Werke*, 2:288–99, is variously referred to as "What Next?" by Nettl; "What Further?" by Schorske; and "The Next Step" by Looker. It was Robert Looker who finally published it in English in his *Rosa Luxemburg: Selected Political Writings* (New York: Grove Press, 1974), p. 148. To complicate things still further, one of Karl Kautsky's articles in opposition to Luxemburg is called "Was Nun?" ("What Now?").

5. It was this Resolution that she used as proof of German proletarian solidarity with the Russian proletariat, in her greetings to the 1907 Congress of the Russian Social-Democratic Labor Party (RSDRP). See Appendix for my translation of the entire speech.

6. Rosa Luxemburg, "Theory and Practice," *Neue Zeit*, 22 and 29 July 1910, in *Gesammelte Werke*, 2:378–420. The first English translation of this article, by David Wolff, was published in 1980 (Detroit: News & Letters). It is this translation I am using here; see p. 35. All page citations in following text are to this translation.

7. Rosa Luxemburg, "Attrition or Collision?" is included in *Gesammelte Werke*, 2:344–77. A translation of the section on Fabius Cunctator is included in Rosa Luxemburg, "Theory and Practice," trans. David Wolff (Detroit: News & Letters, 1980).

8. Rosa Luxemburg, "Our Struggle for Power," *Gesammelte Werke*, 2:530–41.

9. On 29 May 1913, in an article entitled "Die weltpolitische Lage" ("The World Political Situation") in *Leipziger Volkszeitung*, she wrote: "Then came the Hunn campaign in China, to which Wilhelm II sent the soldiers with the slogan: Quarter will not be given, prisoners will not be taken. The soldiers were to wreak havoc like the Hunns so that for a thousand years no Chinese would dare cast squinting, envious eyes on a German." In *Gesammelte Werke*, 2:214.

10. *Protokoll* of the Social-Democratic Party Congress, 1910, pp. 181–82, (Resolution No. 100).

11. "Our Morocco Leaflet," *Gesammelte Werke*, 3:32.

12. Quoted in Olga-Hess Gankin and H.H. Fisher *The Bolsheviks and the World War*, pp. 24–5.

13. The quotations that follow were translated by David Wolff from *Protokoll . . . Jena, 1911* (Berlin: Buchhandlung Vorwärts, 1911). Page citations are to the *Protokoll*. The amendment, signed by Luxemburg, Gustave Hoch and Klara Zetkin, can be found on pp. 162–63; Luxemburg's speech and discussion on pp. 204–07, 247–49, and 348–50.

14. On the question of anti-Semitism as well as the whole question of how the Dreyfus affair affected the SPD in general and Rosa Luxemburg in particular, see Daniel Guerin's Introduction, in his *Rosa Luxemburg: Le Socialisme en France* (Paris: Editions Pierre Belfond, 1971). For an English translation of Luxemburg's article, "The Socialist Crisis in France," see *New International*, July 1939.

15. Peter Nettl, *Rosa Luxemburg*, 2 vols. (London: Oxford Univ. Press, 1966), 1:432.

16. Karen Honeycutt, "Clara Zetkin: A Left-Wing Socialist and Feminist in Wilhelmian Germany" (Ph.D. diss., Columbia University, 1975).

17. The first edition was *Die Frau und der Sozialismus* (Zurich, 1879). A Russian translation of the 55th German edition (Berlin, 1946) was published as *Zhenshchina i sotsializm* (Moscow, 1959), and contained all the revisions made by Bebel up to his death in 1913. Daniel DeLeon translated an American edition, titled *Woman Under Socialism* (New York: Labor News Co., 1904); a Jubilee edition, trans. M. L. Stern, was published as *Woman and Socialism* (New York: Socialist Literature Co., 1910).

18. In 1972, Marx's Notebooks, titled *The Ethnological Notebooks of Karl Marx* (Assen: Van Gorcum, 1972), were finally transcribed by Lawrence Krader, painstakingly footnoted and containing a ninety-page introduction.

III

Marx's and Luxemburg's Theories of Accumulation of Capital, its Crises and its Inevitable Downfall

Luxemburg's isolation of herself from party work, following the German Social-Democracy's rejection of her analyses, both on the question of the General Strike as applicable during the struggles for electoral rights, and the uncompromising anti-imperialism she articulated over the "Morocco Incident," provided time for her to plunge into creating her greatest theoretical work, *Accumulation of Capital (A Contribution to an Explanation of Imperialism).*[1] From her letter to Konstantin Zetkin, at the end of 1911, when she first thought of the work, it was clear that, far from her defeats in the party making her tolerant of the political opportunism permeating it, she was out to discover "the economic roots of imperialism." With her massive 450-page work, she felt she was treading new ground where none, not even Marx, had ever been before. She considered volume 2 of *Capital* to be unfinished, since Marx had died before it was prepared for the printer, and she questioned what Engels had "made out" of the manuscripts left by Marx. Clearly, she felt confident that she was the pupil of Marx who could and did fulfill the task Marx had left "unfinished." As she was later to point out: "It was clearly left to his pupils to solve this problem (like many others) and my *Accumulation* was intended as an attempt in this direction."[2]

Accumulation of Capital was published in 1913. The outbreak of war and the collapse of the Second International were such traumatic experiences that Luxemburg felt all the more confident, when she was able to answer her critics, that she had been right all along. In that spirit, she entitled the work: *Volume II of Accumulation of Capital, or What the Epigones Have Made of It. An Anti-Critique.* (Hereafter, this will be referred to as *Anti-Critique.*)

She was later to describe the four impassioned months in which she wrote *Accumulation* as the "happiest" in her life. As she later wrote to Diefenbach: "Do you know that I wrote the entire 30 galleys in one go in four months— incredible performance—and sent it off to the printer without so much as a further glance through."[3] And, she added, she felt the same intellectual excitement when she wrote her answer to her critics, which she had sent off to Diefenbach for his comments. The point in both cases was that she considered this intellectual probing a great adventure.

The long road Luxemburg traveled to develop from mere agitation to serious theory is important to note. To begin with, she had been pivotal in both of the great debates which determined the direction of Marxism: the first against the first appearance of reformism, and the second against the acknowledged leading orthodox Marxist, Karl Kautsky.

As we saw, she had experienced her flash of genius on the shift in global politics—imperialism—with the Chinese–Japanese war in 1895.[4] Not only that, she warned about its effects *within* the Social-Democracy itself as early as her very first entrance on the German scene. Her 1898 description of the global shift of power was reiterated at the 1900 Congress, where she took issue with a certain pusillanimity she felt on the part of her coleaders in relationship to the war against China. She followed this up in 1905 in the debate on the first Moroccan crisis, where she most concretely spelled it out in the failure of the party to take a principled position against Germany's imperial policies.

In 1907 she spoke in the name of the Russians as well as the Poles at the International Congress in Stuttgart, amending its antiwar resolution so that there would be no doubt that Socialists were pledged to oppose any imperialist war. It is certainly no accident whatever, and it is certainly related to the question of anti-imperialism, that she broke with Kautsky and Bebel. She isolated herself from the party in order to face, ground, and try to resolve the new, fantastic, militaristic, threatening, catastrophic appearance of imperialism. By 1912, when she decided to dig into "the economic roots of imperialism," she had fought, analyzed, and written about colonialism for some fifteen years. Whether one thinks her theory right or wrong, it is utterly fantastic to act as if it can be dismissed as a mere *tour de force* and not a serious theory—that is to say, brilliant but not profound.

Once Luxemburg has stated the problem of reproduction—Section One— she plunges into, not actual history but a detailed history of ideas on the subject. That is to say, the bulk of the work consists of debates with other economists, mostly those Marx had analyzed, from Quesnay and Adam Smith to Sismondi–Malthus vs Say–Ricardo, MacCulloch, Rodbertus and von Kirchmann. Then she turns to "A New Version of the Problem": Struve– Bulgakov–Tugan Baranovski vs Vorontsov–Nikolai Danielson. Whether or not Luxemburg was consciously trying, in dealing with the question of reproduction, to follow what Marx had done with his *Theories of Surplus Value* (which, however, he had relegated to volume 4 of *Capital*), the point is that "history" up to the very last section of the book has not been the history of the day, which she had accused Marx of subordinating to the abstract diagrams, but the history of various debates. It is only with Section Three, "The Historical Conditions of Accumulation," that we get down to history, to the "reality vs theory" that was the purpose of her work.

ENCOUNTER WITH MARX'S THEORY OF EXPANDED REPRODUCTION

Rosa Luxemburg's *Accumulation of Capital* is a critique of Marx's theory of expanded reproduction in volume 2 of *Capital*. The question of the accumulation of capital has been the central theme of political economy. It was the subject of debate between Ricardo and Malthus, Say and Sismondi, Engels and Rodbertus, and Lenin and the *Narodniki* (Populists). Luxemburg occupies a conspicuous but unenviable position in this debate—that of a revolutionist hailed by bourgeois economists as having supplied "the clearest formulation" of the problem of "effective demand" until Keynes's *The General Theory of Employment, Interest and Money.*[5]

Since the publication of volume 2 of *Capital* in 1885, the pivot of the dispute on expanded reproduction has been Marx's diagrammatic presentation of *how* surplus value is realized in an ideal capitalist society. It is necessary to turn to that first. Marx does not let us forget that his premise is that of a closed society, which is capitalistic, i.e., dominated by the law of value, and that the law of value is the law of the world market: "The industrialist always has the world market before him, compares and must continually compare his cost prices with those of the whole world, and not only with those of his home market."[6]

In a word, while Marx excludes foreign trade, he nevertheless places his society in the *environment* of the world market. These are the conditions of the problem.

Marx's famous formulae in part 3 of volume 2 were designed to serve two purposes. On the one hand, he wished to expose the "incredible aberration" of Adam Smith, who "spirited away" the constant portion of capital by dividing the total social production, not into constant capital (c), variable capital (v), and surplus value (sv), but only into v plus s. (The terminology Smith used for v and s was "wages, profit and rent.") On the other hand, Marx wanted to answer the underconsumptionist argument that continued capital accumulation was impossible because of the impossibility of "realizing" surplus value, i.e., of selling.[7]

Marx spent a seemingly interminable time in exposing the error of Smith. That is because it is the great divide, separating both bourgeois political economy *and* the petty-bourgeois critique from "scientific socialism." Smith's error became part of the dogma of political economy because it dovetailed with the *class* interests of the bourgeoisie to have that error retained. If, as Smith maintained, the constant portion of capital "in the final analysis" dissolved itself into wages, then the workers need not struggle against the "temporary" appropriation of the unpaid hours of labor. They need merely wait for the product of their labor to "dissolve" itself into wages. Marx proves the contrary to be true. Not only does c not "dissolve" itself into wages, but it becomes the very instrumentality through which the capitalist gains mastery over the living workers.

In disproving the underconsumptionist theory, Marx demonstrates that there is no *direct* connection between production and consumption.

When Lenin argued with the Russian underconsumptionists, with the Populists, here is how he phrased it:

> The difference in views of the petty bourgeois economists from the views of Marx does not consist in the fact that the first realize in general the connection between production and consumption in capitalist society, and the second do not. (This would be absurd.) The distinction consists in this, that the petty bourgeois economists considered this tie between production and consumption to be a *direct* one, thought that *production follows consumption*. Marx shows that the connection is only an *indirect* one, that it is so connected *only in the final instance*, because in capitalist society *consumption follows* production.[8]

The underconsumptionists construed the preponderance of production over consumption to mean the "automatic" collapse of capitalist society. Where the classicists saw only the tendency *toward* equilibrium, the petty-bourgeois critics see only the tendency *away* from equilibrium. Marx demonstrates that *both* tendencies are there, inextricably connected.

To illustrate the process of accumulation, or expanded reproduction, Marx divides social production into two main departments—Department I, production of means of production, and Department II, production of means of consumption. The division is symptomatic of the class division in society. Marx categorically refused to divide social production into more than two departments, for example, a third department for the production of gold, although gold is neither a means of production nor a means of consumption, but rather a means of circulation. That is an entirely subordinate question, however, to the basic postulate of a closed society in which there are only two classes and *hence* only two decisive divisions of social production. It is the premise that decides the boundaries of the problem. The relationship between the two branches is not merely a technical one. It is rooted in the class relationship between the worker and the capitalist. Surplus value is not some disembodied spirit floating between heaven and earth, but is embodied *within* means of production and *within* means of consumption. To try to separate surplus value *from* means of production and *from* means of consumption is to fall into the petty-bourgeois quagmire of underconsumptionism.

This is fundamental to Marx's whole conception. It cuts through the whole tangle of markets. Marx's point is that the bodily form of value predetermines the destination of commodities. Iron is not consumed by people but by steel; sugar is not consumed by machines but by people. Value may be indifferent to the use by which it is borne, but it must be incorporated in some use-value to be realized. The use-value of means of production, Marx emphasizes, shows how important is "the determination of use-value in the determination of economic orders."[9] In the capitalist economic order, means of production forms the greater of the two departments of social production. And *hence* also of the "market." In the United States, for instance, a large quantity of pig iron is "consumed" by the companies that produce it; a significant "market" for the products of the steel industry is the transportation industry.

It is impossible to have the slightest comprehension of the economic laws of capitalist production without being oppressively aware of the role of the material form of constant capital. The material elements of simple production and reproduction—labor power, raw materials, and means of production—are the elements of expanded reproduction. In order to produce ever greater quantities of products, more means of production are necessary. That, and not the "market," is the *differentia specifica* of expanded reproduction.

Marx proceeds further to emphasize the key importance of the material form of the product for purposes of expanded reproduction by beginning his illustration of expanded reproduction with a diagram showing that, *so far as its value is concerned*, expanded reproduction is but simple reproduction: "It is not the quantity but the destination of the given elements of simple reproduction which is changed and this change is the material basis of the subsequent reproduction."[10]

The difficulty in understanding expanded reproduction lies not in the value form of production, but in the *comparison* of the value with its material form. Marx's view is that in order not to get lost in "a vicious circle of prerequisites"—of constantly going to market with the products produced and returning from the market with the commodities bought—the problem of expanded reproduction should be posed "in its fundamental simplicity." That can be done by a realization of two simple facts: (1) the very law of capitalist production brings about the augmentation of the working population and hence, while part of the surplus value must be incorporated into means of consumption, and transformed into variable capital with which to buy more labor power, labor power will always be on hand; and (2) capitalist production creates its own market—pig iron is needed for steel, steel for machine construction, etc.—and that therefore, so far as the capital market is concerned, the capitalists are their own best "customers" and "buyers." Therefore, concludes Marx, the whole complex question of the conditions of expanded reproduction can be reduced to the following: can the surplus *product* in which the surplus value is incorporated go *directly* (without first being sold) into further production? Marx's answer is: "It is not needed that the latter (means of production) be sold; they can *in nature* again enter into new production."[11]

Marx establishes that the total social product cannot be "either" the means of production "or" the means of consumption; there is a preponderance of means of production *over* means of consumption (symbolically expressed as mp/mc). Not only is this so but it *must* be so, for the use-values produced in capitalist society are not those used by workers or even by capitalists, *but by capital*. It is not "people" who realize the greater part of surplus value; it is realized through the constant expansion of constant capital. The premise of simple reproduction—a society composed solely of workers and capitalists—remains the premise of expanded reproduction.

At the same time, surplus value, in the aggregate, remains uniquely determined by the difference between the value of the product and the value of labor power. The law of value continues to dominate over expanded reproduction. The whole problem of the disputed volume 2 is to make it apparent that realization is not a question of the market, but of *production*. The conflict in production and therefore in society is the conflict between capital and labor. That is why Marx would not be moved from his premise.

LUXEMBURG'S CRITIQUE: REALITY VS THEORY; PHENOMENOLOGY VS PHILOSOPHY

The main burden of Luxemburg's critique of Marx's theory of accumulation was directed against his assumption of a closed capitalist society. She gave this assumption a twofold meaning: (1) a society composed solely of workers and capitalists, and (2) "the rule of capitalism in the entire world."

Marx, however, did not pose the rule of capital in the *entire* world, but its rule in a *single* isolated nation. When Luxemburg's critics[12] pointed this out to her, Luxemburg poured vitriolic scorn upon them. To speak of a single capitalist society, wrote Luxemburg in her *Anti-Critique*,[13] was a "fantastic absurdity" characteristic of the "crassest epigonism." Marx, she insisted, could have had no such stratospheric conception in mind. Nevertheless, as Bukharin pointed out, Luxemburg was not only misinterpreting Marx's *concept*, but misreading the simple *fact*, which Marx had most clearly put on paper: "In order to simplify the question (of expanded reproduction) we abstract foreign trade and examine an isolated nation."[14]

Luxemburg, on the other hand, argued that a "precise demonstration" from history would show that expanded reproduction has never taken place in a closed society, but rather through distribution to, and expropriation of, "non-capitalist strata and non-capitalist societies." Luxemburg falsely counterposed reality to theory. Once she had done so, she failed to see that what she was describing as reality was but the phenomenological manifestation of capital as it invaded underdeveloped lands, while Marx had dived deep into accumulation of capital as it came out of the ever-expanding transformation of variable capital (living labor) into constant capital (dead labor). This is why he called Smith's underestimation of that constant form of capital "an incredible aberration," while Luxemburg simply considered constant capital as no more than "the capitalist language" for something characteristic of all societies. Though she was under no great illusion that the entire surplus value (profit) would be "dissolved" back into wages, as was Smith, there was no place for her to go but to the sphere of exchange and consumption.

Far from being only a phenomenological analysis of his age, Marx's theory was so profound a dialectic of accumulation that, at one and the same time, it disclosed the different forms of revolt and how they revealed the logical development to the point where no alteration in exchange or distribution could fundamentally change anything.

Some of the best writing in Luxemburg's *Accumulation* occurs in her description of the "real" process of accumulation through the conquest of Algeria and India; the opium wars against China; the Anglo–Boer war and the carving up of the African Empire; and the extermination of the American Indian. Although Luxemburg described concretely how the war between the Boers and the English was fought "on the backs of the Negroes," she did not draw any conclusions about the Black Africans being a revolutionary force. That revolutionary role was reserved for the proletariat alone. In her critique of Marx's diagrams she saw his economic categories as only economic, rather than as symbols of the class struggle itself. As we saw, during the 1910–11 debate with Kautsky, Luxemburg's revolutionary opposition to German imperialism's barbarism against the Hereros was limited to seeing them as suffering rather than revolutionary humanity. Yet both the Maji Maji revolt in East Africa and the Zulu rebellion in South Africa had erupted in those pivotal years, 1905–06—although they were known, no doubt, to few other than the imperialists engaged in putting them down.

Luxemburg did hit out passionately against imperialism:

> Just as the American farmer had driven the Red Indian West before him under the impact of capitalist economy, so the Boer drove the Negro to the North. The "Free Republics" between the Orange River and the Limpopo thus were created as a protest against the designs of the English bourgeoisie on the sacred right of slavery. The tiny peasant republics were in constant guerrilla warfare against the Bantu Negroes. And it was on the backs of the Negroes that the battle between the Boers and the English government, which went on for decades, was fought.[15]

Luxemburg had become so blinded by the powerful imperialist phenomena *and* the opportunism it led to in the SPD, that she failed to see: (1) that the oppression of the non-capitalist lands could also bring about powerful new allies for the proletariat, and (2) that, in any case, all this had nothing to do with the problem posed in volume 2 of *Capital* which is concerned with how surplus value is realized in an *ideal* capitalist world. Neither has it anything to do with the "real" process of accumulation, which Marx analyzes in volume 3, for the *real* process of accumulation is a capitalist process or one of *value* production.

Luxemburg, on the other hand, writes that: "The most important thing is that value can be realized neither by workers nor by capitalists *but only* by social strata who themselves *do not produce capitalistically*."[16]

According to Luxemburg, the Russian Marxists were deeply mistaken when they thought that the preponderance of constant capital over variable capital (symbolically expressed as c/v) "alone" revealed the specific characteristic law of capitalist production, "for which production is an aim in itself and individual consumption merely a subsidiary condition." To raise consumption from this subordinate position, Luxemburg transforms the inner core of capitalism into a mere outer covering. To Luxemburg, the relationship of c/v, as we saw, is merely "the capitalist language" of the general productivity of labor. With one stroke Luxemburg is depriving the carefully isolated c/v relationship of its class character. Value production loses the specificity of a definite *historic* stage in the development of humanity. Luxemburg is thus driven to identify what Marxism has considered to be the specific characteristic law of capitalist production—c/v—with "all pre-capitalist forms of production" *as well as* with "the future, socialist organization" (p. 222).

The next inevitable stage is to divest the *material* form of capitalism of *its* class character. Where Marx makes the relationship between Department I, producing means of production, and Department II, producing means of consumption, reflect the *class* relationship inherent in c/v, Luxemburg, at one and the same time, manufactures a third department out of gold, and speaks of the "branches of production" as if it were a purely technical term! In so doing she not only moves away from Marx's level of abstraction but also from the class relations which he was expressing by the division of social production into two and only two departments. No wonder she first deprives the material *form* of capital of its capital content, then discards it because it has no capital content: "Accumulation is not only an inner relation between two branches of production. It is *first of all* a relation between capitalist and non-capitalist surroundings" (p. 297; my emphasis).

Luxemburg has transformed capital accumulation from a substance derived from labor into one whose chief sustenance is an outside force: non-capitalist surroundings. To complete this inversion of the chief source of capitalist accumulation she is compelled to break the confines of the closed society, outside of whose threshold she has already stepped. Her "solution" stands the whole problem on its head, and she now implores us to drop the assumption of a closed society and "allow for surplus value to be realized outside of capitalist production."

This step, she says, will reveal that out of capitalist production could issue "either means of production or means of consumption" (p. 247). There is no law compelling the products of capitalist production to be the one and *not* the other. In fact, states Luxemburg without any awareness of how far she is departing from the method of Marx: "*the material form has nothing whatever to do with the needs of capitalist production. Its material form corresponds to the needs of those non-capitalist strata which make possible its realization*" (p. 247; my emphasis).

Where Marx said that alone the use-value of means of production shows how important is the determination of use-value in the determination of the entire economic order, Luxemburg leaves out of consideration entirely the use-value of capital: "In speaking of the realization of surplus value," she writes, "we *a priori* do not consider its material form" (p. 245). Where Marx shows the inescapable molding of value into use-value, Luxemburg tries violently to separate them, as if surplus value could be "realized" outside its bodily form. The contradiction between use-value and value which capitalist production cannot escape, Luxemburg tries to resolve by dumping the total *product* of capitalist production into non-capitalist areas.

When she got to answer her critics of *Accumulation*, which was completed before the outbreak of World War I, not only had capitalism sunk into its first world war, but the Second International had also collapsed. She further expanded her analysis:

> At first glance, it may appear to be a purely theoretical exercise. And yet the practical meaning of the problem is at hand—the connexion with the most outstanding fact of our time: imperialism. The typical external phenomena of imperialism: competition among capitalist countries to win colonies and spheres of interest, opportunities for investment, the international loan system, militarism, tariff barriers, the dominant role of finance capital and trusts in world politics, are all well known . . . How can one explain imperialism in a society where there is no longer any space for it? It was at this point that I believed I had to start my critique.[17]

Luxemburg was not unaware of Marx's eloquent description of primitive accumulation: "Colonial system, public debts, heavy taxes, protection, commercial wars, etc.—these children of the true manufacturing period, increase gigantically during the infancy of Modern Industry. The birth of the latter is heralded by a great slaughter of the innocents."[18]

However, she insisted on having such "reality" included in the theoretical analysis of the day without any dialectical awareness of how that diverted from Marx's purpose of "discerning the law of motion of capitalism" to its downfall.

For Marx, however, it is production that determines the market. Luxemburg, on the other hand, finds herself in a position where, although she accepts Marxism, she yet makes the market determine production. Once Luxemburg eliminates the fundamental Marxian distinction of means of production and means of consumption as indicative of a class relationship, she is compelled to look for the market in the bourgeois sense of "effective demand." Having lost sight of production, she looks for "people." Since it is obviously impossible for workers "to buy back" the products they created, she looks for other "consumers" to "buy" the products, and she proceeds to blame Marx for not having used that as *his* point of departure. The Marxian formulae, writes Luxemburg, seem to indicate that production occurs for production's sake. As Saturn did his children devour, so here everything produced is consumed internally:

> Accumulation is effected here (the schema)[19] without it being seen even to the least degree *for whom*, for what new consumers does this ever-growing expansion of production take place in the end. The diagrams presuppose the following course of things. The coal industry is expanded in order to expand the iron industry. The latter is expanded in order to expand the machine-construction industry. The machine-construction industry is expanded in order to contain the ever-growing army of workers from the coal, iron and machine-construction industries as well as its own workers. And thus "ad infinitum" in a vicious cycle.[20]

By means of her substitute of the noncapitalist milieu for Marx's closed society, Luxemburg is out to break this "vicious circle." The capitalists, she writes, are not fanatics and do not produce for production's sake. Neither technological revolutions nor even the "will" to accumulate are sufficient to induce expanded reproduction: "One other condition is necessary: the expansion of effective demand."[21] Except to the extent that surplus value is necessary to *replace* constant capital and supply the capitalists with luxuries, surplus value cannot otherwise result in accumulation, cannot be "realized." Or, as she put it, "They alone (capitalists) are in a position to realize only the consumed part of constant capital and the consumed part of surplus value. They can in this way guarantee only the condition for the renewal of production on the former scale."[22]

That the "consumed part of constant capital" is not consumed personally, but *productively*, seems to have escaped Luxemburg's attention. Capital*ists* do not "eat" machines, neither their wear and tear nor the newly created ones. Both the consumed part of constant capital and the new investments in capital are *realized through production*. That precisely is the meaning of expanded reproduction, as Marx never wearied of stating.

Luxemburg, however, instead of speaking of the laws of production based on the capital–labor relationship, has now no other refuge but the subjective motivation of the capitalists for profits. Capitalist production, she writes, is distinguished from all previous exploitative orders in that it not only hungers for profit but for ever greater profit. She asks, in her *Anti-Critique:* how can the sum of profits grow when the profits only wander in a circle, out of one pocket and into another? That is, out of the pocket of the iron producers and into that of the steel magnates into that of the machine-construction industry tycoons. No wonder Marx was so insistent upon establishing the fact that "profit is therefore that disguise of surplus value which must be removed before the real nature of surplus value can be discovered."[23]

Luxemburg, being a serious theoretician, was compelled to develop her deviation to its logical conclusion. Where, to Marx, expansion of production meant aggravation of the conflict between the worker and the capitalist, to Luxemburg it meant "first of all" expansion of demand and of profits. She contended that Marx *assumed* what he should have *proved*—that expanded reproduction was possible in a closed society. With her attention focused on noncapitalist lands, she overlooked that capitalism was developing to a much greater extent *capitalistically* (expansion of machinofacture within the home country) and *between* capitalist countries (e.g., United States and Britain) rather than through "third groups" or between capitalist and noncapitalist countries. All of this was, of course, inextricably bound to "realizing" surplus value whereas, in fact, imperialism was out for surplus profit, ever greater profit.

Luxemburg had left the sphere of production for that of exchange and consumption. There she remained. Having given up Marx's premise, she had no vantage point from which to view these phenomena. She arrived pivotless on the broad arena of the market, asking that the obvious be proved, while "taking for granted" the production relationship which the obvious obscured. Remaining in the market, there was nothing left for her to do but adopt the language characteristic of what she herself, in other circumstances, had called "the merchant mentality."

Luxemburg maintains that, although coal may be needed for iron and iron for steel and steel both for the machine-construction industry and for machines producing means of consumption, the surplus product cannot be reincorporated into further production without first assuming "the pure form of value," which is evidently money and profits: "Surplus value, no matter what its material form, cannot be directly transferred to production for accumulation; it must first be realized."[24]

Just as surplus value must be "realized" (sold) after it is produced, so it must after that reassume both the "productive form" of means of production and labor power as well as means of consumption. Like the other conditions of production, this leads us to the market. Finally, after this has succeeded, continues Luxemburg, the additional mass of commodities must again be "realized, transformed into money." This again brings us to the market, and Luxemburg, closing the door to what she thinks is the "vicious circle" of production for production's sake, opens the doors wide to what Marx called "the vicious circle of prerequisites."[25]

Whether she was betrayed by the powerful historical development of imperialism that was taking place to substitute for the relationship of capital to labor the relationship of capitalism to noncapitalism and to deny Marx's assumption of a closed society; *or* whether she was so weighted down by her false position against national self-determination that she could not see that the absolute opposite to imperialism was not noncapitalism, but the masses in revolt, in the oppressed as in the oppressor country—she could not escape from the false counterposition of theory to reality. In any case, she let go of Marx's total philosophy of revolution, which kept, as one, theory and practice, objective and subjective, economics and politics, philosophy and revolution. Since that, and not different formulae, is what Luxemburg likewise wanted, we must now consider the market, not as against production, but in relationship to crises and the breakdown of capitalism.

CRISES AND THE BREAKDOWN OF CAPITALISM

The dispute between Marx and Luxemburg was, of course, not confined to the limits of the formulae. That was only the outer shell of the inner core of the essential question of the breakdown of capitalism, or the creation of the material foundation for socialism.

Throughout her criticism of the formulae in volume 2, Luxemburg maintains that volume 3 contains *in implicite* the solution to the problem posed "but not answered" in volume 2. By the "implicit" solution Luxemburg means the analysis of the contradiction between production and consumption, and between production and the market. That, however, is *not* what Marx called "the general contradiction of capitalism."

The "general contradiction of capitalism,"[26] writes Marx, consists in the fact that capitalism has a tendency toward limitless production "regardless of the value and surplus value incorporated in it and regardless of the conditions of production under which it is produced." That is why, in "Unravelling the Inner Contradiction," Marx places in the center of his analysis, not the market, but the "Conflict between Expansion of Production and the Creation of Values."

The constant revolutions in production and the constant expansion of constant capital, writes Marx, necessitate, of course, an extension of the market. But, he explains, the enlargement of the market in a capitalist nation has very precise limits. The consumption goods of a capitalist country are limited to the luxuries of the capitalists and the necessities of the workers when paid at value. The market for consumption goods is just sufficient to allow the capitalist to continue his search for greater value. *It cannot be larger.*

This is the supreme manifestation of Marx's simplifying assumption that the worker is paid at value. The innermost cause of crises, according to Marx, is that labor power *in the process of production*, and *not in the market*, creates a value greater than it itself is. The worker is a producer of overproduction. It cannot be otherwise in a value-producing society where the means of consumption, being but a moment in the reproduction of labor power, cannot be bigger than the needs of capital for labor power. That is the fatal defect of capitalist production. On the one hand, the capitalist must increase his market. On the other hand, it cannot be larger.

Luxemburg, however, insists that it is not the problem that is insoluble, but Marx's premise that makes it so. She is prevented from seeing what is most fundamental to Marx because, on the one hand, she has excluded crises as being merely "the *form* of movement but not the movement itself of capitalist economy."[27] On the other hand, because she abandoned Marx's basic premise, she looked at the market not as a manifestation of the production relationship, but as something expendable *outside of* that relationship. To Marx, however, the "market" that can be enlarged beyond the limits of the working population paid at value is the capital market. Even there the constant technological revolutions make the time necessary to *reproduce* a product tomorrow *less* than the time it took to *produce* it today. Hence there comes a time when all commodities, *including labor power*, have been "overpaid."

The crisis that follows is not caused by a shortage of "effective demand." On the contrary, it is the crisis that causes a shortage of "effective demand." The worker employed yesterday has become unemployed today. A crisis occurs not because there has been a scarcity of markets—the market is largest just before the crisis—but because *from the capitalist viewpoint* there is occurring an unsatisfactory distribution of "income" between recipients of wages and those of surplus value or profits. The capitalist decreases his investments and the resulting stagnation of production appears as overproduction. Of course, there is a contradiction between production and consumption. Of course, there is the "inability to sell." But that "inability to sell" manifests itself as such *because of the fundamental antecedent decline in the rate of profit, which has nothing whatever to do with the inability to sell.*

What Marx describes in his analysis of the "general contradiction of capitalism" is (1) the degradation of the worker to an appendage of a machine, (2) the constant growth of the unemployed army, and (3) capitalism's own downfall because of its inability to give greater employment to labor. Since labor power is the supreme commodity of capitalist production, the only source of its value and surplus value, capitalism's inability to reproduce it dooms capitalism itself.

Thus the three principal facts of capitalist production, which are reaffirmed not merely "implicitly" but *explicitly* in the real world in volume 3 are: (1) decline in the rate of profit, (2) deeper and deeper crises, and (3) a greater and greater unemployed army. Luxemburg denies Marx the right to assume that labor power will always be on hand for purposes of expanded reproduction *simultaneously* with assuming a closed capitalist society. "Reality" would show, she writes, that it is the noncapitalist societies which are the "reservoir of labor power." By denying Marx that right she is denying the Marxist theory of population. With a single stroke of the pen Luxemburg frees capitalism from its "absolute general law"—the reserve army of labor—which, says Marx, is all-dominant even when the entire social capital has been concentrated in "the hands of one single capitalist or one single corporation."[28]

This single capitalist society becomes the ideal capitalist society which is the premise of Marx's famous formulae in volume 2. Even in volume 3 where we are introduced to the "real" world, with its bogus transactions, credit manipulations, and all the other complicating factors of a complex society, Marx's vantage point remains the sphere of value production of a closed capitalist society. The main conflict in society, as in production, remains the conflict between capital and labor. It becomes aggravated, not modified, with the expansion of production and expansion of credit, and none of the laws of production, whether reflected in the declining rate of profit, or in the reserve army of labor, are attenuated by market manipulations. Rather the abstract laws themselves come to full fruition.

Marx considered the theory of the declining rate of profit to be "the *pons asini*" of the whole political economy, that which divides one theoretic system from another.[29]

The protracted depression following the 1929 crash silenced the vulgarizers of political economy, who denied that there is such a tendency. However, it was inconceivable to this "new political economy," as it is to all bourgeois, that the decline in the rate of profit comes from the very vitals of the productive system. Marx, based as he was on the capital–labor relationship, saw the decay in capitalist production in the tendency in the *rate* of profit to decline despite the growth in its *mass*. The bourgeois economists, on the other hand, see the decline in the rate not as a result of the organic composition of capital, reflecting the relationship of dead to living labor, but as a result merely of a deficiency in effective demand.

Unfortunately, so did Luxemburg. She held that the tendency for the *rate* to decline is, if not entirely negated, at least strongly counterbalanced by the increase in the *mass* of profit. Therefore, she concludes, we might as well wait for "the extinction of the sun"[30] as to wait for capitalism to collapse through a decline in its rate of profit. On the contrary, she writes, the historic process will reveal the "real" source of capital accumulation and hence the cause of capitalism's downfall when that source will have been exhausted: "From the historic point of view, accumulation of capital is a process of exchange of things between capitalist and pre-capitalist methods of production. Without pre-capitalist methods of production, accumulation cannot take place . . . The impossibility of accumulation signifies from the capitalist point of view the impossibility of the further development of the productive forces and consequently the objective historic necessity for the breakdown of capitalism."[31]

Wherein lay the importance of the imperialist phenomena that Luxemburg said contradicted the Marxist theory and diagrammatic presentation of accumulation? Obviously in the fact that the phenomena brought into view "not only" a closed capitalist society and *its* contradictions, "but also" the non-capitalist strata and societies and its relation to *them*. And not merely "also," but "first of all." And from this "first of all" Luxemburg did not hesitate to draw the logical conclusion that accumulation was "inconceivable in any respect whatever" without these third groups. But if accumulation is "inconceivable" without this outside force, then it is this force, and not labor, which will bring about the downfall of capitalism. The historic necessity of the proletarian revolution falls to the ground. And so does her own theory of the "impossibility" of accumulation without these noncapitalist lands, once the live negative in her theory—the colonial masses—are seen nowhere as revolutionary.

Put otherwise, the dialectic, both as movement of liberation and as methodology, is entirely missing. All these opposites coexist without ever getting jammed up against each other to produce a movement. What Hegel called "comes before consciousness without mutual contact,"[32] Lenin called "the essence of anti-dialectics."[33] *This, indeed, is the nub of Luxemburg's error.*[§]

Luxemburg, the revolutionist, feels the abysmal gap between her theory and her revolutionary activity, and comes to the rescue of Luxemburg, the theorist. "Long before" capitalism would collapse through exhaustion of the non-capitalist world, writes Luxemburg, the contradictions of capitalism, *both* internal and external, would reach such a point that the proletariat would overthrow it.

But it is not a question of "long before." No revolutionist doubts that the *only final* solution of the problem of expanded reproduction will come in the actual class struggle, on the live historic stage, as a result of class meeting class on the opposite sides of the barricades. The question *theoretically* is: does the solution come *organically* from your theory, or is it brought there merely by "revolutionary will." In Marx the granite foundation for socialism and the inevitability of capitalist collapse come from the very laws of capitalist production: capitalism produces wage labor, its gravedigger. The organic composition of capital produces, on the one hand, the decline in the rate of profit, and, on the other hand, the reserve army of labor. The inability of capitalism to reproduce its only value-creating substance sounds the death knell of capitalism.

With Luxemburg, on the other hand, capitalism's downfall comes not from the *organism* of capitalism, but from an outside force: "non-capitalist strata and non-capitalist societies," while the revolution is dragged in by her indomitable revolutionary will. The socialist proletarian revolution, which, for Marx, is rooted in the *material* development of the conflicting forces of capital and labor, here becomes a wish disconnected from the increasing subordination of the laborer to, and his growing revolt from, the capitalist labor process.

By projecting an ideal capitalist society in which the capitalist has absolutely no headaches about markets—everything produced is "sold"[34]—

[§] See "New Thoughts on *Rosa Luxemburg, Women's Liberation, and Marx's Philosophy of Revolution,*" pp. xxxiv–xxxv.—Ed.

Marx proved that the capitalists' search for markets is motivated by the search for greater profits and not because it is absolutely "impossible to realize" the goods produced within the capitalist society. Engels, in trying to show that no kind of different distribution of national capital would change basically the capital–labor relationship, wrote: "The modern state, whatever its form, is an essentially capitalist machine; it is the state of the capitalists, the ideal collective body of all the capitalists. The more productive forces it takes over, the more it becomes the real collective body of all the capitalists, the more citizens it exploits. The workers remain wage earners, proletarians. The capitalist relationship is not abolished; it is rather pushed to an extreme."[35]

Because not even state capitalism would abolish this relationship, but only push it "to an extreme," Marx would not budge from his premise of a society consisting only of workers and capitalists. By being solidly based on the capital-labor relationship Marx sees that the decline in the rate of profit cannot be obviated, either by an increase in the mass of profits or by an increase in the "effective demand" for the extra products created. No matter what the market is, the technology of production is such that the capitalist needs relatively less workers to man the new and ever larger machines. Along with the technology of production, the production relationship is such that surplus value comes only from living labor (variable capital in the process of production), which is now an ever smaller part of total capital. Hence the tendency to decline reveals ever more clearly the *law of surplus value* behind that tendency.

The logical development of this tendency, writes Marx, will reveal that ultimately *not even the full twenty-four hours of labor* would produce sufficient surplus value to turn the wheels of expanded reproduction on a *capitalist* basis: "In order to produce the same rate of profit when the constant capital set in motion by one laborer increases ten-fold, the surplus labor time would have to increase ten-fold and soon the total labor time and finally the full twenty-four hours a day would not suffice even if wholly appropriated by capital."[36]

We have reached the theoretic limit of capitalist production. It is as inextricably connected with labor as is the theory of the abolition of capitalism with the proletarian revolution. That is why an organic part of Marx's theory of accumulation is the mobilization of the proletariat for the overthrow of capitalism. That is why Marx would not be moved from his premise of a closed society. It was the basis not only of volume 2 of *Capital* but of volumes 1 and 3, as well as of his *Theories of Surplus Value*. Moreover, it was the basis not only of his entire theoretical system, but also of all of his revolutionary activity.

While it is true that the specific capitalistic imperialism that Luxemburg was prescient enough to recognize as a new global stage in the mid-1890s was a phenomenon not known to Marx, none has yet matched, much less surpassed, Marx's analysis of what Luxemburg called "the world historic act of the birth of capitalism": "The discovery of gold and silver in America, the extirpation, enslavement and entombment in mines of the aboriginal population, the beginning of the conquest and looting of the East Indies, the turning of Africa into a warren for the commercial hunting of black-skins, signalized the rosy dawn of the era of capitalist production."[37]

Luxemburg's only criticism of this analysis was that Marx handled it as if it were true only of the primitive accumulation of capital and not "the constant epiphenomenon of accumulation." But Luxemburg had precious little strict theory of the *specifics* of accumulation in the era of imperialism, which were new since the days of Marx, such as monopoly and other forms of the fundamental laws Marx had described of the concentration and centralization of capital.

What is worst of all, it must be repeated and stressed, is Luxemburg's failure to recognize that there were any new revolutionary forces in the noncapitalist lands that could become allies of the proletariat. In a word, imperialism becomes simply an "epiphenomenon." All her magnificent descriptions of imperialist oppression have no live Subject arise to oppose it; they remain just suffering masses, not gravediggers of imperialism. When Marx summed up the General Law of Capitalist Accumulation, he left "pure economics"—roots and all—far behind, as he searched for its absolute opposite and found that, whereas that absolute law of capitalism was the creation of an unemployed army, *that unemployed army is capitalism's "gravediggers."*

What Marx is tracing in the historical tendency of capitalist accumulation is what results from the disintegration of capitalism: "From that moment new forces and new passions spring up in the bosom of society . . . "[38] Luxemburg's failure to see that, in what she was trying to trace with imperialism's rise, is the fatal flaw of her work. Luxemburg the revolutionary, tried to save Luxemburg the theoretician, by adding that "long before" capitalism's downfall because of the absence of noncapitalist lands, the proletariat would overthrow it. What stood in the way of the theoretician was not only the theory of accumulation of capital but also her very contradictory position on organization. On the one hand, she had such high confidence in the spontaneity of the masses that she is still often considered no more than a "spontaneist." On the other hand, despite her merciless criticism of the SPD for its betrayal of the proletariat when World War I broke out, and her designation of the Second International as "the stinking corpse of 4 August 1914," she remained a member.

Simultaneously, although the women were the core of her fight against militarism, and all her magnificent antimilitarist battles were central to the concept and actuality of revolution, she kept posing spontaneity/consciousness as if consciousness was exhausted in class struggle instead of self-developing into so total a philosophy of revolution as to be its actuality. The proletariat always did remain force of revolution, but she failed to see other forces of revolution, either in relation to the National Question or new forms of organization, except at the very end of her life, when she headed the Spartacist uprising in 1919 and called for all power to the councils as she became head of the newborn Communist Party of Germany.

NOTES

1. Although this work is now available in English translation, I prefer to use my own translation from the Russian edition (translated from the German by Dvoilatsky, edited by Bukharin, and published in Moscow in 1921), which I consider to be more precise.

It took British academia thirty-eight years to get around to translating and publishing her work (London: Routledge & Kegan Paul, 1951). Neither that accumulation of time nor the accumulation of scholars involved—the translation was by Dr. Agnes Schwarzchild, the prefatory note by Dr. W. Stark, and the fifteen-page Introduction by Joan Robinson—prevented them from leaving out both Luxemburg's subtitle and her own brief introductory note which specified that her "scientific" work "is at the same time tied to the practical, contemporary, imperialist politics." They also left out, through a "technicality," an entire era of Russian dissident history. Thus, in 1913, when she wrote *Accumulation*, Luxemburg had protected from the tsarist regime the name of Nikolai Danielson, the great Russian Populist and translator of Marx's *Capital*, by entitling her chapter 20 dealing with him: "Nikolai—on." By eliminating the dashes and printing it as "Nikolayon," the scholars managed not only to create a nonexistent man, but to eliminate the very specific, reactionary, historic period of tsarist censorship. In 1968, Monthly Review Press published a paperback edition of this work.

2. *The Accumulation of Capital—an Anti-Critique*, ed. Kenneth J. Tarbuck (New York and London: Monthly Review Press, 1972), p. 62. Page citations that follow are to this edition. There has been much confusion between *Accumulation of Capital, a Contribution to the Economic Explanation of Imperialism* (originally published in German in 1913), and *Accumulation of Capital, or What the Epigones Have Made of the Marxist Theory—An Anti-Critique* (originally published in German in 1919). In the text I refer to the first as *Accumulation*, to the second as *Anti-Critique*.

3. Cf. Luxemburg's letter to Hans Diefenbach dated 12 May 1917.

4. With the outbreak of the imperialist war, Luxemburg retraced imperialism's development in the pamphlet she had signed "Junius," the first German pamphlet to appear in opposition to the war. There are many translations and editions of this work; the quotation which follows appears in *Rosa Luxemburg Speaks* (New York: Pathfinder Press, 1970), p. 281:

> England secured control of Egypt and created for itself, in South Africa, a powerful colonial empire. France took possession of Tunis in North Africa and Tonkin in East Asia; Italy gained a foothold in Abyssinia; Russia accomplished its conquests in Central Asia and pushed forward into Manchuria; Germany won its first colonies in Africa and in the South Sea, and the United States joined the circle when it procured the Philippines with "interests" in Eastern Asia. This period of feverish conquests has brought on, beginning with the Chinese-Japanese war in 1895, a practically uninterrupted chain of bloody wars, reaching its height in the Great Chinese Invasion, and closing with the Russo-Japanese war of 1904.

5. M. Kalecki, *Essays on the Theory of Economic Fluctuations* (New York: Russell & Russell, 1939), p. 46.

6. Karl Marx, *Capital* (Chicago: Kerr, 1909), 3:396. Unless otherwise noted, all quotations from the three volumes of *Capital* are to the Kerr editions.

7. When the word "realization" is used in its underconsumptionist meaning of sale, I am here putting it in quotation marks.

8. Lenin, *Sochineniya* (Collected Works), 2:424. I was the first to translate this section on "The Theoretic Mistakes of the Narodniki," the greater part of chap. 1 of Lenin's *Development of Capitalism in Russia*, which had been omitted from the English edition of Lenin's *Selected Works*. My translation was published as "Origins of Capitalism in Russia," *New International*, October 1943, November 1943, December 1943. It is available on microfilm in "The Raya

Dunayevskaya Collection" on deposit with the Wayne State University Labor History Archives, Detroit.

9. Marx, *Theories of Surplus Value*, 2:170 (Russian edition). My translation of sections of vols. 2 and 3 from the Russian are included in "The Raya Dunayevskaya Collection" at Wayne State University Labor History Archives.

10. *Capital*, 2:592.

11. Marx, *Theories of Surplus Value*, 2:170 (Russian ed.).

12. The argument was complicated by the fact that, in the majority, her critics were reformists. She, on the other hand, attacked indiscriminately both the revolutionists and those who betrayed the revolution, labeling all her critics "epigones."

13. Luxemburg, *Anti-Critique*, p. 137.

14. *Theories of Surplus Value*, 2:161 (Russian ed.). See also N. Bukharin, *Imperialism and the Accumulation of Capital* (New York: Monthly Review Press, 1972).

15. Luxemburg, *Accumulation of Capital* (New York: Monthly Review Press, 1968), p. 412. For a description of the Zulu rebellion, see Edward Roux's 1948 study, *Time Longer Than Rope: A History of the Black Man's Struggle for Freedom in South Africa* (Madison: University of Wisconsin Press, 1966). See also my reference to the Maji Maji revolt in *Philosophy and Revolution*, p. 215; and *American Civilization on Trial*, pp. 19, 28-9, where I deal with the Zulu rebellion and other African revolts. On the relationship of ideologies to revolutions in Africa and Asia, see my *Nationalism, Communism, Marxist-Humanism and the Afro-Asian Revolutions*.

16. *Accumulation*, p. 245, Russian edition. (My translation and my emphasis.) Page citations in the following text are to this edition.

17. *Anti-Critique*, pp. 60–61.

18. *Capital*, 1:830.

19. Since Luxemburg herself claimed in the *Anti-Critique* that she had used the mathematical formulae only because Marx had used them, but that they weren't essential, and because these have been written about innumerable times, we have left them out entirely. For anyone interested, see Bukharin's *Imperialism and Accumulation of Capital*, included with Luxemburg's *Anti-Critique* in the Tarbuck edition. In his introduction, Tarbuck sums up many of the books on the formulae.

20. *Accumulation*, p. 229.

21. Ibid., p. 180.

22. Ibid., p. 244.

23. *Capital*, 3:62.

24. *Accumulation*, p. 86.

25. *Theories of Surplus Value*, 2:170 (Russian ed.)

26. *Capital*, 3:292.

27. *Accumulation*, p. 6.

28. *Capital*, 1:688.

29. *Capital*, 3:250.

30. Luxemburg puts this expression in a footnote in *Anti-Critique*, which appears in Tarbuck's edition on p. 77, but I am using my own translation here.

31. *Accumulation*, p. 297.

32. This phrase of Hegel comes during his attack on formal thought which "makes identity its law, and allows the contradictory content which lies before it to drop into the sphere of sensuous representation . . . where the contradictory terms are held apart . . . and thus come before consciousness without being in contact." See *Science of Logic*, vol. 2 (New York: Macmillan Pub. Co., 1929), p. 477; (London: Allen & Unwin, 1969), p. 835. The first was translated by Johnston and Struthers, the second by A.V. Miller.

33. " 'Come before consciousness without mutual contact' (the object)—that is the essence of anti-dialectics . . . Is sensuous representation *closer* to reality than thought? Both yes and no. Sensuous representation cannot apprehend movement *as a whole*, it cannot, for example, apprehend movement with a speed of 300,000 km. per second, but *thought* does and must apprehend it. Thought, taken from sensuous representation, also reflects reality. . . " Lenin, *Collected Works* (Moscow, 1961), 38:228. See also my critique of Roman Rosdolsky's *The Making of Marx's Capital*, "Rosdolsky's Methodology and Lange's Revisionism," in *News & Letters*, January–February 1978.

Permit me to add a personal note, since Roman Rosdolsky has made a category of the fact that, in 1948, he "had the good fortune to see one of the then very rare copies of Marx's *Rough Draft*." (He was referring to the German text of the *Grundrisse der Kritik der politischen Ökonomie [Rohentwurf], 1857–1858*, published by the Marx-Engels-Lenin Institute in 1939 in Moscow.) That year, 1948, was when I first met Rosdolsky; I, too, had been studying the *Grundrisse*. Despite the fact that Rosdolsky was still clinging to a concept of Russia as "a degenerated workers' state," whereas I had developed the theory of state-capitalism in 1941 (when he was still incarcerated in Hitler's concentration camps), our friendship continued for some time. Later, for very different reasons, we each moved to Detroit. By then the differences between us were no longer limited to a single theory, but involved the centrality of dialectics in Marxism. To me, philosophy did not mean dialectics only "in general," but, very specifically, "negation of the negation," which Marx had called "a new Humanism." I held that this was spelled out concretely on 17 June 1953, in the East German revolt against Communist totalitarianism. What had come alive to me was the breakup of the Absolute Idea in the context of second negativity, not just philosophically, but in combat. The whole new movement *from practice* that came alive with that revolt demanded that a totally new relationship of practice to theory be established for a new unity of theory and practice to be achieved. In summing up the Theoretical Idea and the Practical Idea, Hegel had stressed that "each of these by itself is onesided and contains the Idea itself only as a sought Beyond and an unattained goal." I dare say that a great deal more than the question of Hegel was involved in our dispute in 1953, but that was when my break with Rosdolsky became complete. For the development of Marxist-Humanism in the United States, see *The Raya Dunyevskaya Collection: Marxist-Humanism, Its Origin and Development in the U.S., 1941 to Today*, 10 vols. (Detroit: Wayne State University Labor History Archives, 1981). The Collection is available on microfilm.

34. This doesn't mean that Marx forgot either that they had to be "sold" or the constant crises in the world market. As he put it in *Theories of Surplus Value*, 2:510: "The crises in the world market must be regarded as the real concentration and forcible adjustment of all the contradictions of bourgeois economy. The individual factors, which are condensed in these crises, must therefore emerge and must be described in each sphere of the bourgeois economy and the further we advance in our examination of the latter, the more aspects of this conflict must be traced on the one hand, and on the other hand it must be shown that its more abstract forms are recurring and are contained in the more concrete forms."

35. F. Engels, *Anti-Dühring* (Chicago: Charles H. Kerr Pub. Co., 1935), p. 290.
36. *Capital*, 3:468.
37. *Capital*, 1:823.
38. Ibid., p. 835.

IV

From the "National Question" and Imperialism to the Dialectics of Revolution; the Relationship of Spontaneity and Consciousness to Organization in the Disputes with Lenin, 1904, 1917

> ... *cause is the highest stage in which the concrete Notion as beginning has an immediate existence in the sphere of necessity; but it is not yet a subject* ...
>
> Hegel, Science of Logic

THE HALF-WAY DIALECTIC: THE POLISH QUESTION AND INTERNATIONALISM

From her start in the Marxist movement, internationalism was Luxemburg's most distinctive revolutionary mark, as she and Jogiches first emerged on the Polish exile scene in Zurich, broke with the Polish Socialist Party (PPS) and established a new party, the Social Democracy of the Kingdom of Poland (SDKP). Though Luxemburg's adamant, unbending, stubborn, intransigent opposition to the "right of nations to self-determination" in general, and that of Poland, the country of her birth, in particular, flew in the face of Marx's position, she considered her stand the only true, proletarian, internationalist position. At her first appearance at a Social-Democratic Congress in 1896 the young woman lectured the experienced, orthodox leaders of the Second International, the direct inheritors-continuators of Marxism, that they knew nothing at all about the Polish Question, and that their recognition of the PPS, who were no more than "nationalists," if not outright "social patriots," was proof of that.

The objective situation, she maintained, had totally changed since Marx's day, when there was hardly a proletarian movement, much less a revolutionary one. Now, however, there was a revolutionary Marxist movement both in Russia and in Poland. And Poland was not only economically integrated into the tsarist empire, but was more advanced industrially than Russia itself. Over the next two years she continued work on her doctoral thesis, *The Industrial Development of Poland*, which was to prove the point. Though no one agreed with her position on self-determination, she did win recognition from the International for the SDKP as the official Marxist party of Poland. Within four years, the Lithuanian Marxists joined with the SDKP, which thus became SDKPiL.

Luxemburg never let up on her opposition to self-determination of nations before or even during a revolution. When Jogiches, who had collaborated on the original thesis of opposition to the "National Question," felt it nevertheless inappropriate and untimely to show so clearly her opposition to Marx's position on the question at the outbreak of the 1905 Revolution in Poland, she answered: "The fear that I make too much play of our contradiction with Marx seems groundless. The whole thing should, in fact, be taken as a triumphant vindication of Marxism. Our clear 'revision' will impress our youngsters all the more . . . " She added a P.S.: "At worst, any impressions of direct disagreement with Marx could be altered with a little retouching."[1]

Contrary to the belief of anti-Leninists who have written voluminously that the great divide between Luxemburg and Lenin centered on the organizational question, the exit of Luxemburg's adherents from the famous Russian Social-Democratic Congress occurred *not* on the organizational but on the National Question. It is true that she wrote against Lenin on the question of organization, but that was after the Congress, and, again, during the 1917 Revolution. The point here is that, although she did not attend the 1903 Congress, she joined the party in 1906, even though the famous "Point 9" of the party program on self-determination remained exactly what it had been at the 1903 Congress. Revolution was always the life force of her own activities, her principles, her writings. Revolution was the unifying force; which did not mean that she stopped her critical writing; quite the contrary. In 1908–09 Luxemburg worked out her most comprehensive statement in six lengthy articles, which she entitled "The Problem of Nationality and Autonomy."

Just as some anti-Leninists try to make the organizational rather than the National Question the point of division between Lenin and Luxemburg, so others act as if Lenin did not "refute" Luxemburg's 1908–09 thesis.[2] In truth, one of Lenin's greatest contributions is precisely his work on the National Question before and after the war, as well as after he, himself, had come to power. Everyone from Marx and Engels to Kautsky and Bebel, to Plekhanov and Lenin—absolutely everyone in the international Marxist movement outside her own group—opposed her position. Nothing, however, moved her from her opposition.

She began her most comprehensive thesis on the "nationality problem" by taking issue with the Russian stand ("Point 9" of the RSDLP program), "that all nationalities forming the state have the right to self-determination." She admitted that—although "at first glance" it appeared as "a paraphrase of the old slogan of bourgeois nationalism put forth in all countries at all times: 'the right of nations to freedom and independence' "—it was true that the Russian Social-Democracy was also for the class struggle and for revolution. Still, Luxemburg held triumphantly, "It gives no practical guideline for the day to day politics of the proletariat, nor any practical solution of nationality problems." Having reduced the Marxist principle of self-determination to hardly more than "bourgeois nationalism," since "practically" it offers nothing, Luxemburg now proceeded to knock down that straw man. She concluded that self-determination was sheer "utopia": under capitalism it is impossible of achievement, and why would anyone need it under socialism?

When Luxemburg took issue with Marx on the National Question, she raised the point only that it was outdated. The dispute was conducted as if it were merely a question of whether "orthodox" means that one holds that Marx could never be wrong. But it was not a question of whether Marx could or could not be wrong, nor was it that the objective situation could not have changed. It was a question of dialectics, of the methodology in approaching opposites. Any question of dialectic methodology and the relationship of that to the dialectics of liberation, where it had been raised, had been judged "abstract" by Luxemburg. As she searched for new theory to answer new "facts," dialectics of liberation entirely passed her by. Unfortunately, *so did the new forces of revolution in the national struggle against imperialism.*

Luxemburg could not have been in the dark about Marx's position, which was expressed innumerable times in innumerable places, and she argued against it often enough. She may not have known, however, about the 7 February 1882 letter Engels wrote to Kautsky on "Nationalism, Internationalism and the Polish Question."[3] It bears special importance to us here because it was written just a few weeks after Engels had collaborated with Marx on a new preface to the Russian edition of the *Communist Manifesto*, dated 21 January 1882. It has special relevance to the problematic of all discussions about the 1905 Revolution, not only as it was discussed while it was happening, 1905–07, but as it reappeared in the 1910 dispute with Karl Kautsky, when the question was the relationship between "backward" Russia and "advanced" Germany. The 1882 Preface had predicted that a revolution could occur first in Russia and be successful if it "becomes" the signal for proletarian revolution in the West. Naturally, this added impetus to the whole question of Poland, which was then part of the Russian Empire.

Engels's letter to Kautsky reads as follows:

> Polish socialists who do not place the liberation of their country at the head of their program, appear to me as would German socialists who do not demand first and foremost repeal of the socialist law, freedom of the press, association, and assembly . . . It is unimportant whether a reconstitution of Poland is possible *before* the next revolution. *We* have in no case the task to deter the Poles from their efforts to fight for the vital conditions of their future development, or to persuade them that national independence is a very secondary matter from the international point of view. On the contrary, independence is the basis of any common international action . . . We, in particular, have no reason whatever to block their irrefutable striving for independence. In the first place, they have invented and applied in 1863 the method of fighting . . . ; and secondly they were the only reliable and capable lieutenants in the Paris Commune.

It simply was not true, as Luxemburg had argued, that the objective situation had changed so drastically since Marx's time that a new thesis was needed; nor that, in any case, there are "no absolutes" in Marxism. No doubt national self-determination was not "an absolute," but neither was it something limited to the 1840s or 1860s. Marx always had a global vision, and the opposition to Russian tsarism was that it was then the counterpoint of European reaction. When Marx, in delivering the keynote address to the International's celebration of the fourth anniversary of the 1863 Polish uprising, called the Poles "20 million heroes between Europe and Asia," it was not only a question of self-determination of the nation, but a question of *revolutionary potential*. He likewise singled out their role in the Paris Commune.

In a word, to counterpose the class struggle, not to mention revolution, to "the National Question" *as Marx analysed it*, is to transform the reality into an abstraction. Not only did the objective situation in Luxemburg's time not change so drastically on the National Question from what it was in Marx's day, but self-determination as a revolutionary potential demanded a broadening of the very concept of a philosophy of revolution as a totality.

Luxemburg, however, continued to develop her differences both on the question of ideology and on the question of production:

> Any ideology is basically only a superstructure of the material and class conditions of a given epoch. However, at the same time, the ideology of each epoch harks back to the ideological results of the preceding epochs, while on the other hand, it has its own logical development in a certain area. This is illustrated by the sciences as well as by religion, philosophy and art . . . Because the modern capitalist culture is an heir to the continuator of earlier cultures, what develops is the continuity and monolithic quality of a national culture . . .
>
> Capitalism annihilated Polish independence but at the same time created modern Polish national culture. This national culture is a product indispensable within the framework of bourgeois Poland; its existence and development are a historical necessity, connected with the capitalistic development itself.[4]

What is ironic is that, without ever changing her "general" position that "national culture" was "indispensable" to the bourgeoisie, she insisted on the autonomy of the SDKPiL even after they "merged" with the Russian Social-Democracy.

The outbreak of World War I did not stop her opposition to self-determination. Rather, the shock of the betrayal of the Second International deepened her belief that internationalism and "nationalism," including the question of self-determination, were absolute opposites. She mobilized at once to fight the betrayal. Under the pseudonym of Junius, she produced the first great outcry against the betrayal. *The Crisis of the Social Democracy*[5] spoke most eloquently:

> The "civilized world" which looked on calmly while this same imperialism consigned tens of thousands of Hereros to the most horrible destruction, and filled the Kalahari desert with the mad cries of those perishing of thirst and the death rattles of the dying; while in Putumayo, in ten years forty thousand human beings were martyred by a gang of European industrial robber barons, and the rest of a people beaten into cripples; while in China an ancient culture was offered up to all the abominations of destruction and anarchy, under the firebrands and murders of the European soldier-rabble; while Persia helplessly suffocated in the ever-tightening noose of foreign despotism; while in Tripoli the Arabs were bowed to the yoke of capital with fire and sword, their culture and their dwellings alike razed to the ground—this "civilized world" has only today become aware that the bite of the imperialist beast is fatal, that its breath is infamy.

Nevertheless, the Fifth Thesis of the Junius pamphlet states:

> In the era of rampaging imperialism there can be no more national wars. National interests can serve only as a means of deception of betraying the working masses of the people to their deadly enemy, imperialism . . .
> It is true that socialism recognizes for every people the right of independence and the freedom of independent control of its own destinies. But it is a veritable perversion of socialism to regard present-day capitalist society as the expression of this self-determination of nations.

Junius concludes: "So long as capitalist states exist, i.e., so long as imperialistic world policies determine and regulate the inner and the outer life of a nation, there can be no 'national self-determination' either in war or in peace."

Great as the solidarity was that swept the revolutionary internationalists abroad–Lenin included, of course–when they got that antiwar pamphlet from Germany, Lenin (who did not know that Junius was Luxemburg) was shocked to read in the same pamphlet that analysis opposing national self-determination and counterposing to it "the class struggle." It was the exact opposite of his own attitude, not because he was always for the right of nations to self-determination, but because, where previously it had just been principle, now he considered it a matter of the very life of the revolution as well, holding that the struggle for national self-determination could become "one of the bacilli" for a proletarian socialist revolution itself. He wrote:[6]

> In saying that the class struggle is the best means of defense against invasion, Junius applied Marxist dialectics only halfway, taking one step on the right road and immediately deviating from it. Marxist dialectics call for a concrete analysis of each specific historical situation . . . Civil war against the bourgeoisie is *also* a form of class struggle . . . [p. 210].
>
> There is not the slightest doubt that the Dutch and Polish Marxists who are opposed to self-determination belong to the best revolutionary and internationalist elements in international Social-Democracy. How is it, then, that their theoretical reasoning is, as we have seen, just a mass of errors? Not a single correct general argument; nothing but "Imperialist Economism"! [p. 293].

"Imperialist economism" meant subordinating the new "Subject"—the colonial masses who are sure to revolt—to the overwhelming might of the imperialist land. For Lenin, the whole point, always and forever, so to speak, was that: "All national oppression calls forth the resistance of the *broad masses* of the people; and the resistance of a nationally oppressed population always *tends* towards national revolt" (p. 248). It became absolutely imperative to see the single dialectic in revolution and in thought when the Irish rebellion erupted. As he put it: "The dialectics of history is such that small nations, powerless as an *independent* factor in the struggle against imperialism, play a part as one of the ferments, one of the bacilli which help the *real* power against imperialism to come on the scene, namely, the socialist proletariat" (p. 303).

That would have been exactly Luxemburg's point of view if the proletariat had been the mass involved; that, precisely, was what she meant by "spontaneity." But having judged national self-determination to be "bourgeois," having seen the great suffering of the colonial masses but not the dialectic of their creativity, she didn't change her old position. As it happens, Ireland had been the country she used as "proof" for opposing national self-determination, and even before the Easter Rebellion—when Lenin thought that Luxemburg was unaware of Marx's position on the independence of Ireland—Lenin considered her attitude one of "amusing boldness" as he repeated her contrast between herself as "practical" and those favoring national self-determination as "utopian." He wrote: "While declaring the independence of Poland to be a utopia and repeating it *ad nauseam*, Rosa Luxemburg exclaims ironically: why not raise the demand for the independence of Ireland? It is obvious that the 'practical' Rosa Luxemburg is unaware of Karl Marx's attitude to the question of the independence of Ireland."[7]

Now that it was a question not of knowing Marx's position but of needing to confront the imperialist war and the revolt of the colonial masses, Lenin struck out against all, especially the Bolsheviks, who opposed national self-determination, calling their position nothing short of "imperialist economism."

Luxemburg's admirers, adherents and nonadherents alike, are at a loss to explain her position on the National Question; it has been attributed to everything from "factional origins" (she had emerged as a Marxist internationalist revolutionary in the struggle against the Polish Socialist Party's "Nationalism") to, very nearly, calling her position "insanity." "There is no other word for it," wrote George Lichtheim, asking his readers

> to pause here. The subject is loaded with passion. It was the central issue of Rosa Luxemburg's political life . . . It was the one issue on which she stood ready to break with her closest associates and to fly in the face of every authority, including that of Marx. Poland was dead! It could never be revived! Talk of a Polish nation, of an independent Poland, was not only political and economic lunacy; it was a distraction from the class struggle, a betrayal of Socialism! . . . One thing only counted: fidelity to proletarian internationalism as she understood it (and as Marx, poor man, had plainly not understood it). On this point, and on this alone, she was intractable . . . One of the strangest aberrations ever to possess a major political intellect.[8]

The birth of the Third World in our era has made it easy not to fall into the trap of counterposing "internationalism" and "nationalism," as if they were at all times irreconcilable absolutes. In the hands of a revolutionary like Frantz Fanon, the dialectical relationship of the two was beautifully developed by him in expressing the idea, even of an absolute, as if it were a fighting slogan. In *Wretched of the Earth* he wrote:

> History teaches us clearly that the battle against colonialism does not run straight along lines of nationalism . . . National consciousness which is not nationalism is the only thing that will give us an international dimension . . . The natives' challenge to the colonial world is not a rational confrontation of points of view. It is not a treatise on the universal, but the untidy affirmation of an original idea propounded as an absolute . . . For Europe, for ourselves and for humanity . . . we must work out new concepts and try to set afoot a new man.[9]

Even if we do not go out of the historic framework of Rosa Luxemburg's period, Lichtheim's psychologizing is no answer. Instead, we must grapple with the ambivalence of her position on spontaneity and organization, considering it within the context of her total commitment, at one and the same time, both to the spontaneous action of the masses and to the vanguard party.

The difficulty of disentangling is not made easy by the endless series of slanders and myths about Luxemburg's attitude to organization, as if all that was involved was Luxemburg the democrat vs Lenin the dictator. Where these rewriters of history begin with mistitling the very subject of her 1904 critique of Lenin—which she called "Organizational Questions of the Social-Democracy," and which they twisted to read "Leninism or Marxism?"—it is necessary, instead, to follow her own articulation of the question.[10] It is clear enough that she opposed Lenin's concept of organization, but it is equally clear that she was criticizing Germany as well as Russia and holding that each had "equal historic status." Towering above all her criticism, as well as her approval, was not the question of organization but the concept of revolution. Because that was so, the organizational question took a subordinate place throughout the next decade. What did predominate, and what brought her close to Lenin, was the actual 1905 Revolution.

DIFFERENCES WITH LENIN ON ORGANIZATION

The distorters of history try to make it appear as if Luxemburg's opposition to Lenin on the organizational question was total, lasted to her dying day, and signified opposition to the 1917 Revolution. The truth, as we shall see, is that she considered the 1917 Revolution the greatest event in history and attempted to have the same kind of revolution in 1919 in Germany.

Let us begin at the beginning, back in 1904. Luxemburg, at the beginning of "Organizational Questions," cleared the decks of two questions: the need for centralism as against the circle and local-club atmosphere that appeared previously in Russia, and the need for secretive work in an absolutist regime like tsarism. Once that was done, she stressed, as always, the "genius" of the proletariat as creators of actions as well as elaborators of tactics, and the insignificance of central committees: "the limited role of the conscious initiative of the party direction in the formation of tactics—can be seen in Germany and in all other countries" (p. 293).[11]

Luxemburg was not denying the need for centralism and conspiratorial work under an absolutist regime, nor underestimating the organizational difficulties revolutionaries face in such regimes. What she did object to was making a virtue out of necessity and then turning it into a veritable principle. This concept of organization she designated as "ultra-centralist."

She turned directly to what she considered Lenin's main error, the concept that a Social-Democrat is "a Jacobin indissolubly connected with the organization of the class-conscious proletariat." In devoting the next few pages to exposing "Jacobinism" and "Blanquism," Luxemburg concluded that Lenin "forgets that this difference [class consciousness] implies a complete revision of the concept of organization, a whole new content for the concept of centralism, and a whole new conception of the reciprocal relations of the organization and the struggle" (p. 288). She insisted that this cannot simply be dismissed as if class consciousness automatically meant mere opposition to Blanquism as "a conspiracy of a small minority." Quite the contrary.

What she was saying was: If we grant you the truth about the kind of conditions you have to work under, and if we furthermore admit it to be a principle for Marxists to be "centralist" rather than either localized groups or anarchistic, the fundamental question remains: Doesn't the very theory and principle of Marxism demand a total revision of any other concept of organization? Isn't it true that, even when we are for "centralism," it is so different from any kind of capitalistic centralism that we must never forget that what towers over both of these questions is the *relationship* of the organization to the class struggle? We could never be Blanquist, since his concept of conspiratorial organization had no need for mass organization or mass action except on the day of revolution, whereas our concept is that the mass party is not only for the day of revolution, but for the day-to-day activity where class consciousness is every bit as needed.

Furthermore, continued Luxemburg—here answering Lenin's attacks on intellectuals who, he claimed, were the ones who had "need for self education in the sense of organization and discipline"—neither the intellectuals nor the proletariat had need for what Lenin extolled, "factory discipline." Finally, she said, it is fantastic to think that some ultracentralist formula (her expression, not Lenin's) will help fight opportunism and what Lenin calls "the scatter-brainedness and individualism of the intellectuals"; no formula will help that. She was especially critical of Lenin's expression: "It is a question of forging by means of the paragraphs of the organizational statutes, a more or less sharp weapon against opportunism. The deeper the source of opportunism, the sharper this weapon must be." She held that "the attempt to exorcise opportunism by means of a scrap of paper can in fact only affect Social Democracy itself, in that it paralyzes its living pulse and weakens its capacity for resistance, not only in the struggle against opportunist currents but also, more importantly, against the established order. The means turns against the ends" (p. 305).

Lenin's answer (which it is doubtful Luxemburg ever saw, since Kautsky refused to publish it) was that she was speaking in generalities and had not answered a single concrete question, whereas he was being very concrete on the 1903 Congress, which she had not attended. That Congress, he said, would have shown her that not only was he not ultracentralist, but that the ones who were violating simple democratic principles were the Mensheviks, who refused to follow through on the decisions of the Congress and wanted to continue being the head of the organization although they were now the minority.

Although it is true that Lenin and Luxemburg were, indeed, not on the same wave length, the greater truth is that, once the actual revolution broke out in 1905, she not only was closer to Lenin, but everything that flowed from the actual revolution—which she summarized after the revolution in her most famous pamphlet, *The Mass Strike, the Party, and the Trade Unions*—was directed not against Lenin but against the German Social-Democracy. Nevertheless, we can under no circumstances agree with the vanguardists, who, from the opposite point of view than those who try to make a pure democrat out of her, likewise try to reduce her to their size and make a vanguardist of her. The "proof" these epigones offer is this: since Lenin, by sticking to the concrete questions raised at the Congress, proved Luxemburg wrong; and since, in 1919, Luxemburg "followed" Lenin, there is no further need to pay attention to her "abstractions."

On the contrary, Luxemburg's generalizations are relevant for our day and we must examine them. There is absolutely no doubt that not only is there a need for a great deal more democracy, for different tendencies to express themselves, but even for a totally new concept of democracy, like Luxemburg's. And surely it is imperative not to make a virtue out of necessity, which leads one living under tsarism to overstress the need for centralism to oppose it. Furthermore, whereas her expression, "the Marxist conception of socialism cannot be fixed in rigid formulas in any area, including . . . organization" (p. 286), may have left elbowroom for opportunism to continue functioning in a Marxist organization (as witness the fact that the first expression of reformism, Bernstein, was not expelled), it is even truer that Lenin's concept of centralism—which was perverted by Stalin into totalitarianism—makes imperative the need for decentralization.

Luxemburg was absolutely right in her emphasis that the Marxist movement was the "first in the history of class societies which, in all its moments, in its entire course, reckons on the organization and the independent, direct action of the masses" (p. 288). However, she is not right in holding that, very nearly automatically, it means so total a conception of socialism that a *philosophy* of Marx's concept of revolution could likewise be left to spontaneous action. Far from it. Nowhere is this seen more clearly than in the 1905 Revolution, where spontaneity was absolutely the greatest, but failed to achieve its goal.

The question of class consciousness does not exhaust the question of cognition, of Marx's philosophy of revolution. But within the context of the 1904 debate—that is, before the revolution—it is sufficient to limit cognition to organizational relations, and therefore to stress, as Luxemburg did, that the working class must be free "to make its own mistakes and to learn the historical dialectic by itself. Finally, we must frankly admit to ourselves that errors made by a truly revolutionary labor movement are historically infinitely more fruitful and more valuable than the infallibility of the best of all possible 'central committees' " (p. 306). Lenin, of course, denied claiming "infallibility" for any "central committee."

Luxemburg herself very nearly made a fetish out of the principle of a unified party. When Henriette Roland-Holst became so disgusted with the bureaucratization of the Dutch party that she wanted to leave it, Luxemburg wrote to her on 11 August 1908: "A splintering of Marxists (not to be confused with differences of opinion) is fatal. Now that you want to leave the party, I want to hinder you from this with all my might . . . Your resignation from the SDAP [the Dutch Sociaal-Democratische Arbeiderspartij] simply means your resignation from the Social-Democratic movement. This you must not do, none of us must! We cannot stand outside the organization, outside contact with the masses. *The worst working-class party is better than none.*"

Clearly, there was too much organizational Lassalleanism in Luxemburg as there was in Lenin. Neither her critique of Lenin's position, nor the development of her concept of spontaneity in *Mass Strike*, in 1906, had prepared her for the break with Karl Kautsky in 1910–11; what was missing in both at that time was a philosophy of revolution that was as one with their concept of organization.

Thus in 1910–11, when her dispute with Kautsky and Bebel, both on the general strike and on imperialism, became so total that she broke with them, she did not leave the party.

Even when, in 1917, the centrists broke with the SPD and organized the USPD, she joined them, since that was a "mass movement." It is true that both in theory and in activity—even when Spartakus, which is what the Gruppe Internationale became, was a fully organized tendency—she did not organizationally break with the USPD until the actual outbreak of the German Revolution.

It is here, therefore, that we must once again stop at the question of organization and ponder what the ramifications are of answering concrete organizational questions exclusively in generalities. Luxemburg herself may have been satisfied—especially so as the 1905–06 Revolution transformed her small party into a mass organization—with her statement in the *Mass Strike* pamphlet: "A rigid, mechanical, bureaucratic conception will only recognize struggle as a product of a certain level of organization. On the contrary, dialectical developments in real life create organization as a product of struggle."[12]

She certainly proceeded to so glorify mass action as to leave nothing for leadership: "Any action, once unleashed, must move forward." The ultimate goal kept being proletarian class struggle, not theory of revolution: "What is always important for Social-Democracy is not to prophesy and to preconstruct a ready-made recipe for the future tasks. Rather, it is important that the correct historical evaluation of the forms of struggle corresponding to the given situation be continually maintained in the party, and that it understand the relativity of the given phase of the struggle, and the necessary advance of the revolutionary stages toward the ultimate goal of the proletarian class struggle."[13]

She certainly didn't anticipate *counter-revolution from within*, although she was the very one who sensed Kautsky's deep opportunism four full years before the outbreak of World War I. She was so stunned when that war also spelled out the collapse of the Second International that she was said to have contemplated suicide. Lenin, on the other hand, though he was four years late in confronting not just the opportunism of the Socialist International but its outright betrayal of socialism, embarked *at once* and *at one and the same time* in two directions. One was issuing the slogan: "Turn the imperialist war into civil war!" Because they stagified peace and revolution, and did not see that the only way to arrive at genuine peace was through civil war, even revolutionaries rejected it. Lenin, however, never bowed. Nor was he sufficiently impressed with the Zimmerwald and Kienthal antiwar conferences to give up his revolutionary slogan, though it took another four years before it could be transformed into reality.

The other direction Lenin undertook in 1914 was to re-examine his old philosophic ground by turning, instead, to Marx's origins in Hegel. The new comprehension of the dialectic, especially the principle of transformation into opposite, by no means limited itself to the "ultimate"—that is, the socialist revolution. Dialectics became the key concept, the judgment, of every problem—whether that was seeing that a section of the proletariat had itself become transformed into its opposite as the aristocracy of labor, which led Lenin to turn instead to the Easter uprising in Ireland, as a national movement that could become the true bacillus of the proletarian revolution; or whether it was viewing the leaders not only in relation to the masses but to the *dialectics* of revolution. Thus, when any of his Bolshevik colleagues—from Pyatakov to Bukharin—failed to see the dialectics of revolution in the National Question as *movement* and continued to expound the thesis that imperialism had put an end to the National Question and that there could be no successful national revolutions, Lenin did not hesitate to designate their theory as "imperialist economism." Where Luxemburg called for "The Rebuilding of the International," Lenin called for a *new*, a *Third*, International.

Luxemburg's overriding concept— a unified party, a unified International— was in great part responsible for the many false interpretations of her concept of both spontaneity and organization. Where the SPD, before World War I, was forever quoting and attacking Luxemburg's writings on spontaneity, the post–World War II critics were always stressing her 1904 critique of Lenin. In both cases, two opposites that Luxemburg did *not* consider genuine opposites— democracy/dictatorship of the proletariat, and spontaneity/organization— were twisted to make her say what she had not said. Further, her critics both concealed what she did say and didn't bother to ask either her or themselves the burning question: What were the dialectics of revolution? Was spontaneity/ consciousness the equivalent of philosophy and revolution in the full Marxian sense, or did it stop at a Lassallean sense of spontaneity/organization?

When we come to her intransigent, revolutionary antiwar stand, there is certainly not a whiff of affinity between Luxemburg and the SPD and the Second International. So deep, though mechanistic, was her internationalism that she refused to divert in any way to a national-freedom slogan. Thus, when her friend Mathilde Wurm bemoaned the condition of the Jews, she replied:

What do you want with this particular suffering of the Jews? The poor victims on the rubber plantations in Putumayo, the Negroes in Africa with whose bodies the Europeans play a game of catch, are just as near to me. Do you remember the words written on the work of the Great General Staff about Trotha's campaign in the Kalahari desert? "And the death-rattles, the mad cries of those dying of thirst, faded away into the sublime silence of eternity."

Oh, this "sublime silence of eternity" in which so many screams have faded away unheard. It rings within me so strongly that I have no special corner of my heart reserved for the ghetto: I am at home wherever in the world there are clouds, birds and human tears . . . [14]

Lenin, in criticizing Luxemburg's mechanistic view of internationalism that opposed the National Question, called her view a "half-way dialectic." The expression arose from the reorganization of his own former philosophical foundations. In grasping the idea that one cannot reach Absolute Method when "*opposite* determinations . . . come before consciousness without mutual contact," Lenin concluded: "that is the essence of anti-dialectic."

Ironically enough, although Rosa Luxemburg and Lenin were opposites in attitude to philosophy, they were *alike* in failing to relate organization to philosophy. Whereas Luxemburg paid very little attention to philosophy in general, Lenin's profound attention to philosophy in 1914 became an attitude that would, when it affected politics and theory, last until his dying day. But it was never worked out by him in relationship to the party. Put another way, when it was a question of analyzing imperialism—not just in economic terms but related to its opposite, the national revolts—Lenin changed his former positions, reorganizing his own attitude toward the relationship of idealism to materialism.

But there was no such reorganization on the "Woman Question," although it was the women, by their spontaneous act, who had initiated the toppling of the tsarist regime, as will be shown in Part Two. And there was the same lack of reorganization on the question of the party, although here there were many modifications. Yet despite all the modifications in his 1903 concept of the party that he introduced during the 1905 Revolution; despite the fact that in 1917 he actually threatened to resign and "go to the sailors," Lenin still never "rewrote" *What Is To Be Done?* Therein lies the greatest tragedy.

For both Luxemburg and Lenin, once the revolution became actual all other disputes faded into the background. Just as the 1905 Revolution towered high above the 1904 dispute, so the 1917 Revolution once again brought them close together, Luxemburg declaring: "The Russian Revolution is the most over-whelming fact of the World War. Its outbreak, its unparalleled radicalism, its enduring action best give the lie to the catch phrases with which official German Social-Democracy, eager to be of service, at first ideologically cloaked German imperialism's campaign of conquest: phrases about the mission of German bayonets to overthrow Russian tsarism and liberate its oppressed peoples."[15]

She continued to stress that "Freedom only for the supporters of the government, only for the members of one party—however numerous they may be—is no freedom at all. Freedom is always and exclusively freedom for the one who thinks differently." On the other hand, nothing could be more wrong than to think—or more correctly put, to try to make others think—that Luxemburg's criticisms meant opposition to the Russian Revolution.[16] The very opposite was the case:

> Everything that is happening in Russia is comprehensible and an inescapable chain of causes and effects, whose point of departure and keystone are the abdication of the German proletariat and the occupation of Russia by German imperialism. It would be demanding the superhuman of Lenin and his comrades to expect them, under such circumstances, to also conjure up the most beautiful democracy, the most exemplary dictatorship of the proletariat, and a flourishing socialist economy. Through their resolutely revolutionary stand, exemplary energy, and inviolable loyalty to international socialism they truly have accomplished enough of what could be accomplished under such diabolically difficult conditions. The danger begins when they make a virtue of necessity, when they wish henceforth and in all points to theoretically fix the tactics forced upon them by these fateful circumstances and to recommend them for imitation by the international [proletariat] as the model of socialist tactics.

Luxemburg herself gave the best summation of her position:

> The question is to distinguish the essential from the non-essential, the core from the coincidental in the politics of the Bolsheviks . . . In this connection, Lenin and Trotsky with their friends were the *first* to set the example before the world proletariat, and so far they are still the *only ones* who can proclaim with Hutten: I have dared! . . . In Russia the problem could only be posed. It could not be solved in Russia, it can only be solved internationally. And *in this sense*, the future everywhere belongs to "Bolshevism."

All the divisive questions became unimportant once the Russian Revolution broke out. What mattered was the revolution. Luxemburg's criticism of some of the features, especially what she considered insufficient democracy, took secondary place to her hailing the Russian Revolution as the greatest world event and praising the Bolsheviks as the only ones who dared, and who therefore should serve as the beacon light for all.

Within a year came the overthrow of the kaiser and the beginning of the German Revolution. Her commitment to the revolution being total, once action became *the* determinant, Luxemburg plunged in to lead the January 1919 Spartacist revolt, although she had soberly advised against it as both ill-timed and ill-prepared. There was certainly no time to talk of any other organization but the newly created Communist Party of Germany—not when the counterrevolution was moving so murderously fast that in two short weeks it would behead the German Revolution, murdering Luxemburg, Liebknecht, and Jogiches.

NOTES

1. See her letter to Jogiches of 7 May 1905, in *Roza Luksemburg: Listy do Leona Jogichesa-Tyszki*, vol. 2, 1900–1905 (Warsaw: Ksiazka i Wiedza, 1968).

2. See Horace B. Davis's introduction to *The National Question: Selected Writings by Rosa Luxemburg*, ed. Horace Davis (New York: Monthly Review Press, 1976), p. 9. "The Problem of Nationality and Autonomy," translated as "The National Question and Autonomy," is included in this work, along with other fundamental writings by Luxemburg on the National Question. It is not because the United States is so "backward" on theoretical questions that we did not get an English translation of Luxemburg's 1908 work until 1976. Rather, this fundamental work by Luxemburg so flew in the face of reality that it did not evoke translations into other languages. As Lenin once put it: "No Russian Marxist ever thought of blaming the Poles . . . Russians must continue to be for their independence."

3. It was first published by Moscow in 1933 in *Briefe an A. Bebel, W. Liebknecht, K. Kautsky und Andere*. It has been translated among the articles included in *The Russian Menace to Europe*, a collection of articles by Karl Marx and Frederick Engels, selected and edited by Paul W. Blackstock and Bert F. Hoselitz (Glencoe, Ill.: The Free Press, 1952), pp. 116–20.

4. Davis, *National Question*, pp. 253–55.

5. This pamphlet is universally known as the Junius pamphlet, from the signature Luxemburg used. The quotations that follow are from Rosa Luxemburg, *Gesammelte Werke* (Berlin: Dietz Verlag, 1974), 4:161. Trans. David Wolff. The reproduction of this pamphlet in Mary-Alice Waters's *Rosa Luxemburg Speaks* (New York: Pathfinder Press, 1970) contains a most fantastic error in referring to the Hereros doomed to destruction as "tens of thousands of heroes" (p. 326).

6. The quotations that follow are from V. I. Lenin, *Collected Works*, vol. 19 (New York: International Pub., 1942). Paginations in the text refer to this edition.

7. V.I. Lenin, *Selected Works*, 4:274.

8. See George Lichtheim's review of Nettl's biography of Rosa Luxemburg in *Encounter*, June 1966.

9. Frantz Fanon, *Wretched of the Earth* (New York: Grove Press, 1968), pp. 121, 198, 33, 255.

10. It took all the way to 1971 before we got a new and correct translation of this essay in Dick Howard, *The Selected Political Writings of Rosa Luxemburg* (New York: Monthly Review Press, 1971). The more famous and presumptuous is that which was included in the book mistitled *The Russian Revolution and Leninism or Marxism?* (Ann Arbor: Univ. of Michigan Press, 1961), to which Bertram Wolfe added his own introduction.

11. This and other page citations in the text following are to Howard, *Selected Political Writings*.

12. Nettl, *Rosa Luxemburg*, 2:504.

13. "Was Weiter?", *Gesammelte Werke*, 2:288-99. See chap. 2, n. 4 for the many ways this has been translated into English.

14. This letter from Wronke i. P. Fortress, dated 16 February 1917, is found in Stephen Bronner's edition of *The Letters of Rosa Luxemburg* (Boulder, Col.: Westview Press, 1978), p. 178.

15. This and the following quotations from Luxemburg's *The Russian Revolution* can be found in her *Gesammelte Werke*, 4:332-65.

16. Luxemburg never finished the draft of her pamphlet on *The Russian Revolution*, which she had begun in her prison cell, nor did she attempt to publish it. It was published posthumously by her associate, Paul Levi, when he broke with Lenin.

V

War, Prison, and Revolutions, 1914–19

> *... proletarian revolutions ... criticize themselves constantly, interrupt themselves continually in their own course ... deride with unmerciful thoroughness the inadequacies, weaknesses and paltriness of their first attempts ... recoil ever and anon from the indefinite prodigiousness of their own aims, until a situation has been created which makes all turning back impossible, and the conditions themselves cry out: Hic Rhodus, hic salta!*
>
> *Marx,* The 18th Brumaire of Louis Bonaparte

So ingrained was the horror and shock produced by the events of 4 August 1914—when the Socialist Reichstag deputies voted war credits to the Kaiser, and with this betrayal of socialism unloosed World War I—that it became the Global Great Divide for Marxists. The trauma notwithstanding, Rosa Luxemburg, on the evening of that very day, met in her apartment with her closest colleagues to disassociate socialism from the ignominy of that event. When hardly any other than Clara Zetkin (who at once telegraphed her enthusiastic support) answered the three hundred telegrams Luxemburg had sent out to SPD local leaders, she called a conference the following month. It was that one, in September 1914, that worked out the first public disclaimer of the vote for war credits, thus giving notice that there was opposition to the war within Germany. By then Karl Liebknecht had raised his lone voice in the Reichstag, and the public statement was signed: "Karl Liebknecht, Dr. Franz Mehring, Dr. Rosa Luxemburg, Clara Zetkin."

It was the next year, however, before *Die Internationale* appeared as the magazine of the Gruppe Internationale—later to become known as the Spartacists. For its first issue, Luxemburg had written "The Rebuilding of the International," a lengthy and serious analysis of the imperialist war:

On Aug. 4, 1914, German Social-Democracy abdicated politically, and at the same time the Socialist International collapsed ... Kautsky as the representative of the so-called "Marxist center," or in political terms, as the theoretician of the swamp, has for years degraded theory into the obliging hand-maiden of the official practice of the party bureaucrats and thus made his own sincere contribution to the present collapse of the party . . . On Aug. 4, German Social-Democracy, far from being "silent," assumed an extremely important historical function: the shield-bearer of imperialism in the present war.[1]

That was the one and only issue of *Die Internationale* that ever appeared; the magazine no sooner came out than the Prussian authorities confiscated it. Rosa Luxemburg had already been imprisoned, charged with "disobedience to the laws" long before the war broke out, for her anti-militarist activities—specifically, her speech of 16 September 1913, in which she had declared that if the militarists "think we are going to lift the weapons of murder against our French and other brethren, then we shall shout: 'We will not do it!' " Found guilty at her trial on 20 February 1914,[2] she had managed to remain free of jail, on appeal, for almost a full year. Then, suddenly, on 18 February 1915, just as she was preparing to leave with Clara Zetkin for a planning meeting to organize the first international antiwar women's conference, she was arrested.

The other revolutionary socialist women—Zetkin from Germany, Balabanoff from Italy, Krupskaya and Inessa Armand from Russia, and many others—did meet in Bern, and worked out ways for antiwar agitation in their own countries. Martial law had been declared in each belligerent country, and Zetkin found that the Social-Democracy was so involved in the imperialist war that they at once fired her from *Die Gleichheit*, of which she had been editor since its beginning in 1891, and which had become not only a "woman's paper" but the major publication of the radical left. It was recognized as *the* antiwar journal, internationally. By August 1915, Zetkin, too, was arrested.

THE "JUNIUS" PAMPHLET

In her dark and dreary prison, Luxemburg—isolated from everything that was going on outside, even though she had worked out a network for getting some news in and smuggling her writings out—at once set out to write the first comprehensive antiwar pamphlet to come out of Germany. *The Crisis in the German Social-Democracy* has retained its fame to this day, known by the signature she used as *Junius.*[3]

It raised high the banner, not only for internationalism and against imperialist war, but also against the official Social-Democracy: "Shamed, dishonored, wading in blood and dripping with filth, thus capitalist society stands . . . And in the midst of this orgy a world tragedy has occurred: the capitulation of the social democracy" (p. 262).

Far from being only agitation, the pamphlet traced capitalism's historical development for the past fifty years, that is to say, ever since it had destroyed the Paris Commune, and started on its imperialist course. Luxemburg had always felt that the Chinese-Japanese War of 1895 had signalled a shift in global power, which indeed led up to the First World War. Her main stress, however, was on German imperialism, from the "Morocco incident" on: "Whole peoples are destroyed, ancient civilizations are levelled to the ground, and in their place profiteering in its most modern forms is being established . . . The present world war is a turning point in the course of imperialism . . . " (p. 325).

As against the "stinking corpse" of the SPD, Luxemburg pointed to the revolutionary nature of Marx's Marxism and the revolt of the workers themselves: "The theoretical works of Marx gave to the working class of the whole world a compass by which to fix its tactics from hour to hour, in its journey toward the one unchanging goal . . . Historic development moves in contradictions, and for every necessity puts its opposite into the world as well. The capitalist state of society is doubtless a historic necessity, but so also is the revolt of the working class against it" (pp. 263, 324-25).

It is on these two grounds that the "Theses on the Tasks of International Social Democracy," which followed the Junius pamphlet, were based, as they propounded the following principles: "The class struggle against the ruling classes within the boundaries of the bourgeois states, and international solidarity of the workers of all countries, are the two rules of life, inherent in the working class in struggle and of world-historic importance to it for its emancipation" (pp. 330-31).

At the same time, Luxemburg repeated her opposition to national self-determination on the ground that it would be a return to "nationalism": "In the present imperialistic milieu there can be no wars of national self-defense. Every socialist policy that depends upon this determining historic milieu, that is willing to fix its policies in the world whirlpool from the point of a view of a single nation, is built upon a foundation of sand" (p. 305).

This first great antiwar pamphlet—which was, at one and the same time, propagandistic in the bravest sense, seriously theoretical, and straight out of Germany itself—was more than just a breath of fresh air for isolated antiwar Marxists the world over. It was the genuine opening of a new epoch, of a new path to revolution. Lenin was among those heaping praise upon the pamphlet for its courage; but he felt strongly that it was worked out in isolation. He did not know that "Junius" was Rosa Luxemburg when he wrote: "Junius' pamphlet conjures up in our minds the picture of a *lone* man who has no comrades in an illegal organization accustomed to thinking out revolutionary slogans to their conclusion and systematically educating the masses in their spirit . . . "[4]

Marxists from the day of Marx had always felt that criticism was pivotal to clarification and development of ideas. Just as Luxemburg had felt it important to criticize the Russian Revolution while hailing it as the greatest event, so Lenin, in introducing his criticism, wrote: "It would be a very deplorable thing, of course, if the 'Lefts' began to be careless in their treatment of Marxian theory, considering that the Third International can be established only on the basis of unvulgarized Marxism" (p. 207). We have dealt previously with his criticism, especially on the National Question, both as principle and as it related to one of the struggles against imperialism. He felt that unless one was most specific—that is to say, *named* the betrayers like Kautsky—Luxemburg's magnificent exposé of the imperialist war would sound merely agitational, instead of becoming a call to transform this imperialist war into a civil war. That, of course, was not her slogan.

Whereupon Lenin singled out what he considered her greatest error, hitting at it in the same manner in which he attacked his own Bolsheviks on the same question in the same period of 1916: " . . . when Junius lays particular emphasis on what to him is the most important point: the struggle against the 'phantom of national war, which at present dominates Social-Democratic policy', we cannot but agree that his reasoning is correct and quite appropriate. But it would be a mistake to exaggerate this truth; to depart from the Marxian rule to be concrete; to apply the appraisal of the present war to all wars that are possible under imperialism; to lose sight of the national movements *against* imperialism . . . " (p. 202).

As we saw in the previous chapter, Lenin accused Junius of applying Marxist dialectics "only halfway, taking one step on the right road and immediately deviating from it. Marxist dialectics call for a concrete analysis of each specific historical situation . . . Civil war against the bourgeoisie is *also* a form of class struggle . . . " (p. 210).

Luxemburg remained isolated, confined in jail for the rest of the war. She experienced ever worsening conditions, and violent changes of mood. But she was never without many projects she intended to carry out—whether that meant she had to invent the means of writing, as witness the letter she wrote in urine on a page from a book of French poems[5]; or that she could return to serious theoretical work. Here is one of her letters to Mathilde Jacob that was smuggled out: "After two weeks I got my books and permission to work—they didn't have to tell me twice. My health will have to get used to the somewhat peculiar diet, the main thing is that it doesn't prevent me working. Imagine, I get up every day at 5:40! Of course by 9 at night I have to be in 'bed', if the instrument I jack up and down every day deserves the name."[6]

The clandestine work of Spartakusbund would hardly have been able to continue while Luxemburg was in prison had it not been for Jogiches. Her other colleagues were also antiwar and for revolution but had little talent for clandestine work. Thus it was that Jogiches, who had up to then shown little interest in the German party except insofar as its work impinged on the work of the Polish party, now emerged as the leader of the German Left Opposition. He wrote the circulars of the Spartakusbund, arranged for their printing and circulation, and continued with all of the work needed to keep the Tendency together, including being the conduit to Luxemburg—both in getting her theoretical work out and in trying to ease her life in prison.

On 28 July 1916, Luxemburg sent Dietz, the party publisher, the following plan of what she intended to do for the duration of the war:

> 1. A complete work on economics with the title *Accumulation of Capital*, consisting of the original work together with an appendix, an *Anticritique*, and
> 2. A series of entirely popular essays under the collective title, *Introduction to Political Economy*, and
> 3. I am in the process of translating the Russian book by Korolenko, *History of my Contemporary*, into German.[7]

The fact that Dietz rejected the entire idea did not stop her from doing the work: she worked out her *Anticritique* and decided to publish her *Accumulation of Capital* as a single totality, translated the Korolenko work, and wrote a brilliant analysis of nineteenth-century Russian literature as the introduction to that work. Just as in 1911, when she was most isolated in the party because of her break with Kautsky and had at the same time painted a magnificent self-portrait and plunged into the writing of her greatest theoretical work, so now, in prison, Luxemburg studied her titmice and songbirds *and* achieved her highest theoretical writing. That does not mean that she was insensitive to her conditions. In March 1917 she wrote to Diefenbach: "Each day that I have to spend here becomes a minor mountain to be wearily climbed, and every little thing irritates me grievously. In 5 days, fully 8 months of the second year of my solitude will have come to an end. Then, surely, like last year, a revival will occur of its own, especially since Spring is coming."[8]

It was not spring, however, that made her spirits climb so high and made her feel so confident that she was ready to battle the whole world, Marx included. She had finished her *Anticritique*, and when she sent it to Diefenbach (the second person to read it), she quoted Mehring as having called it "Simply a work of genius, a truly magnificent, ravishing achievement!" She herself felt that the work "will certainly outlive me. It's much more mature than *Accumulation* itself; its form is extremely simple, without any accessories, without coquetry or optical illusions, straightforward and reduced to the barest essentials; I would even say 'naked,' like a block of marble. This is, in fact, where today my taste lies. In theoretical work, as in art, I value only the simple, the tranquil and the bold."[9]

Into the dark dungeon came a most brilliant and inspiring light—news of the March 1917 Revolution in Russia. So historic was the achievement, so great was the overturn of the tsarist regime, so magnificent was the first revolution to emerge out of the imperialist war, that it lighted up Luxemburg's life. As she put it in April in a letter to Marta Rosenbaum: "Of course the marvels in Russia are like a new lease on life for me. They're a saving grace for all of us. I only fear that you all do not appreciate them enough, do not recognize sufficiently that it is our own cause which is winning here. It *must* and *will* have a salutary effect on the whole world, it must radiate outwards into the whole of

Europe; I am absolutely certain that it will bring a new epoch and that the war cannot last long."

In her pamphlet on "The Russian Revolution," Luxemburg's praise went hand in hand with her opposition to anything that would infringe on democracy: "Socialist democracy begins simultaneously with the demolition of class rule and the construction of socialism."[10]

A new epoch was indeed dawning. 1917 was not only March, it was November as well. And it included not just the overthrow of the tsar, but the conquest of power by the Bolsheviks. Luxemburg was absolutely and firmly for it. "Yes, dictatorship! But this dictatorship consists in the *manner of applying democracy*, not in its *elimination*," she wrote in "The Russian Revolution." So anxious was she to stress that it was "a first proletarian revolution of *transition*, world-historical in significance," that she had written to Luise Kautsky on 11 November 1917, that if the Russians "will not be able to maintain themselves in this witches' sabbath," it would not be "because statistics show that economic development in Russia is too backward, as your clever husband has figured out, but because the social democracy in the highly developed west consists of pitifully wretched cowards who, looking quietly on, will let the Russians bleed themselves to death . . . " Her point was that it must be supported, extended by the world proletariat, especially the German proletariat. As she was to put it in "The Russian Revolution," "In Russia the problem could only be posed, it could not be solved." In a word, it was the first step in the world revolution and could be saved only if it became the world revolution.

On one point in that pamphlet she seemed to support the SPD: "It is a well known and indisputable fact that without a free and untrammeled press, without the unlimited right of association and assemblage, the rule of the broad masses of the people is entirely unthinkable." This critique of the dismissal of the Constituent Assembly in Russia was a few months later seen differently in her own revolution. There she declared the national assembly to be a "bourgeois assembly," "a counter-revolutionary stronghold" against the genuine democracy contained in her slogan "All power to the Workers, Soldiers and Peasants Councils."

"THE GERMAN REVOLUTION HAS BEGUN"

At the end of October 1918, a mutiny at the Kiel naval base, where, in August 1917, the first mutiny of the war had occurred, precipitated the collapse of the imperial regime. By 9 November, the waves of strikes that had broken out in November coalesced to become the general strike in Berlin. The German Revolution had begun. The kaiser fled. That same day the revolutionary masses reached the prison gates of Breslau and freed Rosa Luxemburg, who promptly repaired to the town square and addressed the mass meeting. Workers Councils sprang up in all major cities. Soldiers Councils appeared everywhere at the front, and Sailors Councils at naval bases. On 11 November, Spartakus issued a special supplement to their new paper, *Rote Fahne*, which this time was most concrete, with a fourteen-point program ranging from the demand for immediate peace to a call for elections of Workers and Soldiers Councils and the slogan: "All power to the Soviets!"

At once the counterrevolution began with the unified SPD–USPD call for still one more parliament: a National Assembly.

Just as, from the very first issue of the antiwar paper *Die Internationale*, the Spartacists had tightly related their positive program to the need for "unmercifully thorough derision of [their] own inadequacies and weaknesses" and "moral fall since August 4," so the very first issue of *Rote Fahne* called for "the strictest self-criticism and iron concentration of energy in order to continue the work," now that the revolution had begun.[11]

This focal point for both the call for rebuilding the International and for starting the revolution was a way of not ever separating ends from means: "The path of the revolution follows clearly from its ends, its method follows from its task. All power in the hands of the working masses, in the hands of the workers' and soldiers' councils, protection of the work of revolution against its lurking enemies—this is the guiding principle of all measures to be taken by the revolutionary government."[12]

Rote Fahne kept up a daily, unceasing attack on "the petty-bourgeois illusion" that the Kautskys and Hilferdings tried to perpetrate with their call for a national assembly: "These profound Marxists have forgotten the ABCs of socialism. They have forgotten that the bourgeoisie is not a parliamentary body, but a ruling class in possession of all means of economic and social power."

Spartakus also issued a special pamphlet in those two intense months of 1918, which they entitled *What Does the Spartakus Bund Want?* This made it clear that only the "elimination of all parliaments" and "election of workers' councils in all Germany" could achieve the "abolition of all class discrimination, orders and titles, complete legal and social equality of the sexes," "expropriation of property and takeover of all public transport," and "maximum 6-hour workday."[13]

Luxemburg's inexhaustible energy did not flag for a single second from the moment she was released from prison and began her first meetings—public and organizational—to the writings, to the demonstrations, to the strikes, to the editing of the papers, to still more strikes and still more demonstrations. Her eloquence, her passion, her *practicing* "the revolution is everything, all else is bilge," were all compressed in those two-and-a-half months of freedom before she was murdered.

The red thread that runs through it all is, of course, the abolition of capitalism and the creation of socialism. There was no middle road. It was either barbarism or socialism. The one thing that distinguished the Spartacists however, from what the Bolsheviks called for and prepared to achieve—conquest of power—was articulated as follows:

> The Spartacus League refuses to share governing power with the errandboys of the bourgeoisie, i.e., with Scheidemann, Ebert, *et al* . . .
> The Spartacus League will also refuse to take power merely because Scheidemann, Ebert, *et al* ruin themselves . . .
> The Spartacus League will never assume governing power in any way other than through the clear, unambiguous will of the great majority of the proletarian mass in all Germany, never in any way other than on the strength of the masses' conscious agreement with the views, aims and methods of struggle of the Spartacus League . . .
> The victory of the Spartacus League is not at the beginning but at the end of the revolution: it is identical with the victory of the great millions-strong masses of the socialist proletariat . . . [14]

These were the first articulations of the revolution in *What Does The Spartakus Bund Want?* By the end of December, the Spartakus Bund was joined by Karl Radek's Bremen Radicals, Borchardt's Internationalists, and other Marxists who had refused to join USPD, to form a new communist party. We have reached the last two weeks of Luxemburg's life, the culmination of all her activities, the historic speech to the Founding Conference of the Communist Party of Germany.[15] Let's listen to her speak: "Great historic movements have been the determining causes of today's deliberations . . . To those who participated in the revolution of 9 November, and who nonetheless shower calumnies upon the Russian Bolshevists, we should never cease to reply with the question: 'Where did you learn the alphabet of your revolution? Was it not from the Russians that you learned to ask for workers' and soldiers' councils?' " (p. 405).

And of course she drew the Great Divide between the betrayal of 4 August 1914 and 30 December 1918, when the Congress opened, stressing especially the 1872 edition of the *Communist Manifesto*, in which Marx had called attention to the fact that what the Paris Commune showed was that the "working class cannot simply lay hold of the ready-made state machinery and wield it for its own purposes, but must smash it" (p. 406). Luxemburg concluded:

> But we have now reached the point, comrades, when we are able to say that we have rejoined Marx, and that we are once more advancing under his flag . . .
> First and foremost, we have to extend in all directions the system of workers' councils . . . We have to seize power, and the problem of the seizure of power assumes this aspect; what, throughout Germany, can each workers' and soldiers' council achieve? [Bravo!] There lies the source of power . . .
> The masses must learn how to use power, by using it. There is no other way . . . The workers, today, will learn in the school of action. [Hear! Hear!] Our scripture reads: in the beginning was the deed [pp. 425, 426].

The deed had hardly begun, however, as the strikes mounted, soldiers and sailors councils—especially the latter: the People's Naval Division—surrounded the Reich's chancellory and held the government captive until 5 January, when two hundred thousand workers marched in Berlin against the Eberts and Scheidemanns, who, allied with the old imperial Supreme Army Command, tried to restore discipline in the Security Police by dismissing the USPD Police Chief Eichhorn, who had been with the workers. The "Spartakus Week," which began with the occupation of the *Vorwärts* building, was a spontaneous outburst from below, with which Luxemburg, though opposed to it as ill-timed and ill-prepared, nevertheless totally aligned herself. She would not abandon the mass movement; they led the way.

The counterrevolution, on the other hand, was armed to the teeth. Ebert had appointed Noske as Defense (sic) Minister. They did not even dare to call upon the troops in Berlin to participate in the planned massacre. Instead, Noske, from his headquarters in Dahlem, marched in with three thousand troops (with more columns following from the hinterlands), shot their way into the building, killing 100, wounding innumerable others, and fired up the lynch campaign against Luxemburg and Liebknecht that had gone on unabated for weeks. But Luxemburg would not stop her activity at all, much less stop her criticism of the "demagoguery and clap-trap of 'unity'." She never failed to credit the masses with the ability to recoup:

> The leadership has failed. But the leadership can and must be created anew by the masses and of the masses. The masses are the decisive factor; they are the rock upon which the final victory of the revolution is erected. The masses were abreast of events; they have turned this "defeat" into one of those historical defeats which are the pride and strength of international socialism. And thus the future victory will blossom from out of this "defeat."[16]

These are the last words from her lips: " 'Order reigns in Berlin!' You stupid lackeys! Your 'order' is built on sand. Tomorrow the revolution will rear its head once again, and, to your horror, will proclaim, with trumpets blazing: *I was, I am, I will be!*"[17]

The date was 14 January. The lynch campaign of the Social-Democracy had come to a climax and the Freikorps was its executioner. The very next day, 15 January, Luxemburg was dragged out of her house, beaten, shot in the head. Her body was thrown into the Landwehr Canal. It was May before her body was discovered, so mutilated that it was beyond recognition.

After her murder, *Rote Fahne* continued unabated, under Jogiches's direction, as he waged a relentless campaign to find the murderers of Luxemburg and Liebknecht and to expose the fact that the SPD was protecting—and indeed, had inspired—those murderers. Those critical days were spent also in gathering Luxemburg's writings to assure they would not be destroyed. Within six weeks, Jogiches too was murdered, on 10 March.

The German Revolution that was thus beheaded had enough energizing creativity left in the thousands upon thousands of working men and women to reappear, not just once more in 1921, but also again in 1923, before it was finally crushed.

By the time the Russian Revolution and its workers' state likewise got transformed into its opposite—state capitalism—and Depression put an end to "pure" private capitalism only to end at the monstrosity of Nazism, Luxemburg's theory of the breakdown of capitalism—Socialism or Barbarism—came alive again. Indeed, she comes alive every time we are in a deep new crisis. Nowhere was this more true than with the birth of a Third World, a new generation of western revolutionaries fully disillusioned with vanguardism, and a totally new Women's Liberation Movement busily digging out the true history of womankind. Philosophy still may have been lacking, but history has original ways of illuminating the thought of its time.

NOTES

1. Robert Looker, ed., *Rosa Luxemburg: Selected Political Writings* (New York: Grove Press, 1974), pp. 197–99.

2. Luxemburg's remarkable speech is included as an appendix in J.P. Nettl, *Rosa Luxemburg*, 2 vols. (London: Oxford Univ. Press, 1966), 2:488–92.

3. This is included in several collections. The page citations in the following text are to the translation in *Rosa Luxemburg Speaks*, ed. by Mary-Alice Waters, pp. 257–331.

4. Lenin, *Collected Works*, 19:213. The page citations in the text following are to this edition.

5. Nettl includes in his biography, *Rosa Luxemburg*, a reproduction of this secret letter from Luxemburg to Fanny Jezierska. Plate 14.

6. Nettl, *Rosa Luxemburg*, 2:621.

7. Ibid., 2:620 n.

8. Bronner, *The Letters of Rosa Luxemburg*, p. 182.

9. Ibid., p. 185.

10. In *Gesammelte Werke*, 4:363.

11. Looker, *Luxemburg*, pp. 205, 253.

12. Ibid., p. 254.

13. The pamphlet was published as an article in *Rote Fahne*, 14 December 1918.

14. Looker, *Luxemburg*, pp. 285–86.

15. The excerpts from this speech that follow are taken from the translation used in Mary-Alice Waters, *Rosa Luxemburg Speaks*, and page citations in the text are to this edition.

16. Rosa Luxemburg, "Order Reigns in Berlin," *Rote Fahne*, 14 January 1919. As translated in Looker, *Luxemburg*, pp. 305–06.

17. Ibid., p. 306.

PART TWO

The Women's Liberation Movement as Revolutionary Force and Reason

... see to it that you stay human ... Being human means joyfully throwing your whole life "on the scales of destiny" when need be, but all the while rejoicing in every sunny day and every beautiful cloud. Ach, I know of no formula to write you for being human ...

Rosa Luxemburg

A work is never beautiful, unless it in some way escapes its author.
D. H. Lawrence

Life itself becomes too dear,/So vast are one's dreams.
Louise Michel

The whole movement of history is, on the one hand, the actual act *of creation—the act by which its empirical being was born; on the other hand, for its thinking consciousness, it is the* realized and recognized *process of development.**

Karl Marx, 1844

---

*I am using my own translation of "Private Property and Communism," which appeared as Appendix A in the first edition of my work *Marxism and Freedom* (New York: Bookman, 1958), p. 293.

VI

An Overview by Way of Introduction; the Black Dimension

Because it is our age which has forced upon the world consciousness the truth that Women's Liberation is an Idea whose time has come, it is necessary to turn backward and forward in time as well as to look globally at this phenomenon. Neither the urgency of our time, nor space, will permit us to turn as far back as 1647, when the first Maids' Petition to the British Parliament asked for "liberty every second Tuesday"; or even to Wollstonecraft's "Vindication of the Rights of Woman," 1792. But we must begin with 1831, both because of its relevance to today, and because of the events that happened that year—in particular the greatest slave revolt in United States history, led by Nat Turner,[1] who held that the idea of freedom is present in every slave so tempestuously that "the same idea prompted others as well as myself to this undertaking." It was the same year that a Black woman, Maria Stewart, became the first American-born woman, white or Black, to speak publicly.

Here is what Maria Stewart said:

> O ye daughters of Africa, awake! awake! arise! no longer sleep nor slumber but distinguish yourselves. Show forth to the world that ye are endowed with noble and exalted faculties... How long shall the fair daughters of Africa be compelled to bury their minds and talents beneath a load of iron pots and kettles? ... How long shall a mean set of men flatter us with their smiles, and enrich themselves with our hard earnings: their wives' fingers sparkling with rings and they themselves laughing at our folly?[2]

When it comes to the question of woman, it was not only the voice of the working woman, or that of the Black dimension, that was not listened to. The same held true of the middle-class woman Margaret Fuller, whose intellect had been recognized as serious but who was still considered merely as a sort of "handmaiden" of the Transcendentalists.

Now that we have her full story,[3] it is clear that as a feminist she was an original, and that as an activist she was so far from the rarified atmosphere of Brook Farm as to have become a participant in the 1848 Italian Revolution, where she took a partisan as her lover. Whether or not Vivian Gornick is correct in her conclusion that "had she lived, Margaret Fuller would have become one of the first important American Marxists,"[4] the point is that Margaret Fuller judged herself to "have become an enthusiastic Socialist."[5]

A WORLD-HISTORIC MOMENT

Objectively, though the United States had experienced no social revolution in 1848, a revolution in women's liberation did occur that year. The Woman's Rights Convention at Seneca Falls, N.Y., disclosed a new force for revolution. Women throughout the world heard it. From St. Lazare prison in Paris, to which they had been sentenced for their activities in and after the revolution of 1848, Jeanne Deroin and Pauline Roland sent greetings in 1851 to the Second National Woman's Rights Convention, held in Worcester, Mass. On behalf of that convention, Ernestine Rose declared: "After having heard the letter read from our poor incarcerated sisters of France, well might we exclaim, Alas, poor France! where is thy glory? where the glory of the Revolution of 1848?"[6]

The 1840s had been filled with revolutionary ideas as well as actual revolutions. Thus, in 1843, Flora Tristan was the first to call for a Workers' International of men and women; in her book, *Union Ouvrière*, she stressed the need "to recognize the urgent necessity of giving to the women of the people an education, moral, intellectual and technical . . . [and] to recognize in principle, the *equality of right* between men and women as being the sole means of establishing *Human Unity*."[7] The very next year, typhoid fever deprived us of this exciting utopian revolutionary. In that same year, however, 1844, Marx discovered a whole new continent of thought and of revolution, with his now-famous Humanist Essays.

It took a revolution—the Russian Revolution of November 1917—to dig out these 1844 Manuscripts from the musty, closed Second International archives. Once they were published, the shock of recognition was not just that they were great writings, but writings that disclosed so profound an Idea of Freedom that it transcended both time and place, that is to say, the Germany of the 1840s. The genius Marx could articulate such a philosophy of revolution, not because he was a prophet, but because he dived so deeply into human relations that he came up with this concept of Man/Woman:

> The infinite degradation in which man exists for himself is expressed in this relation to the *woman* as the spoils and handmaiden of communal lust. For the secret of the relationship of man to man finds its *unambiguous*, definitive, *open*, obvious expression in the relationship of *man to woman*, and in this way the *direct, natural* relationship between the sexes. The direct, natural, necessary relationship of man to man is the *relationship of man to woman* . . . From the

character of this relation it follows to what degree *man* as a *species* has become *human* . . . [8]

Which is why Marx concretized each human relationship as a "to be" instead of a "to have": "Each of his human relations to the world—seeing, hearing, smell, taste, feeling, thought, perception, experience, wishing, activity, loving . . . in place of all the physical and spiritual senses, there is the sense of possession, which is the simple alienation of all these senses . . . The transcendence of private property is, therefore, the total *freeing* of all the human senses and attributes." But for "the wealth of human needs [to] take the place of the wealth and poverty of political economy," a total uprooting is needed.

The Marxist philosopher Herbert Marcuse, when these Essays were published in Germany in 1932, perceived the pivotal point of philosophy, its integrality with actual revolution. He entitled his review "The Foundation of Historical Materialism,"[9] and traced how embedded in Marx's philosophic critique was his theory of revolution. As he put it, "we are dealing with a philosophic critique of political economy and its philosophical foundation as a theory of revolution" (p. 3). Furthermore, Marcuse continued: "This does not mean that Hegel's 'method' is transformed and taken over, put into a new context and brought to life. Rather, Marx goes back to the problems at the root of Hegel's philosophy (which originally determined his method), independently appropriates their real content and thinks it through to a further stage" (p. 4). Marcuse devoted forty-five pages to detail each of Marx's Essays, and not only as philosophy but as practical and revolutionary analysis related to the whole human existence.

And yet . . . and yet . . . missing from Marcuse's comprehensive analysis was any reference whatever to the Man/Woman relationship, which Marx made so central in the essay "Private Property and Communism." That essay covered a great deal more than the two topics in the title. What was involved in Marx's opposition to private property was very far removed from a question of "property." Rather, as he made clear over and over again, his opposition to private property was due to the fact that it "completely negates the *personality* of man . . . "

And to make absolutely sure that his readers did not find still other ways of either fragmenting or "collectivizing" the individual, Marx ended the essay with a warning that "communism, as such, is not the goal of human development, the form of human society."

Just as even a Herbert Marcuse missed hearing the crucial Man/Woman concept, so all too many Women's Liberationists today do not perceive the Black dimension as Reason in our age. Those who deny today that the idea of revolution and that exciting Black dimension were both crucial in establishing the first Woman's Rights Convention not only have forgotten that today's

Women's Liberation Movement likewise arose out of the Black dimension, but have failed entirely to grasp what is the root of theory, its true beginning. Take something as simple as a name—that of Sojourner Truth—and compare it to what we today think of as an accomplishment when we use, not our husbands' names, but our "maiden" names. When Isabella became free and wanted to throw away her slave name, she included her entire philosophy in her new name. It is true that she attributed to God the reason for her name, saying that when she wanted to have nothing to do with her slave past and asked God for advice as to a name, "He" told her to sojourn the world over and reveal the truth to the people. But the fact is that her name tells us more than just the fact that she had broken with male domination.

Or for that matter, consider how she silenced the clerics at the meeting who were booing her. She asked them "Do you believe in Christ?" and added, did the clerics know where Christ came from? She proceeded to tell them: "from God and a woman! Man had nothing to do with Him!"

Naiveté? Then consider the "generalship" of a Harriet Tubman, be it as conductor of the Underground Railroad, or in her activity behind the lines of the confederacy during the Civil War.

These historic facts of a Harriet Tubman or a Sojourner Truth[10] are not the only manifestations of Black activity in and influence upon the early women's rights struggle and the Civil War; thousands were involved. The turning point for American Black women was reached in 1867, after the Civil War, when even the most revolutionary Abolitionists, like Frederick Douglass and Wendell Phillips, refused to collaborate with the women in their fight for suffrage on the grounds that this was "the Negro hour." Sojourner Truth hit back at her own leader, Frederick Douglass, calling him "short-minded." In that, Harriet Tubman joined. Not only did they separate from their Black male leaders and align with the white women, but it became clear that "short-minded" was more than an epithet. Rather, it was a new language—the language of thought—against those who would put any limitations to freedom.

In four more years, the world was to become witness to the greatest revolution of men and women for a totally new, classless society: the Paris Commune. Why, may we ask, did it take nearly a century to learn all the facts of the breadth of women's actions, and why, even now in our age, did it take a Resistance woman, Edith Thomas, to discover, i.e., to seriously and comprehensively present, the women Communards as revolutionaries and as thinkers—many of whom were friends of Marx—in *The Women Incendiaries*?[11]

Nor should we forget—even though, for space, we must skip many of the labor struggles—that the American labor struggles, with very active participation by women, had been continuous since the very first National Labor Union was established in the U.S. and affiliated with the First International. Indeed, when Zetkin proposed to the 1910 Second International Women's Conference that an International Women's Day be adopted, it was an act of solidarity with the organizing struggles of the American garment workers who had erupted in the "Uprising of the 20,000" the year before. Six days after the first IWD was celebrated in March 1911, the infamous sweatshop Triangle Fire took the lives of 146 workers, most of whom were young women, and Rose Schneiderman organized no less than 120,000 workers in the funeral march—not just to mourn but to declare solidarity with all unorganized women workers.[12]

INDIVIDUALISM AND MASSES IN MOTION

Instead of inventing some mythical highpoint for the "Woman Question" to reach, let us realize that we are, at one and the same time, confronted with two seemingly opposite facts—that the individuality of each woman liberationist is a microcosm of the whole, and yet that the movement is not a sum of so many individuals but *masses in motion*. This does not mean that original characters have not emerged. Rosa Luxemburg was certainly an original,[13] and not because of her multidimensionality, or even her great revolutionary achievements, though in both instances she made great contributions that remain as ground for our age. No, it is that such an original character as Luxemburg, instead of being simply "one in a million," combines yesterday, today and tomorrow in such a manner that the new age suddenly experiences a "shock of recognition," whether that relates to a new lifestyle or the great need for revolution here and now.

Take such a question as why Luxemburg, out of the blue, while she was in the dungeons, suddenly invoked the image of the queen of the Amazons, in a letter to Mathilde Wurm. Her reference to Penthesilea was, no doubt, not to the Greek legend in which Penthesilea is killed by Achilles, but rather as the German dramatist Heinrich von Kleist reversed the legend, so that it was Penthesilea who killed Achilles. All this Luxemburg made relative to the need for revolutionaries to attack not only those who capitulated to the war, but the "Centrists" who devised theories for the capitulators:

> I'm telling you that as soon as I can stick my nose out again I will hunt and harry your society of frogs with trumpet blasts, whip crackings, and bloodhounds—like Penthesilea I wanted to say, but by God, you people are no Achilles. Have you had enough of a New Year's greeting now? Then see to it that you stay *human* . . . Being human means joyfully throwing your whole life "on the scales of destiny" when need be, but all the while rejoicing in every sunny day and every beautiful cloud. Ach, I know of no formula to write you for being human . . . [14]

It is this need to throw one's whole life on the scales of destiny; it's this passion for revolution; it's the urgency to get out of prison confinement and open entirely new vistas; in a word, it's the need for what Luxemburg called "staying human," that characterized the whole of her vision for a new society. It put the stamp on all she did and ever hoped to make real. And it created so totally different a direction for women's liberation that it makes it possible for our age to first understand it fully—in a great measure more fully than she, herself, was conscious of.

What illuminates the contributions both of an original character and of the masses in motion is the way those masses in motion uproot the old and create the new. Let us, therefore, turn to see it in two very different locales and historic periods.

Take Africa, whose history, especially as it concerns women, has hardly been touched. We are first now beginning—without knowing the full story, even now—to hear about one of the great events that happened in 1929, which entered Great Britain's imperial history as the "Aba riots," but which the Africans named "The Women's War."[15] This event, hidden from history, involved tens of thousands of Igbo women, who organized demonstrations in Calabar and Owerri provinces in southeastern Nigeria, against both British imperialism and their own African chiefs, whom they accused of carrying out the new British edict to tax women. These women, without any help from their own men, combined forces across tribal lines and began their protests, called "making war," or "sitting on a man."[16]

This was by no means an individual act, but a traditional Igbo way of expressing revolt; it involved masses of women, meeting at an agreed time and place (in this case the hut of the Warrant Chiefs), dancing, and singing scurrilous songs that detailed the women's grievances and insulted the chiefs (including questioning their manhood) and banging on the men's huts with the pestles they used for pounding yams. Traditionally, this might last all night and day until an apology came and the man mended his ways. In the 1929 Women's War[17] it continued through November and December.

It was serious enough, and British imperialism feared it sufficiently to forget that women had not previously been fired on. This time they brought out the troops, murdering fifty women and wounding fifty others. The women, however, had won their point, and the taxes were not imposed. It was clear that though the event had women leaders—Ikonia, Nwaunedie, Narigo—*this grass-roots leadership had emerged out of the collective action of Igbo women.*[18]

The greatest of all events were the March and November 1917 Russian Revolutions. We saw in the last chapter how very conscious Luxemburg was of those revolutions and how totally she practiced the principles of proletarian revolution in her call for the revolution in Germany. However, the last chapter did not describe in any detail the March Revolution, which was initiated by women. It was initiated, on International Women's Day, against the advice of all tendencies—Mensheviks, Bolsheviks, Anarchists, Social-Revolutionaries. Those five days that toppled the mighty empire demonstrate that it is never just a question of leaders, no matter how great. Rather, it is masses in motion.

In the continuing imperialist war, which had wrought such havoc and brought such misery to the Russian masses, the various left organizations thought it right to celebrate International Women's Day at a regular meeting. As it happened, the Bolsheviks' printing press broke down and they could not even issue a leaflet, but the *mezhrayontsy*[19] group did address a flysheet to the working women who opposed the war. However, the women of the Vyborg textile factory categorically refused to limit themselves to a closed meeting.

Despite the advice of all political tendencies, they went out on strike, fifty thousand of them. The next day they appealed to the metal workers, led by the Bolsheviks, who then joined the strike: now there were ninety-thousand out. Someone cried, "To the Nevsky!" and the demonstration was joined by a mass of other women, not all of them workers, but all demanding "Bread!" Whereupon that slogan was drowned out with, "Down with the war!" By this time, the third day of the strike, there were two hundred and forty thousand strikers; the Bolsheviks issued a call for a general strike. The police opened fire and some fell dead, but the Cossacks had not yet unleashed their fury against the strikers. The women went up to the Cossacks to ask whether they would join them. They did not answer but, wrote Trotsky, "the Cossacks did not hinder the workers from 'diving' under their horses. The revolution does not choose its paths: it made its first steps toward victory under the belly of a Cossack's horse. A remarkable incident!"[20]

On the decisive fifth day, the prisons were opened and all political prisoners were freed. At the same time, the mutinous troops descended on the Tauride Palace. "Thus dawned upon the earth the day of destruction of the Romanov monarchy."[21] By November the Kerensky government was also overthrown and the Bolsheviks took power on 9 November.

* * *

Having viewed the relationship of Man/Woman as Marx's concept, integral to a philosophy of revolution; as it appears in the Women's Liberation Movement, as revolutionary force and reason; and at different historic periods, we can see that it is not just a question of then and now—that is to say, of contrasting historic periods. Rather, time is now to be considered as Marx defined it: "Time is space for human development." Rooted in such a concept, we want to take a second look at Luxemburg as original character, as revolutionary theorist, and as feminist: although she might sometimes appear as a reluctant feminist, she is always a revolutionary.

NOTES

1. "Nat Turner's Confession" appears as an appendix to John H. Clarke, ed., *William Styron's Nat Turner: Ten Black Writers Respond* (Boston: Beacon Press, 1968).

2. Bert James Loewenberg and Ruth Bogin, eds., *Black Women in 19th Century American Life* (University Park, Pa.: Penn State University Press, 1967).

86   The Women's Liberation Movement as Revolutionary Force and Reason

3. Bell Gale Chevigny, *The Woman and the Myth* (Old Westbury, N.Y.: Feminist Press, 1976). In Larzer Ziff's profound study of classic American literature, *Literary Democracy: The Declaration of Cultural Independence in America* (New York: Viking Press, 1981), Ziff includes a chapter on Margaret Fuller (pp. 146–64) which deserves serious study. He first quotes Fuller's statement in her 1845 work, *Woman in the Nineteenth Century:* "Let it not be said wherever there is energy or creative genius, 'She has a masculine mind.' " He then develops his view of her "vigorous independence of mind" as inseparable from the fact that she had become a revolutionary in Italy and was returning to the United States "to work for the next revolution." The chapter ends with: "Such exhilaration at attaching passion to intelligence, will to action, self to history, was on the ship with her when she arrived off Fire Island. Kindled in Europe it was drowned within sight of the American strand."

4. Vivian Gornick, *Essays in Feminism* (New York: Harper & Row, 1978), p. 212.

5. Chevigny, *The Woman and the Myth*, p. 490.

6. Miriam Schneir, ed., *Feminism* (New York: Random House, 1972), p. 91.

7. G.D.H. Cole, *A History of Socialist Thought*, 5 vols. (London: Macmillan & Co., 1956), 1:186.

8. There have been several translations by now of the 1844 Manuscripts. The best known are those by Martin Milligan, Erich Fromm, T. Bottomore, and Loyd Easton and Kurt Guddat. I am using my own translation, however, which is the first one that was published in English, as an appendix to my *Marxism and Freedom* (New York: Twayne Pub., 1958). These essays are further discussed in chap. 9. Emphasis in original.

9. This 1932 essay by Herbert Marcuse first appeared in English translation in 1972 in *Studies in Critical Philosophy* (London: New Left Books). Pages cited in text following are to this edition.

10. See especially Earl Conrad, *Harriet Tubman* (New York: Paul S. Erikson, 1943), and *Narrative of Sojourner Truth*, an Ebony Classic (Chicago: Johnson Pub. Co., 1970).

11. Edith Thomas, *The Women Incendiaries* was published in France in 1963 and in English translation in the U.S. in 1966 (New York: George Braziller), but is long out of print. So far there has been no paperback edition.

12. Many histories have been inspired by the Women's Liberation Movement, but Eleanor Flexner's *Century of Struggle* (1959), remains the most comprehensive. For a detailed account of the Triangle Shirtwaist Fire, see Leon Stein, *The Triangle Fire* (New York: Lippincott, 1962) and Corrine J. Naden, *The Triangle Shirtwaist Fire* (New York: Franklin Watts, 1971). Union WAGE (Berkeley, California) issued two pamphlets in 1974 by Joyce Maupin, *Working Women and Their Organizations* and *Labor Heroines, Ten Women Who Led the Struggle*. See also *Working Women for Freedom* by Angela Terrano, Marie Dignan and Mary Holmes (Detroit: Women's Liberation–News & Letters, 1976).

13. When Herman Melville wrote of the "original character" in literature, he stressed that they are "almost as much of a prodigy there, as in real history is a law-giver, a revolutionizing philosopher, or the founder of a new religion." See Herman Melville, *The Confidence Man* (New York: Holt, Rinehart and Winston, 1964), pp. 260–61, from which I have also taken the quotation at the beginning of the next chapter.

14. This letter, written 28 December 1916, is included in *Briefe an Freunde*, Benedikt Kautsky, ed. (Hamburg: Europäische Verlagsanstalt, 1950), pp. 44–6.

15. See Judith Van Allen, "Aba Riots or Igbo Women's War?", *Ufahamu* 6: no. 1 (1975). An elaborated version also appeared in *Women in Africa*, Nancy Hafkin and Edna Bay, eds. (Stanford, Cal.: Stanford Univ. Press, 1976).

16. An exciting historical "forerunner" of the practice of "sitting on a man" is found in Marx's *Ethnological Notebooks* (p. 116), where Marx is summarizing Morgan's findings: "*The women were the great power among the clans, as everywhere else.* They did not hesitate when occasion required, '*to knock off the horns,*' as it was technically called, from the head of a chief, and send him back to the ranks of the warriors. *The original nomination of the chiefs also always rested with them.*"

17. "Women's War" is not as unusual a phenomenon as patriarchal histories would have us think, whether we are dealing with the dramatic fictional Greek *Lysistrata* or, as legend would have it in the land of Luxemburg's birth, with the 1863 Polish revolt against tsarism, which was likewise referred to secretly as "Women's War." In the preface to her *Comrade and Lover: Rosa*

Luxemburg's Letters to Leo Jogiches (Cambridge, Mass.: MIT Press, 1979), Elzbieta Ettinger refers to this 1863 revolt.

18. See James S. Coleman, *Nigeria: Background to Nationalism* (Berkeley: Univ. of California Press, 1958) for an early, comprehensive study of Nigeria.

19. *Mezhrayontsy* is the Russian word for "inter-borough" and was the name used by a small but important group headed by Trotsky, which included such leaders as Lunacharsky, Pokrovsky, Ryazanov and Yoffe. They joined the Bolshevik organization just before the November revolution.

20. Leon Trotsky, *History of the Russian Revolution* (New York: Simon and Schuster, 1932–37), p. 105.

21. Ibid., p. 123.

VII

Luxemburg as Feminist;
Break with Jogiches

"Quite an original":...for original characters in fiction, a grateful reader will, on meeting with one, keep the anniversary of that day... Their rarity may still the more appear from this, that, while characters, merely singular, imply but singular forms so to speak, original ones, truly so, imply original instincts. In short, a due conception of what is to be held for this sort of personage in fiction would make him almost as much of a prodigy there, as in real history is a law-giver, a revolutionizing philosopher, or the founder of a new religion...

Herman Melville, The Confidence Man

Luxemburg rightly refused to be pigeonholed by the German Social-Democracy into the so-called Woman Question, as if that were the only place she "belonged," although she was a theoretician and the editor of a Polish paper as well as an activist when she arrived in Germany. Unfortunately, too many in the Women's Liberation Movement of today reveal their attitude to be the opposite side of the same coin by disregarding this great revolutionary because she allegedly had "next to nothing" to say on women.

Another reverse put-down on the "Woman Question" is to act as if Luxemburg's friendship with Clara Zetkin—who is recognized by all as the founder of women's liberation as a *working class, mass movement*, as well as theoretician and editor of the greatest mass circulation women's newspaper to this day—was a "burden" to Luxemburg.[1] In any case, it was not the "Woman Question" but the fight against reformism that had brought Luxemburg and Zetkin together; this does not mean, however, that Luxemburg left women's liberation to Zetkin, nor did Zetkin simply "follow" Luxemburg. The truth is that their revolutionary comradeship held for all positions for two long decades—from the fight against revisionism to the fight against militarism, from the fight against the bureaucratization of the trade unions to the antiwar struggle, and, of course, to the revolution itself.

There is no doubt that Zetkin was nowhere as profound a thinker as Luxemburg, but there is also no doubt that she was a genuine revolutionary. She *chose* to concentrate on women's liberation, on organizing working-class women, thus becoming a model not only for the German movement but for the Russian women's struggle from Kollontai on; indeed, for the struggle the world over, including that in the United States. She rightly had an international reputation, based on both her activity and her theory on the "Woman Question."

It becomes necessary, therefore, first to set the record straight: not only for straightening out the facts, but also for grasping what *new* stage of feminism was involved as it moved from total concentration on working women's rights to opposing the capitalist system in its entirety.

Despite the fact that Luxemburg had already won the editorship of a Social-Democratic paper, she no sooner arrived in Germany in 1898 than she was immediately confronted with the fact that the male members were not ready to grant to her the same powers as to her male predecessor. Her complaint to Bebel, who was her friend at that time, did not help the situation, and in a few months she resigned. The fact that she did not make this part of the "Woman Question," did not mean that she did not record it in her own mind as such. Quite the contrary. Her friendship with Clara Zetkin was deeply rooted in their common struggle against revisionism, but Luxemburg also collaborated in the autonomous women's movement, which Zetkin headed, and frequently wrote for *Gleichheit (Equality)*, which Zetkin edited.

Luxemburg was quietly engaging herself in the "Woman Question" in her first 1902 organizational tour, as we have already seen.[2] In an article for *Leipziger Volkszeitung* that same year, she wrote: " . . . with the political emancipation of women a strong fresh wind must also blow into its [Social-Democracy's] political and spiritual life, dispelling the suffocating atmosphere of the present philistine family life which so unmistakably rubs off on our party members too, the workers as well as the leaders."[3]

Note the year, 1902; it is a full ten years earlier than the writers on Luxemburg acknowledge that she had written anything on women, and it took all the way to our era before even that 1912 speech on women's suffrage was translated into English.[4]

The 1905 Revolution was as great a turning point in Luxemburg's life as in history itself. Her whirlwind of activities and energizing participation in the ongoing revolution are well enough known. The exhilaration of also being with her lover in that period may not be quite as well known but was by no means kept hidden. But once one confronts the fact that the highpoint of their relationship led to its end, we hear one long story of just how "strictly" personal this matter was. The fact that Luxemburg did keep it private is no help to anyone grappling with it. The greater truth of shying away from any serious analysis, however, is *not* due to its "strictly personal" nature. There surely was gossip galore surrounding the break up, and the reasons given for it ranged from a simplistic "triangle" attribution to slanderous insinuations that the sharp difference between the openness of Luxemburg's activities and the more disciplined behavior of such a consciously organization person as Jogiches led the *Okhrana* to discover their whereabouts and arrest them. The true reason others shy away from analysis, to this writer, is not so much the personal nature of their relationship as it is the failure to understand their attitudes to the ongoing revolution, insofar as their individual organizational tasks were concerned.

SOCIAL REVOLUTION AND
LUXEMBURG'S PERSONAL BREAK WITH JOGICHES

Heretofore, Luxemburg, who had very little interest in organization, and Jogiches, who was "all organization," did not find this difference to be in any way divisive of their love relationship. There was one letter from Paris in which Luxemburg asked for more specific data on internal disputes or factions, but the matter was not pursued.[5] It is clear that once she reached Germany, she was acting independently on the question of organization as well as theoretically. Further, she asked Jogiches to stop "baring your teeth," since his Polish–Russian organizational ideas, which concerned a little group of "seven and a half," simply were not applicable to a mass organization like the German. In no case did it in any way interfere with their intimate relations.

Things changed altogether when both were participating in an ongoing revolution. When Luxemburg first reached Poland at the end of 1905, nothing seemed to have changed. She seemed happiest because she was both part of an ongoing revolution and with her lover. Subtly, however, something was changing, changing radically. For one thing, her appreciation for the spontaneity of the masses was not just theory; the organizational consequence was fantastic: spontaneity had transformed their small organization into a mass party! Heretofore, Luxemburg had analyzed spontaneity as the revolutionary way to oppose trade union bureaucracy, without in any way lessening her belief in the need for a vanguard party. Where "masses" had before meant, for her, mass party, such as the German Social-Democracy, now, seeing *masses in motion* doing nothing short of shaking the tsarist empire exhilarated her beyond anything she ever felt in the German Social-Democracy. She now had proof that it was not she but the masses in motion who were "a land of boundless possibilities." In a word, it was not only intellectually and as pamphleteer that she was reaching new heights, but organizationally. No doubt, she no longer considered Jogiches's organizational expertise as sacrosanct, but we have no record of their dispute on the subject of needed underground work under tsarism and needed openness in revolution. What we do know is that the tensions led to a breakup of their intimacy, without in any way breaking up their revolutionary political activity.

On revolution, as on the Man/Woman relationship, it's all too easy for Marxists to quote abstractions rather than to dig deep into the dialectic of the concrete. And women in the Marxist movement find it a great deal easier to quote how serious Clara Zetkin was on the Man/Woman relationship at the founding of the Second International in 1889, when she addressed it thusly: "Just as the male worker is subjugated to the capitalist, so is the woman by the man, and she will always remain in subjugation until she is economically independent." But when it comes to the effect of the Man/Woman relationship, not only in economic but in personal terms as well as in terms of revolution, they just bow out.

And yet it was there, *just there*, that something new was emerging. A birthtime of history manifests itself not only in great social changes but in original characters, and Luxemburg was an original. Her further self-development was reaching new heights without leaning on Jogiches for either theory or organization. A new historic period had been reached—and differences in the attitude to revolution appeared, not because one wished to play a different "role" than the other, but because the revolution is an overwhelming force that brooks no "interference" from anyone. Luxemburg needed to be free, to be independent, to be whole.

The revolution, for Luxemburg, was an overpowering force; imprisonment had not dampened her ardor, and, although her questioning of Jogiches's authority organizationally did not dampen her love for him, it was precisely then—after the imprisonment *and separation* from Jogiches—that she was most creative. In herself, she found a rare fusion of the political, the personal, and, yes, the organizational. For one thing, the first product of that historic event and experience, the 1905 Revolution—its summation in *The Mass Strike*—became her greatest pamphlet, an analysis that would remain as ground for the 1919 German Revolution. It was written while Jogiches was still in prison, and Luxemburg was in Kuokkala, where Lenin and other Bolsheviks were endlessly discussing the revolution they had just lived through and which they still believed would be revived.

Until then, Jogiches had occupied an important role in editing Luxemburg's manuscripts, but his hand is nowhere to be seen in this work. Whether one has this or a different interpretation of the relationship of the revolution to their relationship to each other, the period in which it happened cannot be rewritten. The fact that both Luxemburg and Jogiches were such objective politicos that they acted as one at the next (1907) Congress—where Bolsheviks, Mensheviks, and all the other tendencies met to draw conclusions and draw up perspectives for the future—does not and cannot restore the former Man/Woman relationship, nor change the ground rules, either of the Man/Woman called Luxemburg and Jogiches, or of revolution. After the breakup with Jogiches, Luxemburg herself put it most succinctly, when she wrote: "I am only I, once more, since I have become free of Leo."[6]

To scrupulously follow Luxemburg's life, in revolution or out, leaves no doubt whatsoever that, no matter how intense her love for Jogiches was, including even the fact that both were revolutionaries with the same theoretical and political goal, no cataclysmic change in her relationship with Jogiches would any longer direct her life.

How could anyone conclude, then, as Nettl does, that "At the beginning of 1907 a major upheaval took place in her affairs, perhaps the most important in her whole life. Her relationship with Jogiches underwent a complete change and with it her entire outlook on life and people." How could anyone designate the period of Luxemburg's great, independent self-development as "The Lost Years—1906–1909?" That is Nettl's title for Chapter 9 of his biography of Luxemburg. These were the years in which Luxemburg summarized the events of the revolution so fundamentally that she expected the party to apply them to the German scene. The party didn't. But, for Luxemburg, they remained the universal form of revolution.

This was also the period when she was her most brilliant self in two critically important conferences—the RSDRP in London and the Second International Congress in Stuttgart. In London she elaborated her position on the 1905 Revolution as initiating new twentieth-century revolutions and not just repeating what Marx had achieved in 1848. And at Stuttgart, so important was she to the *world* Left that the entire Russian delegation—Lenin, Trotsky, Martov (on this all the tendencies acted as one)—authorized her to speak in their name on the crucial antiwar amendment. Furthermore, 1907 comprised not only those historic happenings, but also that of the Socialist Women's Conference, where she reported on the work of the International Socialist Bureau in a way that would hardly have pleased its members. She had also introduced Lenin to Zetkin, who influenced him enough that he based his reports in the Russian press on Zetkin's report in *Gleichheit*.

Finally, it was the period when she became the only woman leading theoretician at the prestigious Party School. She attributed her work on the *Accumulation of Capital* to her experience at the school.

There is no doubt of course that her love for Jogiches had been intense, and that this relationship was more than just an intellectual partnership "with erotic overtones." There is equally no doubt that the breakup of the love relationship neither changed their joint revolutionary political work to their very deaths, nor put an end to Luxemburg's self-development. Quite the contrary. Her greatest intellectual accomplishments occurred after the break.

To say that her whole life was changed because of the breakup is a typical male attitude, i.e., thinking that a woman's life stops when the break in a love relationship occurs. It does not help us to understand Luxemburg either as a revolutionary theoretician or as a most original character in her personal life, a personal life that ventured on many uncharted courses.

THE ROAD TO REVOLUTION; THE ROAD TO FEMINISM

The Women's Conference that was held in 1907, the year of both London and Stuttgart Congresses, was attended by fifty-nine women representing fifteen countries. Everyone, from Balabanoff, who represented Italy, to Kollontai, who represented Russia, accepted the leadership of Luxemburg and Zetkin and considered *Gleichheit* as the coordinating center for them all. Kollontai[7] did not exaggerate when she said that the conference "made an enormous contribution to the development of a working women's movement along Marxist lines." Independent, autonomous women's groups did begin functioning in other countries.

The Conference succeeded in maintaining autonomy despite the fact that they were by then supposed to be subordinated to the International Congress. The manner in which this was accomplished was typical of Luxemburg. In reporting on the ISB work, she created "amusement," first by referring to the fact that, since she was "the only one of the fair sex" on the Bureau, she could assure them that "the only comrades who hold . . . a high opinion of the International Bureau are those who know its workings from very far off." She created further amusement when she said, "I'm going to let you in on another little secret." This turned out to be a description of "four years of painful disappointment in the activity of the International Bureau." All these disparaging remarks were made with one goal in mind, to let the women know that only "you will create this moral center of the International out of yourselves; and I can only admire Comrade Zetkin that she has taken this burden of work upon herself." In a word, she was asking them to reject moving the International Socialist Women's Bureau to Brussels, where the ISB was centered, and instead to remain in Stuttgart with the editor of *Gleichheit*.[8]

This principle became central in 1910–11 when the break with Kautsky and Bebel occurred over the question of both general strike and the "Morocco Incident," and *Gleichheit* was an outlet for Luxemburg's revolutionary views. Indeed, it later became *the* antiwar organ when World War I broke out and the International betrayed—which is the reason the leadership removed Zetkin from its editorship and then changed its character as well as its name.

The general revolutionary struggle during this period and the establishment of the first International Women's Day made 1911 central both for Women's Liberation and for Rosa Luxemburg. Because, however, Luxemburg refused to make any reference to what we would now call male chauvinism, during the hectic debates with Kautsky and Bebel, the two sets of activities remained in separate compartments. No doubt she did not know the specifics of what went on in the letters between Bebel and Kautsky quoted in chapter 2, as they tried to reduce the sharp political differences to a "Woman Question"; she was positive that their opposition to her had very little to do with that and everything to do with their sharp move away from Marxism. Nevertheless, just as she wrote to Luise Kautsky in 1907 and asked her "to keep active" in the women's movement, so in 1911 she wrote to her: "Are you coming for the women's conference? Just imagine, I have become a feminist! I received a credential for this conference and must therefore go to Jena."[9]

March 1911 marks the first celebration of the International Women's Day that Clara Zetkin had proposed to the Second International. In Germany it was the height of the socialist women's struggle for suffrage. To coincide with the first International Women's Suffrage Conference that year, two and a half million leaflets demanding the vote for women were distributed, and tens of thousands of women demonstrated throughout Germany.

Nor did the activity stop in 1911; it reached its climax in 1912, and, as is clear from Luxemburg's important speech on women's suffrage that year, it was not just a struggle for suffrage. Just as her activity in the 1905 Revolution was by no means exhausted in her manifesto's call for "full emancipation for women," so her "tactical struggle" for women's suffrage was related both to the general strike and to revolution itself. Her speech concluded: "The present forceful movement of millions of proletarian women who consider their lack of political rights a crying wrong is such an infallible sign, a sign that the social bases of the reigning system are rotten and that its days are numbered . . . Fighting for women's suffrage, we will also hasten the coming of the hour when the present society falls in ruins under the hammer strokes of the revolutionary proletariat."[10]

Once again, everything merged into proletarian revolution, but always thereafter, woman as revolutionary force revealed its presence. Moreover, before that presence became as massive as it was in the antiwar activities when World War I broke out, and all the way to the 1919 Revolution, Luxemburg remained an activist in socialist feminism. Thus, a few months before the outbreak of World War I, she was still writing on the need for women's suffrage, emphasizing the importance of proletarian women:

> For the propertied bourgeois woman, her house is the world. *For the proletarian woman the whole world is her house . . . Bourgeois women's rights advocates want to acquire political rights* in order to participate in political life. The proletarian women can only follow the path of the workers' struggles, the opposite to winning a foot of real power through primarily legal statutes. *In the beginning was the deed for every social ascent . . .* The ruling society refuses them [women] access to the temple of its legislation . . . but to them the Social Democratic party opens wide its gates.[11]

Those doors were quickly shut when the war actually broke out and *Gleichheit* continued its antiwar propaganda, making it clear that it was not just antiwar rhetoric before a war, but putting their lives on the line after war had been declared. By then there were 210,314 women workers in the Free Trade Unions and no less than 175,000 women belonged to the SPD. The circulation of *Gleichheit* had jumped to 125,000 and the antiwar work of the women went on not only nationally but internationally. Indeed, the first international antiwar conference was organized by women. It was to be held in Holland in early March and Luxemburg was to accompany Zetkin to make the final arrangements, but on 18 February 1915, the evening before their planned departure, Luxemburg was thrown into jail.[12]

The tremendous antiwar activity, which had to be carried on illegally, did not stop even after Zetkin, too, was arrested in August. Early in 1915 the chauvinist SPD leadership had been made to realize that they had to reckon with the mass opposition of revolutionary women. One incident gives the flavor of the subjective as well as the objective situation:

It was the day the Executive Committee of the SPD was meeting on the food crisis. They refused to allow a hundred women protesters into the meeting to air their grievances, whereupon the women burst into the meeting, cursing the male Social-Democrats. One of the leaders, Philip Scheidemann, described the meeting as follows:

Ebert (while ringing his bell): "What do you wish here?"
First woman: "We came here to speak."
Ebert: "Are you all members?"
Many women (shouting): "Yes indeed, and able, not like you."
Ebert: "If you are members, you must know we have parliamentarian order at our discussions."
Chorus of Women: "Ah, now we will speak! You have nothing to say!"
Ebert: "I forbid you to speak."[13]

Ebert had to adjourn the meeting, but found the stairs and corridors were filled with many more women who had arrived by then.

Rosa Luxemburg was not there, of course; she was in prison. But she never rested from producing not only leaflets but the first great theoretical antiwar pamphlet to come out of Germany, which she called *The Crisis in the German Social Democracy* and signed, "Junius."

Clearly, the demonstrations that developed in Germany were not only for bread but for freedom, as is seen in the fact that the majority of the women in the antiwar movement continued their activity into the November 1918–January 1919 Revolution. With the first day of the revolution, the gates of the prison were opened for Luxemburg.

The tremendous movement of women active in the illegal antiwar work was not limited to Germany; it was international throughout the war. It was during Luxemburg's imprisonment that she had written that blistering letter to Mathilde Wurm in which she invoked the name of Penthesilea. But it wasn't for purposes of the "Woman Question." It was, as always, for revolution. No sooner was Luxemburg freed from jail than she at once plunged into the ongoing revolution, creating a theory of revolution that incorporated the

Russian experience and made it distinctly Luxemburgian.

With the beheading of the German Revolution, the women's movement was likewise stifled. The fact that the women had participated massively in revolutionary antiwar work did not assure a totally different stage for women once the revolution was beheaded.

In Russia, where the revolution had succeeded, and the women had started on a very new road to women's equality, it was but a few years until that first workers' state was transformed into its opposite—the infamous, Stalinist, state-capitalist society. And that retrogression was seen most actively in the abolition of Zhenotdel.[14] Retrogression was total under Nazism, and hardly any better under Stalinism. The long march for women's liberation had to be resumed, and new beginnings found. Though many new starts did begin in the 1930s and more in the 1940s, and at no time more strongly than in the immediate post-World War II world, Women's Liberation *as movement* did not re-emerge until the mid-1960s.

NOTES

1. See Henriette Roland-Holst, *Rosa Luxemburg: ihr Leben und Wirken* (Zurich: Jean Christophe Verlag, 1937). It was originally published in Dutch in 1935.

2. See chap. I.

3. *Gesammelte Werke*, 1(2):185.

4. Howard, *Selected Political Writings*, p. 216.

5. In this letter (included in Bronner's collection and dated "probably 3/25/1894"), Luxemburg writes: "Your chivalrous explanation that I should not worry about practical things, since they surely will have been settled without bothering me, can only be given by a person *who does not know me at all*. Such an explanation might suffice for Julek [Marchlewski] so that he wouldn't worry since he has weak nerves, but for me such a procedure—even with the addition, 'my poor little bird'—is insulting to put it mildly."

6. Nettl, *Rosa Luxemburg*, 1:383.

7. There have been several recent studies of Alexandra Kollontai. The most comprehensive is Richard Stites, *The Women's Liberation Movement in Russia: Feminism, Nihilism and Bolshevism, 1860–1930* (Princeton, N.J.: Princeton Univ. Press, 1978). See also Cathy Porter, *Alexandra Kollontai* (New York: Dial Press, 1980).

8. See *Gesammelte Werke*, 2:233–34.

9. Letter to Luise Kautsky, in ed. Luise Kautsky, *Letters to Karl and Luise Kautsky*.

10. Howard, *Selected Political Writings*, p. 222.

11. Rosa Luxemburg, "Die Proletarierin" ("The Proletarian Woman"), in *Gesammelte Werke*, 3:411–12.

12. A postcard sent to her on 28 February 1915 conveyed the resolution that had been passed at the Women's Day Meeting of the Socialist Party at Coshocton, Ohio. It read: "Be it resolved that we convey to Comrade Luxemburg our sincere sympathy with her attitude toward the present European war and that we express our admiration for her uncompromising devotion to revolutionary principle when the socialist movement of nearly all Europe was being corrupted by capitalist and nationalist influences." It is on deposit at the Hoover Institute of War, Peace and Revolution, Stanford University, Cal.

13. From Philip Scheidemann's *Memoiren Eines Sozialdemokraten* (Dresden: Carl Reissner, 1930), 1:333, as quoted by William Peltz in an address delivered at the Conference on the History of Women, College of St. Catherine, St. Paul, Minn., 24–25 October 1975.

14. There have been several studies of the Working and Peasant Women's Department of the Communist Party in Russia, known as *Zhenotdel*. The most comprehensive one, which is not limited to just that period, and which is scholarly in every aspect, including the life and activities of Kollontai, is Stites, *The Women's Liberation Movement in Russia*.

VIII

The Task That Remains To Be Done:
The Unique and Unfinished
Contributions of Today's Women's
Liberation Movement

The Women's Liberation Movement that burst onto the historic scene in the mid-1960s was like nothing seen before in all its many appearances throughout history. Its most unique feature was that, surprisingly, not only did it come out of the left but it was *directed against it*, and not from the right, but *from within the left itself.*

Class oppression and discrimination against women had heretofore naturally produced the struggle against capitalism and its oppressive, alienating regime, but where until now women's oppression was attributed to capitalism's patriarchal nature, this time the women directed the male-chauvinist epithet at the male left.

Where, heretofore, racism and sexism had both been laid totally at the feet of the exploitative class regime, this time accusations of sexism were pointed at the Black males—indeed, at its most left wing, the Student Non-Violent Coordinating Committee (SNCC), during its organizing of southern Blacks.

Where, heretofore, internal tensions between the sexes were judged to be "personal," now the cry was, "the personal *is* political." There were no areas left untouched, from politics (now designated as *Sexual Politics*)[1] to love relationships; from the right to abortion on demand to gay and lesbian rights;[2] from demonstrations against the Miss America pageant to guerrilla theater against the system itself. Nor did the new movement leave uncriticized the women of the old left who had kept silent both on their own "personal questions" and on the left's male chauvinism.

None could question the women liberationists' credentials as opponents of the exploitative, racist, alienating system—whether we take, as our starting point, the year 1965, when the first charges of sexism surfaced in SNCC;[3] or the year 1967 when Redstockings and the New York Radical Women, who emerged from the white left, had expressed their total hatred for anything "male dominated," not just as "man-haters" but as theorists of "consciousness raising"; or the year 1969, when the strongest presence came out of the Students for a Democratic Society (SDS). Beyond any doubt, the centerpoint was the demand for freedom from male domination, for women's autonomy, for decentralized existence, free of any and all male presence.

THE NEW VOICES

Individually and collectively, the cry was loud, clear, and multifaceted:

Don't tell us about discrimination everywhere else; and don't tell us it comes only from class oppression; look at yourselves.

Don't tell us that "full" freedom can come only the "day after" the revolution; our questions must be faced the day before. Furthermore, words are not sufficient; let's see you practice it.

None of your "theories" will do. You will have to learn to hear us. *You will have to understand what you hear. It's like learning a new language. You will have to learn that you are not the font of all wisdom—or of revolution. You will have to understand that our bodies belong to us and to no one else—and that includes lovers, husbands, and yes, fathers.*

Our bodies have heads, and they, too, belong to us and us alone. And while we are reclaiming our bodies and our heads, we will also reclaim the night. No one except ourselves, as women, will get our freedom. And for that we need full autonomy.

We will not open an escape route for you by pointing to the middle-class nature of Betty Friedan's The Feminine Mystique. *Outside of the fact that the trivialization of housework is also demeaning to the "well-paid" housewife, we haven't seen you involved in the struggle of the domestic workers. Our movement didn't begin with* The Feminine Mystique *in 1963. In 1961 we were on the Freedom Ride buses with you, got beat up and thrown in jail, and found that the Black women in Mississippi had organized "Woman Power Unlimited."*[4]

Stop telling us, even through the voices of women (of the old left), how great the German Socialist Women's Movement was. We know how many working women's groups Clara Zetkin organized and that it was a real mass movement. We know how great the circulation of Gleichheit *was, and that we have nothing comparable to it. We demand, nevertheless, to be heard, not only because your implication seems to be that we had better hold our tongues, but because her superiority in organizing women on class lines left hidden many aspects of the "Woman Question," most of all how very deep the uprooting of the old must be. And we also know that none of them, Zetkin and Luxemburg included, had brought out the male chauvinism in the party. They had followed the men in considering that nothing must be done to break up the "unity" of the party by diverting to "strictly personal, strictly feminist" matters rather than be lumped with the bourgeois women.*

Now let us ask you: Is it accidental that the male leaders in the SPD so easily plunged into those malodorous, male-chauvinist remarks when Luxemburg broke with Kautsky and Bebel? And could it be accidental that the male Marxists of this day, with and without female support, first resisted the establishment of an autonomous women's movement and now try very much to narrow it by forever bringing out the priority of the party, the party, the party? There is the rub.

Too many revolutions have soured, so we must start anew on very different ground, beginning right here and now. Under no circumstances will we let you hide your male-chauvinist behavior under the shibboleth "the social revolution comes first." That has always served as excuse for your "leadership," for your continuing to make all decisions, write all leaflets, pamphlets, and tracts, while all we do is crank the mimeo machine.

Finally, the most important thing we must all learn to hear are the voices of the Third World. The real Afro–Asian, Latin American struggles—especially of women—are not heard in the rhetoric at the Tri-Continental Congresses, but in the simple words of people like the Black woman who spelled out what freedom meant to her: "I'm not thoroughly convinced that Black Liberation, the way it's being spelled out, will really and truly mean my liberation. I'm not so sure when it comes time 'to put down my gun' that I won't have a broom shoved in my hands, as so many of my Cuban sisters have."[5]

The Women's Liberation Movement of this age is, indeed, at a different stage, a very different stage. It has raised altogether new questions and made new contributions, and has done so globally. Within the United States the depth and breadth of the movement is seen in the struggles of Chicana feminists, North American Indian women, and Puerto Rican women, who were among the very first to organize their own groups. And globally, it can be seen whether we start with an outright revolution, as in Portugal in 1974–75; or with the demonstration for abortion rights in Italy in 1976, when a hundred thousand women marched and brought down the government. We can take the mass demonstrations in England in 1977; or the protest that same year at the fortieth United Auto Workers anniversary celebration in Flint, Michigan, where the banner unfurled—"1937–1977, The Struggle Continues"—honored the Women's Emergency Brigade that had been crucial to the creation of the CIO.[6] We can look at the continuing critical activities of the women in South Africa in 1978 against apartheid;[7] or we can go to 1979 and once again confront an outright revolution, this time in Iran. No matter where we look, there is no doubt, whatever, that so powerful is the idea of women's liberation today that women are speaking out everywhere—including the Moroccan feminist, Fatima Mernissa, who has exposed the role played by the Muslim religion in women's dehumanization by pointing out how the Koran's concept of woman has been used "to give a divine stamp to female exploitation."[8]

The seventy-fifth anniversary of the first Russian Revolution brought a new emphasis to that revolution because what was muted in 1905—its impact on the East, Persia especially—became the focal point in 1980, with the unfolding revolution in Iran. We had, in fact, been seeing it in daily headlines, because Iranian opponents of the Shah kept referring to the 1906 Constitution they would model themselves after, whereas the Iranian women who had participated in the revolution were marching for their full freedom, and some were recalling a very different aspect of the 1906–11 Iranian Revolution—that which had created, for the very first time anywhere in the world, a women's soviet (anjumen).[9] The fact that, for the moment, the Iranian women have lost out all over again makes it imperative to take a deeper look at the Women's Liberation Movement.

Naturally, certain issues, because of their long neglect and present urgency, begin to dominate over all others, and the one that acted as a unifying force was the right to abortion on demand. Why is there any need to play that down as "secondary"? Just take a look at the mass movement which that demand produced, like the hundred thousand women who marched in Italy in 1976, and on this very issue at one and the same time brought down the Christian Democratic government and delivered a body blow to the Communist Party. While there has been no such similar development in the United States, there have been important new directions begun; and although, in the United States, the movement took on a predominantly bourgeois cast, with the National Organization for Women (NOW) and *Ms.* magazine in the forefront, new links have been forged with both Black and labor.[10]

Of course, the Women's Liberation Movement has made mistakes as its participants have moved away from the vanguardist organizations, not because they "burned bras," but because like the rest of the post–World War II generation they fell into the trap of the existential Other and considered Man the enemy. That attitude of simply turning the other side of the coin reached its most fantastic stage with what could be called the history of the absurd. It is seen in Gerda Lerner who denigrated her magnificent documentary, *Black Women in White America*, calling it "a detour," and proceeded to the supposedly main road of "women-centered" analysis: "What would the past be like if man were regarded as woman's Other?" Far from "Placing Women in History," *The Majority Finds Its Past* wrenched women out of it.[11]

Far from Black being a detour, we know that it has been the keystone of all of American history. The first Woman's Rights Movement arose on the shoulders of the Blacks; that is to say, in working with Blacks against slavery, middle-class American women learned the value of organizations and established the first Woman's Rights Movement. And just as the Sojourner Truths and Harriet Tubmans learned to separate from what they called their "short-minded" leaders who would not fight for woman's suffrage in the "Negro hour" of fighting for Black male suffrage, so the new Women's Liberation Movement arose from participation in the Black freedom struggles of the '60s, and the Black women, in turn, made their own declaration.

"We are often asked the ugly question, 'Where are your loyalties? To the Black movement or the feminist movement?' " is the way a spokeswoman for the National Black Feminist Organization put it when the NBFO was organized in 1973. "Well, it would be nice if we were oppressed as women Monday through Thursday, then oppressed as Blacks the rest of the week. We could combat one or the other on those days—but we have to fight both every day of the week." The NBFO's Statement of Principles declared: "We will encourage the Black community to stop falling into the trap of the white male Left, utilizing women only in terms of domestic or servile needs. We will remind the Black Liberation Movement that there can't be liberation for half a race."[12]

The movement had been reminded of that long before, in action, when the First National Conference for a United Front Against Fascism, called by the Black Panther Party in 1969, had tried to pre-empt the time scheduled for a panel on Women's Liberation to allow Communist theoretician Herbert Aptheker to continue to talk long past his allotted time. The shouting, clapping women made it clear that they had no intention of being silenced; their panel proved the best part of the whole conference.[13]

It was not only that it had been treated as "accidental" that women were among the earliest leaders of the Black movement—from Rosa Parks, who had initiated the whole Black Revolution in the South in 1955 by refusing to give up her seat to a white man, to Fannie Lou Hamer, whose work had been ground for the critical Mississippi Freedom Summer. It was that a woman like Gloria Richardson, the recognized leader of the movement in Cambridge, Maryland, had been told by the male SNCC leadership to step back when they arrived on the scene, because "nobody would accept a woman as leader." Not only did these Black women not "step back," but scores of other Black women rose to lead further struggles and to demonstrate that women's liberation included not only those groups who called themselves that, but Welfare Rights mothers and nurses aides marching in Charleston, South Carolina, for better conditions, and cleaning women in New York in their sixties and seventies who complained that men were being paid more and, when asked what they thought about Women's Liberation, replied, "We *are* women's liberationists."

Color is that exciting dimension which signalled a new Third World not only in the United States but throughout the world. In East Timor, Rosa Muki

Bonaparte organized the Popular Organization of Timorese Women (OPMT) as a group within Fretelin in 1975, when the East Timorese people were trying to end 446 years of Portuguese rule. She declared: "The ideology of a system in which women are considered as 'inferior beings' has submitted Timorese women to a double exploitation: A general form, which applies without distinction to both men and women, and which manifests itself by forced labor, starvation salaries, racism, etc... Another form of a specific character, directed to women in particular."

The objectives of the OPMT were "the total destruction of all forms of exploitation" and "to restore to women the position and rights due to them in the new society which we are building through revolution."[14]

In the Congo, the women formed a Union for the Emancipation of the African Woman, whose aims were: (1) "to struggle against all backward customs which shackle women"; (2) "to promote the participation of women in all national endeavors"; and (3) "to raise the level of awareness of women to involve her in the economic life of the country." The Zulu woman's rebellion against polygamy, too, was called "sister to women's liberation."[15]

PHILOSOPHY AS ACTION: NEW REVOLUTIONARY
PATHS TO LIBERATION VS THE TRAP THAT LIES IN WAIT

To this writer, despite all the new depth and scope and global dimension of the new Women's Liberation Movement today, the most serious errors of not only bourgeois but of socialist feminists are that they, at one and the same time, have disregarded Rosa Luxemburg as a revolutionary and as a feminist, *and*, above all, have helped those men who have tried to reduce Marx to a single discipline, be that as economist, philosopher, anthropologist, or "political strategist." The truth is, however, that Marx, at all times—in theory as in practice, and in practice as in theory—was a revolutionary. Failure to grasp that essential fact makes it very nearly impossible not to fall into the trap of a post-Marx Marxist like Hal Draper, whose ambition to influence the Women's Liberation Movement was strong enough to have him separately publish "Marx and Engels on Women's Liberation,"[16] a chapter he had pulled out of the context of his projected many-volumed study, *Karl Marx's Theory of Revolution*.[17]

It is Draper's essay about which Sheila Rowbotham, the author of that most serious, comprehensive, historic work, ranging over three hundred years, *Women, Resistance and Revolution*, had written: "This is a very useful summary of what Marx and Engels wrote about women." Although she is independent enough of Marx to call Marx and Engels "a couple of bourgeois men in the nineteenth century," she has only one criticism of Draper's "summary": "It doesn't really point out problems and inadequacies of what they [Marx and Engels] wrote." It is because Sheila Rowbotham was reducing Women's Liberation to an "organizing idea" (with which we will deal later) that she fell into the trap Draper had set for the Women's Liberation Movement. Her latest work, *Beyond the Fragments*, which has gained great popularity, has not freed her from tail-endism to the vanguard party concept.[18]

Whether it is out of sheer ignorance, or out of willful disregard of Lawrence Krader's historic *transcription*[19] of Marx's *Ethnological Notebooks*—which reveal, in everything from length to content to scope, that they are very far removed from the so-called "Abstract" that Engels included in *The Origin of the Family*—Draper holds that *The Origin of the Family* by Engels "should be considered the joint work of both men."

This question, which has disoriented the Marxist movement since the death of Marx, will be developed in full later in this book (Part Three). Here, because many in today's Women's Liberation Movement have likewise fallen into that mire—which has kept them from seeing how totally new and almost visionary is Marx's concept of Man/Woman, and discovering how it could become ground for those contributions to be developed by our own age—we must discuss the two worst "Engelsianisms," which Draper repeats endlessly, as he roots himself heavily in *The Origin of the Family*.

1. "The world historic defeat of the female sex,"[20] which Engels grounds in a transition from matriarchy (or at least matrilineal descent) to patriarchy, *is no expression of Marx's*. Marx rejected biologism whether in Morgan, Darwin, or those Marxists from whom Marx felt it necessary to separate himself so sharply that he used the expression: If that is Marxism, "I am no Marxist."[21]

2. "The world historic defeat" is related, in turn, to the so-called "primordial division of labor between the sexes," which can conveniently put freedom off until the millenium. Again, it is *not* Marx's concept; even where Marx said that the first division of labor was sexual (in 1845 in *The German Ideology*, which he and Engels wrote together), it was perceived as not just personal but *social*. Marx then developed the concept that the most serious division in humanity's development was that between country and city. He ended by showing that the most fundamental division of all, the one which characterized *all class societies*, and none more so than capitalism, is the division between mental and manual labor. This is the red thread that runs through all of Marx's work from 1841 to 1883. This is what Marx said must be torn up root and branch. But of that Great Divide, so critical to our age, there is not a whiff in Draper.[22]

The questions of sexual relations, forms of marriage, and the family are certainly pivotal, and even if one wishes to skip over the 1844 *Economic–Philosophic Manuscripts*, especially so on the question of that fundamental relationship of Man/Woman, there is plenty of other evidence about Marx's disgust with bourgeois monogamy and its double standard, all of which needed total uprooting in any new society.

Marx strongly opposed patriarchy, calling for the "abolition" of the patriarchal family. He held: "The modern family contains in embryo not only slavery (*servitus*) but serfdom also, since from the very beginning it is connected with agricultural service. It contains within itself, *in miniature*, all the antagonisms which later develop on a wide scale within society and its state." And "all the antagonisms" extended from "ranks" that began in communal life and led to the division between the chieftain and the masses, class divisions in embryo, "*in miniature.*"

Engels appears to have had a unilateral instead of a multilateral attitude to the question of the development of Man/Woman. It is true that it was great, in 1884, to stress the manner in which woman had always been oppressed since her "world historic defeat," how different it had been in "matriarchal" society, and how socialism would be the re-establishment of primitive communism on a higher scale. Or, as Engels italicized Morgan's judgment as the very final sentence of his whole book, "*It will be a revival, in a higher form, of the liberty, equality and fraternity of the ancient gentes.*" But the fact is that Engels's writing there is neither very dialectical nor comprehensive when it gets fixed on the family.

Marx, on the contrary, showed that the elements of oppression in general, and of woman in particular, arose from *within* primitive communism, and not only related to change from "matriarchy," but beginning with the establishment of ranks—relationship of chief to mass—and the economic interests that accompanied it.

So far is Draper, however, from comprehending Marx's revolutionary concepts, that he dismisses Marx's monumental discovery of a whole new continent of thought and revolution by declaring that the historic essays we now know as the *Economic–Philosophic Manuscripts* of 1844 are nothing more than the "lucubrations of this new-fledged socialist." And so bent is he on reducing Marx's view of the Man/Woman relationship to hardly more than an "echo" of Fourierism[23] that he writes of Marx paying "homage to Fourier" not only when he is talking about "Marx's Early Views (1842–46)," but even in 1868 in Marx's letter to Dr. Ludwig Kugelmann (12 December 1868): "Great progress was evident in the last Congress of the American 'Labour Union' in that, among other things, it treated working women with complete equality . . . Anybody who knows anything of history knows that great social changes are impossible without the feminine ferment."

This is not the young Marx, nor even the mature author of the *Grundrisse*. It is the Marx who, the year before, had finally published his greatest theoretical work, *Capital*. Two decades had elapsed since Marx had issued the world-shaking *Communist Manifesto* and plunged directly into the 1848 Revolutions. This is the Marx who was the head of the First International Working Men's Association, writing about a new stage in working class development in the United States after the Civil War and the struggle for the shortening of the working day.

It was the establishment of the National Labor Union with its call for the equality of women (indeed, it was electing them to decision-making positions)[24] that inspired Marx's letter to Dr. Kugelmann. Marx had devoted no less than eighty pages of *Capital* to the struggles for the shortening of the working day, and the bulk of that chapter dealt with the oppression of women and children. Now Marx saw something happening across the ocean on the subject and he called Dr. Kugelmann's attention to the women being invited to join the First International. That letter also reported the historic fact that the First International had elected Madame Harriet Law to the highest ranking body, the General Council.

Marx, both in theory and in fact, in historical accounting as well as in the economic conditions of oppression of women, had been most active as well as theoretically involved in developing his early concept of the Man/Woman relationship. Far from it being just a concept—as was shown by the fact that the women in the First International were not just members but also part of the leadership—Marx was for the autonomous existence of women both in his organization and elsewhere. Thus he had sent Elizabeth Dmitrieva to organize a women's section of the First International in Paris. It was she who became the organizer for the *Union Des Femmes*, and who told the Executive Committee of the Commune: "At this hour, when danger is imminent . . . the entire population must unite to defend the Commune," which stood for "the annihilation of all privilege and all inequality." Justice was to be for all without the distinction as to sex, which had been maintained by the "necessities of the antagonism upon which the governing classes' privilege had rested."[25]

* * *

As we saw, Women's Liberation is by no means restricted to any one period or any one country; and, of course, much happened in the period before Luxemburg and Zetkin, especially in the period when Eleanor Marx[26] was active in every phase from organizing the unorganized gas workers to translating Ibsen's *A Doll's House* and playing the role of Nora in it. But we must concentrate on today.

Let us focus first on Portugal. A most exciting part of the Portuguese Revolution was the new concept of *apartidarismo* (nonpartyism), raised by Isabel do Carmo, chairwoman of the Revolutionary Party of the Proletariat/ Revolutionary Brigades (PRP-BR). A contradiction that appeared at the same time was, in this writer's view, an actual development. It is the different concept between two women revolutionaries, one a feminist—Maria Barreno— and the other a Marxist—Isabel do Carmo—whose preoccupation could hardly be said to be the women's movement. With two other Marias, Maria Barreno wrote a magnificent book, *New Portuguese Letters*, published in English as *The Three Marias*.[27] At the same time, she created a new form of literature in which a "Letter" exposed patriarchal society stretching through the ages, and accepted "the Marxian concept of the socialist philosophy."[28] She attributed her release from prison, however, not to the revolution that followed, but to the international Women's Liberation Movement, which conducted a campaign for her freedom.

As for Isabel do Carmo, she had raised the most important question of all, which was by no means limited to the "Woman Question": *apartidarismo*. She didn't recognize that women's liberation was a question that could not wait until "after the revolution." However, both do Carmo and Barreno had faced the crucial question: *what form* of organization is the one needed to achieve freedom in our state-capitalist age, which has seen a *counter*revolution emerge out of the greatest of all proletarian revolutions, the Russian Revolution of 1917.

A still different level of discussing the same question, form of organization, permeated the whole Women's Liberation Movement as the question of "decentralization." The demand for small informal groups is not to be disregarded as if it were just a question of not understanding the difference between small and large, and that large is better. Nor can this demand be answered in our bureaucratic age by attributing to Women's Liberationists a deep-down belief in private property, petty home industry, and "of course" Mother Earth. Nothing of the kind. The demand for decentralization involves the two pivotal questions of the day; and, I might add, questions of tomorrow, because we are not going to have a successful revolution unless we do answer them. They are, first, the totality and the depth of the necessary uprooting of this exploitative, sexist, racist society. Second, the dual rhythm of revolution: not just the overthrow of the old, but the creation of the new; not just the reorganization of objective, material foundations but the release of subjective personal freedom, creativity, and talents. In a word, there must be such appreciation of the movement from below, from practice, that we never again let theory and practice get separated. That is the cornerstone.

We can see the same insight in China, specifically in Yenan after the Long March, where so many new avenues were opened by Mao Tse-tung (on the question of woman, he was supposed to have been the most advanced). This was the period when the American feminist and revolutionary socialist, Agnes Smedley, was writing from within China to further the revolutionary cause. Her magnificent *Portraits of Chinese Women in Revolution*[29] touched many of the same questions that were raised by the best-known Chinese feminist, Ding Ling, whose "Thoughts on March 8"[30] dealt directly with the Man/Woman relations in Yenan itself, especially those of leaders and their wives. Ding Ling's prescient, succinct, and profound expression, that women married to leaders were like "Noras who came home"—the moral being that, like Ibsen's heroine who rejected her *Doll's House*, once you slam the door behind you, you must leave it slammed—must surely come to mind with renewed power when we witness Jiang Qing, Mao's widow, in the courtroom in 1981.[31] Ding Ling's essay, "Thoughts on March 8," and other writings of women revolutionaries were translated into Farsi by an Iranian woman, and published as a pamphlet entitled *Woman as Reason and as Force of Revolution*, after the women had marched in Iran on International Women's Day, 1979, against the retrogressive laws introduced by Khomeini.[32]

Not to see how very pivotal the Man/Woman relationship is as *concept*; to attempt to reduce Women's Liberation to "an organizing idea," as Sheila Rowbotham does, is, to this author, but the other side of the coin of what Lenin did in 1902, when he *seemed* to reduce Marxism to an organizing idea, adding further that his was the only type of organization that was truly vanguard. To do that in 1981 does not exactly answer the burning questions of the day. Furthermore, Lenin had the saving grace of making revolution integral to all his concepts. Social revolution does come first, *provided* it is not—indeed revolution cannot be—without Women's Liberation or behind women's backs, or by using them only as helpmates.[§]

It will not do to rewrite history, and it certainly will not help, in digging into the 1917 Russian Revolution or the 1919 German Revolution, to repeat the same 1902 answer (as both Stalinists and Trotskyists do)—"the party, the party, the party"—and then to claim that, because Luxemburg did not have "a vanguard party" and Lenin did, that that alone explains the success of the Russian Revolution and the failure of the German. If that is all there is to it, how does one explain the transformation of that first workers' state into its opposite, the state-capitalist monstrosity we know today? No, that glib, fetishistic answer will not do, especially since there was enough life left in the German Revolution, even after it was beheaded, to have been followed by two others, which likewise failed. No one should know this better than the Women's Liberationists of our era, who, from all these different vantage points, have raised the question of decentralization, *apartidarismo*, new forms of organization which are not elitist and which do not separate practice from theory.[§]

For precisely this reason we must turn to Marx—the whole of Marx. Without his philosophy of revolution, neither Women's Liberationists nor the whole of humanity will have discovered the ground that will assure the success of the revolution.

NOTES

1. Kate Millett, *Sexual Politics* (New York: Doubleday & Co., 1970), was one of the first to expose the male chauvinism in literature, from D.H. Lawrence to Norman Mailer.
2. For a recent collection of essays that deal with "Radical Perspectives on Gay Liberation," see Pam Mitchell, ed., *Pink Triangles* (Boston: Alyson Pub., 1980).
3. See the report by Case Hayden and Margaret J. King in *Liberation*, 1965.
4. This was recorded by the Marxist–Humanist women, Black and white, who participated in

§ See "New Thoughts on *Rosa Luxemburg, Women's Liberation, and Marx's Philosophy of Revolution*," pp. xxxv–xxxvi.—Ed.

those Freedom Rides, in Mary Hamilton, et al., *Freedom Riders Speak for Themselves* (Detroit: News & Letters, 1961), pp. 22–24. This pamphlet is cited in the Smithsonian Institution's album, *Voices of the Civil Rights Movement* (Washington, D.C., 1980).

5. Doris Wright, "A Black Woman Writes," *News & Letters*, August–September 1971.

6. The demonstration became the highpoint of the film, *With Babies and Banners*, produced by the Women's Labor History Film Project, and nominated for an Academy Award in 1978.

7. For more on Black women in South Africa, see Phyllis Ntantala, *An African Tragedy* (Detroit: Agascha Productions, 1976), and Hilda Bernstein, *For Their Triumphs and for Their Tears* (London: International Defense & Aid Fund for Southern Africa, 1975).

8. Fatima Mernissa, "Veiled Sisters," *New World Outlook*, April 1971, pp. 36–39. See also Doris Wright, "Black Women Oppose Oppression in Many Lands," *News & Letters*, February 1972, which covered the flanks of the feminists' argument by pointing out: "Mohammed himself granted Muslim women what the Napoleonic Code did not grant French women until the late 1950s—the right to possess property and to administer it without any interference from her husband." She then continued, "To underscore the intensity of the Muslim woman's predicament, the Algerian writer, Fadela M'Rabet reports that the rate of suicide among young girls who refuse arranged marriages and seclusion has risen drastically since the end of the revolution." See also Neda, "An Iranian Woman Speaks: Women and Religion in Iran," *News & Letters*, October 1979; and Tatyana Mamonova's appeal for support of the Russian Women's Movement and her critique of its "Christianization," *News & Letters*, January –February 1981.

9. In W. Morgan Shuster's *The Strangling of Persia (A Personal Narrative)* (1912; reprint ed., New York: Greenwood Press, 1968), the historic role of the women is revealed by the mere description of what happened:

> The Persian women since 1907 had become almost at a bound the most progressive, not to say radical, in the world. That this statement upsets the ideas of centuries makes no difference. It is the fact . . . During the five years following the successful but bloodless revolution in 1906 against the oppression and cruelty of the Shah, a feverish and at times fierce light shone in the veiled eyes of Persia's women, and in their struggles for liberty and its modern expressions, they broke through some of the most sacred customs which for centuries past had bound their sex in the land of Iran [pp. 191–92].

This was discussed in my Political–Philosophic Letter, "Iran: Unfoldment of, and Contradictions in, Revolution" (Detroit: News & Letters, 1979), which was subsequently translated into Farsi by young Iranian revolutionaries. See also Lois Beck and Nikki Keddie, eds., *Women in the Muslim World* (Cambridge, Mass.: Harvard Univ. Press, 1978).

10. Although it quickly became bureaucratized at its very founding in 1974, the formation of the Coalition of Labor Union Women (CLUW) did reveal that even such male-dominated unions as the AFL-CIO and the UAW had been forced to make a gesture toward the growing Women's Liberation Movement. Groups such as Union WAGE (Union Women's Alliance to Gain Equality) have worked directly with rank and file working women in attempts to organize the unorganized. Most recently, the office workers have begun to organize nationally around a new union called District 925—a play on "9-to-5," the working hours of most office workers.

11. The Women's Liberation Movement inspired a veritable explosion of histories of women, including everything from studies such as Eleanor Flexner's *Century of Struggle* (New York: Atheneum, 1973) to works on Russia like Richard Stites's *The Women's Liberation Movement in Russia* (Princeton, N.J.: Princeton Univ. Press, 1978) and Atkinson, Dallin and Lapidus' *Women in Russia* (Stanford, Cal.: Stanford Univ. Press, 1977); and from Kate Millett's *Sexual Politics* (New York: Doubleday, 1970) to Sheila Rowbotham's *Women, Resistance and Revolution* (New York:Random House, 1972). For a work that concentrates on women as hidden not only from history but from philosophy, see Terrano, Dignan and Holmes, *Working Women for Freedom* (Detroit: Women's Liberation–News & Letters, 1976).

12. Margaret Sloan, as reported in *Detroit Free Press*, 28 January 1974.

13. See report, "Women Face United Front," *News & Letters*, August–September 1969.

14. Molly Jackson, "E. Timor women revolutionaries speak to our struggles today," *News & Letters*, October 1976.

15. See Doris Wright's article, "Black Women Oppose Oppression in Many Lands," *News & Letters*, February 1972, in which she is quoting Rebecca Reyher, who has spent many years living among the Zulu women.

16. Hal Draper, "Marx and Engels on Women's Liberation," *International Socialism*, July–

August 1970. It was also reproduced in *Female Liberation—History and Current Politics*, Roberta Salper, ed. (New York: Alfred Knopf, 1972).

17. Draper explains his goal to have been "a full and definitive treatment of Marx's political theory, policies, and practice," but since that was "unattainable," since politics has come to have a narrow meaning, and since there is a need to go "beyond the indispensable 'grand theory' . . . It is to bend the stick the other way that this work is titled *Karl Marx's Theory of Revolution* rather than *Political Theory*, which might be interpreted too narrowly." See Hal Draper, *Karl Marx's Theory of Revolution* (New York and London: Monthly Review Press, 1977), pp. 11–12.

18. See Sheila Rowbotham, *Women's Liberation and Revolution* (Bristol, England: Falling Wall Press, 1972, expanded in 1973), p. 6. This is the "extensive, descriptive bibliography" to which Rowbotham refers in *Women, Resistance and Revolution*. See also *Beyond the Fragments* by Sheila Rowbotham, Lynn Segal and Hilary Wainwright (London: Merlin Press, 1979).

19. Krader, *Ethnological Notebooks*. It is important to emphasize that this is a transcription because Krader reproduced Marx's exact words without interfering in any way with the content, presenting his own views in a full introduction. The same is true for what he published as an appendix to *The Asiatic Mode of Production* (Assen, The Netherlands: Van Gorcum, 1975), Marx's work on Kovalevsky.

20. Frederick Engels, *The Origin of the Family, Private Property and the State*, 1972 edition, p. 120. See Eleanor Leacock's peculiar interpretation of this expression in her introduction to this edition, p. 42.

21. This oft-repeated phrase was used by Marx against many who called themselves "Marxists," including his sons-in-law, one of whom he considered "the last disciple of Bakunin" and the other "the last of the Proudhonists." Engels reported that these "self-styled 'Marxists' " often provoked Marx to say: "one thing is certain, that I am no Marxist." See Rubel's *Marx Without Myth*, p. 329.

22. Draper keeps stressing, when he refers to "the world-historic defeat of the female sex," that it "cannot be changed basically simply by ideological (including psychiatric) exhortation," thus reducing today's fight for total liberation to the merely "ideological," and then further reducing ideology to "psychiatric exhortation." His cynicism is revealed even more when he adds—parenthetically, of course—to his statement that the totality of the change needed in the Man/Woman relationship holds under "all" circumstances: "(That would be so even without the Pill.)"

23. Contrast this to Simone de Beauvoir's *The Second Sex*, where she shows that Fourier "confused the emancipation of women with the rehabilitation of the flesh, demanding for every individual the right to yield to the call of passion and wishing to replace marriage with love; he considered woman not as a person but only in her amorous function" (p. 103). Totally opposite to Fourierism is the penultimate paragraph of de Beauvoir's entire work, that very same paragraph from Marx on the Man/Woman relationship.

24. Two of the best known were Kate Mullaney, president of the Troy Collar Laundry Workers, who was appointed assistant secretary and national organizer for women, and Augusta Lewis, a leader in the typographical union.

25. Edith Thomas, *The Women Incendiaries*, p. 67. This magnificent book has an entire chapter devoted to the Union des Femmes.

26. There are two excellent biographies of Eleanor Marx: Chushichi Tsuzuki, *The Life of Eleanor Marx* (Oxford: Clarendon Press, 1967), and Yvonne Kapp, *Eleanor Marx*, 2 vols. (New York: Pantheon Books, 1972). Yvonne Kapp's is especially important both because it is the most comprehensive and because it deals with the state of Karl Marx's documents. For an article written by Eleanor Marx in 1886 on "The Woman Question," see *Green Mountain Quarterly*, February 1976.

27. The very first sentence of the book reads: ". . . Granted, then, that all of literature is a long letter to an invisible other. . . . " See Maria Isabel Barreno, Maria Teresa Horta, and Maria Velho da Costa, *The Three Marias: New Portuguese Letters* (New York: Doubleday & Co., 1974).

28. See her speech given at Berkeley, California, as recorded in *News & Letters*, April 1975.

29. Agnes Smedley, *Portraits of Chinese Women in Revolution* (Old Westbury, N.Y.: Feminist Press, 1976) is a collection of stories and sketches drawn from Smedley's books, newspaper reports, and magazine articles from 1933 to 1937. The Feminist Press has also reissued her autobiographical novel, *Daughter of Earth*.

30. Ding Ling's "Thoughts on March 8" is available from the Femintern Press, Tokyo, Japan.

It first appeared in the *Jiefang Ribao* (*Liberation News*) (Yenan, China), 9 March 1942. It was used in the campaign against Ding Ling, who was purged from the Chinese Communist Party in 1957 for criticizing the views of the party on marriage and love at the time of the Hundred Flowers campaign.

31. Elsewhere I have analyzed both Jiang Qing and the trial of the so-called Gang of Four. See my pamphlet, *Sexism, Politics and Revolution in Mao's China* (Detroit: Women's Liberation–News & Letters, 1977), and my article, "China's 'Gang of Four' Trial Charade and the So-Called Cultural Revolution" in *News & Letters*, March 1981.

32. This Farsi pamphlet, *Woman as Reason and as Force of Revolution*, includes, as appendices to my writings on women's liberation, both "Woman's Suffrage and Class Struggle," by Rosa Luxemburg, and "Thoughts on March 8," by Ding Ling.

PART THREE

Karl Marx—From Critic of Hegel to Author of Capital and Theorist of "Revolution in Permanence"

IX

Marx Discovers a New Continent of Thought and Revolution

> *Necessity is an evil, but there is no necessity to live under the control of necessity. Everywhere the paths to freedom are open . . .*
> Marx, Doctoral Thesis, *1841*

> *The chief defect of all hitherto existing materialism—that of Feuerbach included—is that the thing (*Gegenstand*), reality, sensuousness, is conceived only in the form of the object (*Objekt*) or of contemplation (*Anshauung*), but not as human sensuous activity, practice, not subjectively. Hence it happened that the* active *side, in contradistinction to materialism, was developed by idealism—but only abstractly . . . Hence, he does not grasp the significance of "revolutionary," of "practical-critical" activity.*
> Marx, Theses on Feuerbach, *1845*

1. A PRELIMINARY NOTE ON THE DIALECTIC: IN MARX OF THE EARLY 1840s; IN LUXEMBURG, 1902; IN LENIN, 1914

The now-famous 1844 *Economic-Philosophic Manuscripts*, the core of which was Marx's critique of the Hegelian dialectic, were unknown to Rosa Luxemburg. It took a near century—and the Russian Revolution—before it was possible to pry those Humanist Essays out of the vaults of the Second International. Lenin, without knowing about them, was the only Marxist who felt the compulsion to grapple seriously with Marx's rootedness in the Hegelian dialectic when World War I brought with it the collapse of the Second International.

Hegel's *Science of Logic* opened so many new vistas for Lenin that he concluded: "It is impossible fully to grasp Marx's *Capital*, and especially its first chapter, if you have not studied through and understood the *whole* of

Hegel's *Logic*. Consequently, none of the Marxists for the past ½ century have understood Marx!!"[1]

And after he concluded his Abstract of Hegel's *Science of Logic*, Lenin summed up his new concept of dialectics by hitting out against "the father of Russian Marxism," Plekhanov: "Plekhanov wrote probably nearly 1,000 pages (Beltov + against Bogdanov + against Kantians + basic questions, etc., etc. on philosophy [dialectic]). There is in them *nil* about the Larger Logic, *its* thoughts (i.e., dialectic *proper*, as a philosophic science) nil!!"[2]

The emphasis that Lenin put on "dialectic *proper*, as a philosophic science" separated him from all other post-Marx Marxists, not only up to the Russian Revolution but also after the conquest of power. When he wrote to the editors of the projected new journal, *Under the Banner of Marxism*, asking them to consider themselves the "Materialist Friends of the Hegelian Dialectic," he stressed that they should let Hegel speak for himself, and should quote his writings extensively. What was most manifest of what he had gained from the 1914–15 Hegel studies was that the Hegelian dialectic needs to be studied "in and for itself." He articulated this most daringly in his 1915 essay, "On Dialectics": " . . . clerical obscurantism (= philosophical idealism), of course, has *epistemological* roots, it is not groundless; it is a *sterile flower* undoubtedly, but a sterile flower that grows on the living tree of living, fertile, genuine, powerful, omnipotent, objective, absolute human knowledge."[3]

What stands out in Lenin's Abstract of Hegel's *Science of Logic* is the length of time he spent in the Doctrine of Notion, especially as its last chapter reached *the* turning point of absolute negativity in the Absolute Method. Again, he stopped to quote Hegel: "In the absolute method the Notion *preserves* itself in its otherness, and the universal in its particularisation, in the Judgement and in reality . . . " Then Lenin concluded: "This extract is not at all bad as a kind of summing up of dialectics."[4]

The reason Hegelian dialectics was so alive to Lenin was not due entirely to the profundity of his study. Rather, it was the objective world situation—the capitalist crisis that brought about the simultaneity of World War I and the collapse of *established* Marxism—which led the revolutionary materialist, Lenin, to single out the Absolute Method of the idealist philosopher, Hegel. With absolute negativity, Lenin worked out a political transformation into opposite: "Turn the imperialist war into civil war."

That Lenin kept his direct encounter with the Hegelian dialectic—his Abstract of Hegel's *Science of Logic*—to himself, however, shows the depth of the economist mire into which the whole Second International, and not just the German Social-Democracy, had sunk; revolutionaries stood on the same ground!

As for Marx's 1844 Manuscripts, they were not published in Lenin's time. They first came to light eight years after Luxemburg's murder.[5] Some of Marx's early works had, however, become known when Mehring published them in 1902. Luxemburg's review, as well as Mehring's introduction and editorializing, only prove how all-pervasive was the mechanical materialism of all the post-Marx Marxists, and how characteristic it was not only of the reformists but of revolutionaries as great as Luxemburg and Mehring. To *all* Marxists, Lenin included in the *pre*-1914 period, the dialectic remained an abstraction. This was so despite Luxemburg's sharp rejection of Bernstein's demand that the dialectical scaffolding be removed from Marxism, and despite her emotional evocation, in *Reform or Revolution*, of the dialectic as "the intellectual arm with the aid of which the proletariat, though materially under the yoke of the bourgeoisie, is yet enabled to triumph over the bourgeoisie. For it is our dialectical system that . . . is already realizing a revolution in the domain of thought." Nowhere is the lack of concreteness in Luxemburg's attitude to the dialectic seen more clearly than in the essay "From the Legacy of Our Masters."[6]

It is true that at the end of the essay, Luxemburg comes to the defense of Marx's "a priori formulation," underlining the fact that it was indeed "derived" out of "*a deductive schema of the proletarian class struggle and victory!*" and further insisting that "only when he had the Ariadne-thread of historical materialism in his hand, did he find his way through the labyrinth of everyday facts of modern society to the scientific laws of its development and downfall." Clearly, she has not forgotten her enemy, the reformists, and retains the passion for the dialectic when she is attacking *them*.

Unfortunately, it is retained *only* when she is attacking them—that is, when she brings in the relevance of the Marxian dialectic to the existing (1902) situation in Germany. And she does so only when Marx has already named the class struggle and the proletariat as the gravedigger of capitalism. Until that point (and the specific point cited was from the 1844 Introduction[7] to Marx's *Critique of Hegel's "Philosophy of Right"*), Luxemburg—far from sensing anything revolutionary in Marx either in his 1841 Doctoral Thesis or even in the openly revolutionary journalism that followed it on the question of censorship and freedom of the press—spoke of the "painful inadequacy of his [Marx's] idealistic world conception," as if the birth of Marx's whole new continent of thought was simply a question of materialism vs idealism. Insofar as she saw most of those early Essays, it was Mehring she credited with shaping those "totally diverse and unconnected youthful writings of Marx" into a logical order, claiming that it was Mehring who "teaches us to understand and love Marx" despite the "motley, disjointed fragments of Marx's intellectual activity," expressed in a "wild, half-understood tongue."

Even when she saw that it was "the cutting weapon of the Hegelian dialectic which allowed him [Marx] to make such a splendid critical butchery" of the Prussian government's views on censorship and wood theft, Luxemburg wrote: "It was only the *dialectic*, the *method* of thought that was of service to him here." Clearly, far from seeing in the dialectic a dialectic of liberation, she saw it merely as a tool. That is the level to which *established* Marxism had reduced dialectical methodology.

In an essay on "Stagnation and Progress in Marxism"[8] Luxemburg took issue with critics who called Marx's writings outdated, holding instead that "our needs are not yet adequate for utilization of Marx's ideas." Luxemburg was right when she related what is remembered and what is forgotten of Marx's writings to the specific stage of class struggle and what Marx*ists* judged to be "practical" or useful for that stage.

She was wrong, however, when she wrote:

> Though that theory is an incomparable instrument of intellectual culture, it remains unused because, while it is inapplicable to bourgeois class culture, it greatly transcends the needs of the working class in the matter of weapons for the daily struggle. Not until the working class has been liberated from its present conditions of existence will the Marxist method of research be socialized in conjunction with other means of production, so that it can be fully utilized for the benefit of humanity-at-large, and so that it can be developed to the full measure of its functional capacity.

Luxemburg's judgment of Marx's new continent of thought as just "a weapon in the class struggle," "a method of research," and "an instrument of intellectual culture," needed by the "party of practical fighters"—as if all that was needed was practice, practice, practice—was the near-fatal error of *all* Marxists after the death of Marx. To grasp it at its root, rather than as if it were just characteristic either of Luxemburg or Germany in the early twentieth century, it is necessary to begin at the beginning, directly with Marx's closest collaborator, without whom we would not have had either volumes 2 or 3 of *Capital*—Frederick Engels.

Here is a Marxist who did not, at least not when he spoke of Marxism in general and not in specifics, delimit Marx's contribution to "method of research." Here is Marx's closest collaborator, who could be considered, in some fundamental respects, a cofounder of Historical Materialism. He was certainly the most devoted of Marx's colleagues, and consciously tried only to follow Marx's "bequests."

Moreover, Engels was modest enough not to allow the movement to behave as if *he*, Engels, were Marx. He not only stressed that Marx was a "genius" while the rest were at best "talented"; he correctly maintained that though Marx and he were moving in the same direction independently of each other, he considered that "the fundamental proposition" that formed the basis of the *Communist Manifesto* had been worked out by Marx "some years before 1845." In a word, Engels stressed that Historical Materialism had been discovered by Marx as early as 1843, when he first broke with bourgeois society; that all the development of the decades since was but an extension of "the nucleus" of everything that we identify with Marxism—from Historical Materialism and the economic laws of capitalism to the Marxian dialectic of the class struggle and revolution, with its global dimension both of the downfall of capitalism and the creation of a new class-*less* society.

And yet, and yet, and yet . . . First came Engels's own work, *The Origin of the Family, Private Property, and the State*, which he considered the fulfilling of a "bequest of Marx." Then, after the publication of volume 2 of *Capital* in 1885, came a new introduction to the 1888 English edition of the *Communist Manifesto*, in which Engels took the liberty of footnoting the historic, majestic first sentence—"The history of all hitherto existing society is the history of class struggles"—by adding the words: "That is, all *written* history." Engels went on to explain, in a long digression, the "discoveries" of prehistory, which had "first then" become known, and to recommend *The Origin of the Family* to all readers. The truth, however, is that Marx had been aware of all these discoveries when he wrote the 1882 Preface to the Russian edition of the *Communist Manifesto*, and, far from changing the historic statement, had instead projected the possibility of a revolution in Russia ahead of any in technologically advanced Western Europe.

Thus Engels muted the dialectical flow of the challenge to all Marx held to be the "prehistory" of humanity, whose true development would first unfold after the overthrow of capitalism.

Luxemburg's disgust with the orthodox SPD leadership did not extend to a perception of how total was the lack of comprehension of Marx's philosophy of revolution that would extend far beyond any single question, be it nationalism or the Morocco incident. Her profound sensing of the opportunism within the German Social-Democracy, which led to the 1910–11 break with Kautsky, was not made into the kind of universal that others could recognize and accept.

Indeed, she herself did not realize that the SPD had deviated from Marx, and not just on tactical grounds; that the course needed to be reversed to reconnect with Marx's philosophy—that is, the actuality of revolution—and to make that philosophy the solid ground of the new, the *totally* new. But to feel the *presence* of something totally new that was the absolute opposite of imperialism required not only economic and political analyses, but live subjects who are creatively struggling, instead of just suffering, and *therefore* can become what Lenin called the "bacilli of proletarian socialist revolution."

There is but one dialectical conceptual framework, an indivisible whole which does not divide economics and politics from Subject: masses in motion—a living, feeling, thinking, acting whole. Therefore, in Marx's new continent of thought, history was not just "economic periods" but masses *making* history. Because a single dialectical course determines the objective and subjective forces, the dialectic of Marx's philosophy of revolution allowed Marx's theory of history to transform historic narrative into historic Reason.[9] It is this which eluded Luxemburg when she very nearly dismissed the "stagnation of Marxism" on the ground that Marx's heirs were "practical fighters."

Far from dialectics being an abstract question, it is this which impinges on

Marx's philosophy of revolution. Is it Marx who wasn't a "Marxist" so long as he was still a "philosopher"? Was "scientific socialism" achieved only after Marx, as Luxemburg put it, "developed himself into a practical, political *fighter*" (her emphasis); only after he discovered the class struggle, wrote the *Communist Manifesto* announcing a proletarian revolution, and finally plunged into economic studies and discovered "the scientific, economic laws" of capitalist development and collapse? The answer to this is no such simple matter as citing that even when *Capital* was already on the presses, Marx still proudly acknowledged authorship of his early work, *The Holy Family*, writing to Engels that when Dr. Kugelmann handed it to him and he reread it, he was "pleased to say there was nothing to be ashamed of."[10] No, it is nothing that simple. Rather, what is involved is the whole question of a dialectic of thought, of liberation, the revolutionary nature of Historical Materialism.

To see *that* dialectic, it is important not to view Marx and Engels as one. Even after the highest point of their collaboration, in the 1848 Revolutions and their joint *Address to the Communist League* on "revolution in permanence" in 1850, Marx wrote to Engels (1 August 1856) about a contemporary commentator: "What is so very strange is to see how he treats the two of us as a singular: '*Marx and Engels says*' etc."

Marx could not possibly have known that precisely such an artificial "merger" of the two would so characterize the thinking of post-Marx Marxists, that the new and the original of what Marx's Marxism *is* becomes blurred. After Marx's death, Engels, fearing that this might happen, felt compelled to record—in nothing less important than the 1883 Preface to the German edition of the *Communist Manifesto*: "The basic thought running through the Manifesto [i.e. Historical Materialism] belongs solely and exclusively to Marx." Engels repeated the thought in the 1888 Preface to the English edition, and expanded on it to show that whereas he had "independently progressed" towards such a position, as was shown by his *Condition of the Working Class in England*, the truth was that when he "again met Marx at Brussels in the Spring of 1845, he [Marx] had it already worked out, and put it before me in terms almost as clear as those in which I have expressed it here."

The reference is clearly to the years 1843–44 when Marx had broken with the bourgeoisie and had produced the writings we now know as the *Economic–Philosophic Manuscripts*. They were the years when, as an economist, Engels was considerably more advanced than Marx, who had had hardly any knowledge or practice, as Marx himself put it, "in material matters." None of this, however, limited Marx's vision of *total, social revolution,* the opening up of a totally new continent of thought. This should have directed, but did not, the new generation to see that there is nothing abstract about philosophy—not about Marx's philosophy of revolution.

The question that concerns us here is this: Could Rosa Luxemburg's near tone-deafness on philosophy have had an impact on the attitude to the theory of revolution in general, and to the 1919 German Revolution in particular? This is not asked in order to pass hindsight off as foresight, but because our age's problematic gnaws at us. Since it is a fact that Rosa Luxemburg never wavered, while the Second International betrayed the revolution; since Luxemburg enthusiastically embraced, participated in, and led the 1919 Revolution, the question remains: is the revolutionary act sufficient to reestablish for our age the Marxism of Marx?

It becomes imperative to dig into the Marxian dialectic from the start of his adult life to his concept of permanent revolution, not only as he formulated it at the conclusion of the 1848–49 Revolutions, but as he expressed it in the last years of his life, when he worked on the *Ethnological Notebooks*, made three drafts of an answer to Zasulich, and wrote the Preface to the 1882 Russian edition of the *Communist Manifesto*. (This period is developed later, in Chapter XII, section 2.) Our age, which has the great advantage in that we finally are in possession of nearly *all* of Marx's works, has the possibility of penetrating the totality of the Marxian philosophy of revolution through all its stages of development.[11]

We will focus here on the two most controversial periods: the first and last decades of Marx's life. It is not that we intend to skip over the most productive period of Marx's life; because his greatest theoretical work, *Capital*, is seen most fully in the French edition of 1875, the consideration of *Capital* as well as of the *Grundrisse* (which was unknown until our own age) is integral to the last seven years. It is in that period that we will confront *Capital* and the dialectic of liberation—and not just as "economic laws."

The first decade after his break with bourgeois society saw not only the concretization of Marx's Promethean vision in the *Critique of the Hegelian Dialectic* and the *Communist Manifesto* but the projection of "the revolution in permanence." We will, in fact, turn back to 1841, when Marx completed his doctoral dissertation, to view the ground on which Marx stood as he left the university and turned to the real world.

The last seven years of Marx's life saw not only the most profound articulation of the organization question in the *Critique of the Gotha Program* and the French edition of *Capital*, which had foreseen our state-capitalist age and deepened the significance of the fetishism of commodities, but the *Ethnological Notebooks*. Only recently transcribed, these *Notebooks* reveal, at one and the same time, the actual ground that led to the first projection of the possibility of revolution coming first in underdeveloped countries like Russia; a reconnection and deepening of what was projected in the *Grundrisse* on the Asiatic mode of production; *and* a return to that most fundamental relationship of Man/Woman which had first been projected in the 1844 Essays.

While Engels did not know these Essays, he did know at least one part of the *Ethnological Notebooks*—the one on Morgan's *Ancient Society*, on which he thought he was basing, as a Marx legacy, his *Origin of the Family*. Now that we have the *Notebooks*, we can see what a chasm there was between Marx and Engels on that most fundamental Man/Woman relationship.

2. PROMETHEUS BOUND, 1841–43

The path to Marx's discovery of the new continent of thought and revolution in 1844 started out at the university as he worked on his doctoral dissertation, "The Difference between the Democritean and Epicurean Philosophy of Nature."[12] The very first sentence of the foreword to this 1841 thesis criticized the form in which it appeared: "The form of this treatise would have been on the one hand more strictly scientific, on the other hand in many of its arguments less pedantic, if its primary purpose had not been that of a doctor's dissertation" (p. 29). Academia, very obviously, was not the ground Marx desired for presentation of either the ancient Greek philosophers that were his subject or, what is more important, that which actually impelled his choice of topic—the desire to illuminate the contemporary post-Hegelian period by examining a parallel age in the history of Greek philosophy, the post-Aristotelian period.

What interests us here is neither the philosophies of Epicurus and Democritus, nor Marx's erudite pioneering analysis,[13] but rather the originality and radical departure of thought Marx was making for his own period. In the very same paragraph in which Marx claimed he was only filling out "details" in regard to Epicurus and Democritus (whom he says Hegel had already dealt with "in the admirably great and bold plan of his history of philosophy from which alone the history of philosophy can in general be dated [pp. 29–30]"), he nevertheless also states that "the giant thinker was hindered by his view of what he called speculative thought *par excellence* from recognizing in these systems their great importance for the history of Greek philosophy . . . " (p. 30).

The key word is *history*, and though the contemporary history that was pulling at the student Marx was here stated as if it were only the history of thought, the nonmuted form in which it was expressed in his so-called Notes[14] makes it clear that it was actual history—the crisis in contemporary Germany in reality as well as in thought. And because that was so, it was both Hegel and the living Left Hegelians (of whom he was one) that Marx was challenging. His point was that it is insufficient simply to show that the master has accommodated himself to reality. One must analyze the accommodation not merely to expose it, but in order thereby to discover the inadequacy of the principle which *compelled* that accommodation. Only in that way could the critique produce an advance in knowledge which would create the possibility of a new beginning.

It is true that Marx would not work out that new beginning until he had broken with bourgeois society, as he had already broken with religion and Prussian censorship, and until he discerned the working class as Subject. But, philosophically, there is no doubt where he was headed, as he contrasted practice to theory and developed his most original interpretation of *praxis*. That was to remain his unique category for breaking both with "idealism" *and* "materialism."

Marx held that because Hegel's philosophy was not the unity of reason and reality that it claimed to be—at least in the present period of crisis—there was a total diremption of the two separate totalities. Reality and Reason confronted each other with hostility: "This duality of philosophical self-consciousness appears finally as a double trend, each side utterly opposed to the other" (p. 86).

Feeling the need not only to attack the one *and* the other, but also to find "the energizing principle" for a new beginning, Marx wrote: "It is a psychological law that the theoretical mind, once liberated in itself, turns into practical energy . . . But the *practice* of philosophy is itself *theoretical*. It is the *critique* that measures the individual existence by the essence, the particular reality by the Idea" (p. 85).

Marx discerned a similar critique of the existing society and its gods in Greece in Epicurus's opposition to the "tyranny of religion" and passion for the freedom of thought. It was that which drew Marx to Epicurus; and it was on that principle of freedom of thought that Marx started working out a history of the world. Let us keep in mind that Marx achieved all this "self-clarification" before his entry into the real world and his fight against Prussian censorship and for freedom of the press. It was the lack of what he called the "energizing principle" in Democritus that sharpened Marx's distance not only from that ancient Greek philosopher but from his own colleagues among the Young Hegelians who refused to turn their eyes to the world of practice. Instead, basing himself on actual history, Marx posed the advice of Themistocles, who, "when Athens was threatened with destruction, tried to persuade the Athenians to abandon the city entirely and found a new Athens at sea, in another element."[15]

Marx himself had not yet discovered "another element," a new beginning, a Subject; but that is what he was searching for—and Freedom was the ground. To discern the direction in which he was headed, all we have to do is start at the beginning and see that, already in his doctoral dissertation, Marx had singled out Prometheus as the greatest of all martyrs in the philosophic calendar. He ended his foreword with a quotation, in the original Greek, from Aeschylus's *Prometheus Bound*, in which Prometheus answers Hermes, the servant of the gods:

> Be sure of this, I would not change my state
> Of evil fortune for your servitude.
> Better to be the servant of this rock
> Than to be faithful boy to Father Zeus.

Marx's *Notebooks* made it clear that it was neither just the Greek myth nor ancient Greek philosophy that concerned Marx. It was contemporary German philosophy and a new ground for post-Hegel Hegelianism: "As in the history of philosophy there are nodal points which raise philosophy in itself to concretion . . . so also there are moments when philosophy turns its eyes to the external world . . . As Prometheus, having stolen fire from heaven, begins to build houses and to settle upon the earth, so philosophy, expanded to be the whole world, turns against the world of appearance. The same now with the philosophy of Hegel" (p. 491).

This Promethean vision did not allow room for any stagifying, as Marx left the university and became, first, a correspondent for and, then, the editor of, *Rheinische Zeitung*. It wasn't a question of becoming a journalist rather than a philosopher. Marx remained a philosopher who was a practicing revolutionary journalist. Thus his articles against Prussian censorship projected the question of freedom of the press in so profound a manner that they remain a model for today: "Freedom is so much the essence of man that even its opponents realize it . . . No man fights freedom; he fights at most the freedom of others. Every kind of freedom has therefore always existed, only at one time as a special privilege, at another time as a universal right."[16]

In turning to what he called "material matters"—be it his defense of the correspondent on the plight of the Moselle peasants, his own articles in defense of the peasantry and in opposition to the innumerable Prussian laws on wood theft, or his analysis of daily events—Marx was brought into conflict with the Prussian state. No matter what the topic, his revolutionary spirit was so predominant that no amount of bourgeois explanation convinced the Prussian censors not to threaten banning the paper. Marx felt compelled to leave the *Rheinische Zeitung*.

3. PROMETHEUS UNBOUND, 1844–48

What to do? First and foremost, Marx broke with bourgeois society—not, however, to join what he considered vulgar communism, much less to remain part of the Left Hegelians. In 1842, a chasm had developed between Marx and those who kept up purely abstract debates, be the subject religion, political questions, or relations to the masses. He had maintained his relationship with Feuerbach, whose theoretical achievements he admired, though by no means uncritically.[17] Marx returned to his own study to work out his own thoughts, this time in the form of a *Critique of Hegel's "Philosophy of Right"*. *Praxis* was the pivotal word which was to govern Marx's whole adult life; for him criticism was always a critique not alone of thought but of the objective world, and always it was aimed at the transformation of the status quo. No sooner had Marx finished the *Critique* than he decided to revise it, and for the proposed revision wrote an Introduction. It was this which had won Luxemburg's enthusiasm and which has to this day remained a beacon light for even those Marxists who reject any whiff of the Hegelian dialectic that pervades it, since it does, for the first time, specify the proletariat as the revolutionary class: "As philosophy finds its material weapons in the proletariat, so the proletariat finds its spiritual weapons in philosophy; and once the lightning of thought has struck deeply into this naive soil of the people, the emancipation of the Germans into men will be accomplished."[18]

The break with the bourgeois state and bourgeois political philosophy was but the first step as Marx proceeded to Paris, not only to the study of both the French Revolution and political economy, but also to relate to workers, attend workers' meetings, and become practical in the Marxian sense of "practical-critical-revolutionary."

Two very opposite developments occurred in Paris. On the one hand, Marx made his final break with all the Young Hegelians, Feuerbach included. On the other hand, a totally new, and this time life-long, collaboration began with Engels. But neither of these developments occurred until the fall of 1844. The year was the most eventful not because of objective developments, but because of the type of subjective self-development that initiated a genuine birth-time of history and thought that Marx called a new Humanism and that was later to be called Marxism.

The year 1844 began with the one and only issue of the *Deutsche-französische Jahrbücher* which contained the two essays Marx had completed the year before—the Introduction to his *Critique of Hegel's "Philosophy of Right"* and the essay "On the Jewish Question"—both of which reflected a great leap forward from the break with bourgeois society and Hegel's political philosophy. It also contained Feuerbach's Thesis on the reformation of philosophy, which so impressed Marx that he thought he could convince Feuerbach to come to Paris and share his enthusiasm for new relations with the workers: "You have to have participated in one meeting of the French workers to be able to believe the virgin freshness and nobility among these workworn men" (Letter to Feuerbach, 11 August 1844).

It may be that Marx himself was not fully aware of all that was stirring in him, now that he had found a Subject. That Subject—labor—became the turning point for the rest of Marx's life. It emerged as, at one and the same time, he studied the *enragés* in the French Revolution (he was planning to write a study of the Convention), and met the workers of the period. His break with bourgeois society had not stopped either with the break with religion or the break with Hegel's Philosophy of the State and Law and bureaucracy.[19] It was Marx's concept of Alienated Labor which broke through all criticism. *That* discovery changed all else. *That* "self-clarification," stretching from April to August, disclosed the inner connection between philosophy and economics, philosophy and politics, subjective and objective; it created a new beginning, a new totality of theory and practice.

What we may call "the self-determination of the Idea," Historical Materialism, which was born out of his concept of Alienated Labor, was the culmination of the critique Marx began in 1841 when he was telling his Young

Hegelian colleagues that it was not enough to criticize Hegel for "accommodating" to the Prussian state, that what was needed was to discover the principle in Hegelian philosophy that led to that accommodation. Only in that way could one transcend the inadequacy in so genuinely historic a way as to create a new ground for a philosophy of freedom. Freedom was the bones and sinew, the heart and soul, the direction for totally new beginnings.

One of the very few post-Marx Marxists who had grasped the fact that Marx had recreated the Hegelian dialectic before he openly broke with bourgeois society was Mikhail Lifshitz. In his book, *The Philosophy of Art of Karl Marx*,[20] he traces the Hegelian inheritance from Marx's 1841 doctoral thesis on Epicurus to *Capital*, concluding that Marx's "reflections upon the ancient world show that the historical analogies permeating the works of 1841–42 remained with the mature Marx . . . he never renounced this inheritance" (p. 89). Because Lifshitz refused to separate a "theory of aesthetics" from the totality of Marx's philosophy of history, holding tight to the integrality in Marx's world view, he introduces Marx's dominant concept of *"Revolution in Permanenz"* (p. 49) into his analysis of Marx's 1841–42 doctoral dissertation and early articles on freedom of the press.

Each of the major topics of the 1844 Manuscripts[21]—Alienated Labor, Private Property and Communism, Critique of Hegel's Dialectic and Philosophy as a Whole—was in the process of growing together into a single body of thought, a philosophy of revolution.

Philosophy pervades the whole; not only is the critique of philosophy "philosophical," but so is the analysis of the political economy. The struggle against private property is the struggle not only against the alienation of the product of labor but against the alienation of the very activity of labor as any kind of self-development.

"Political economy," writes Marx, "proceeds from labor as the real soul of production and nevertheless attributes nothing to labor, everything to private property . . . when man speaks of private property, he believes he has only to deal with a fact outside man. This new posing of the question already includes the resolution." But it took a Marx to find that resolution and to spell it out as a social revolution.

Marx's analysis of labor—and it is that which distinguishes him from all others, not only the tendencies in Marx's day, from which he had to break, but the Socialists and Communists of our day—goes much further than the economic structure of society. His analysis goes not only to class relations, but to actual human relations.

What is wrong with the other critics is that they speak of labor as an abstraction instead of seeing that labor under capitalism "materializes itself in an inhuman way . . . "

What Marx objects to in Hegel is this: "The *philosopher* who is himself an abstract form of alienated man establishes himself as the *yardstick* of an alienated world." Marx tells us not to forget that Hegel stands "on the basis of political economy." Marx calls Hegel's *Logic* "the *money* of the spirit, the abstract expression not only of thought but of life." But as against classical political economy, which stopped at private property, and as against Feuerbach, who saw nothing positive in Hegel's concept of "negation of negation," as if the expression were hardly more than a play on words, Marx wrote: "To the extent that it holds fast the *alienation* of Man—even if Man appears only in the form of Spirit—to that extent *all* elements of criticism lie hidden in it and are often already *prepared* and *worked out* in a manner extending far beyond the Hegelian standpoint . . . The greatness of Hegel's *Phenomenology* . . . is the dialectic of negativity as the moving and creating principle . . . "

Marx argued that Hegel had thrown a mystical veil over the actual movement of history, turning man into a form of consciousness. He concluded that only when we have "actual corporeal Man, standing on firm and well-rounded earth, inhaling and exhaling all natural forces," will we actually get the deep internal dialectic and first be able to transcend, *historically* transcend, the Hegelian dialectic (which nevertheless remains the source of all dialectic), *and* classical political economy, *and* vulgar communism. Marx considered that type of communism "the logical expression of private property." He wrote: "This type of abolition of private property is . . . only a retrogression . . . a *sham* universality."

"Only by the transcendence of this mediation, which is nevertheless a necessary presupposition," he concluded, "does there arise *positive* Humanism beginning from itself."

This is the reason Marx never forgot individualism: "We should especially avoid establishing society as an abstraction, opposed to the individual. The individual *is the social entity*."

Labor was not only Marx's point of departure but his point of return: " . . . *the whole of what is called world history* is nothing but the creation of man by human labor." For human labor to be that type of activity, alienated labor must be abolished. It will be the fully mature Marx in volume 3 of *Capital* who will articulate this as "human power . . . is its own end."[22]

Let us now turn back for a moment to those who describe the Essays as merely "idealistic" (and anthropological idealism at that, as "proven" by such words as "species being") and "Feuerbachian," not to mention "being under the influence of" a limitless series of "sources," as if Marx had not acknowledged the authorship of others. It is ironic that those who hold these views are the very ones who point to Paris as the place where Marx "finally" turned to "material matters" and associated with workers and French socialists.

There is no doubt at all, as we saw from the letter to Feuerbach, about Marx's exhilaration at meeting the workers, nor is there any doubt about his profound study of the French Revolution. Revolution was the talk all over

Paris, with all its German refugees, in the year of the Silesian weavers's revolt. But far from remaining a "Feuerbachian," Marx was led to break with Feuerbach *and* with Ruge *and* with the anarchists. The dividing line was—*precisely*—the analysis of these revolts.

Here is how Marx explained why he held that "the Silesian uprising began where the French and English insurrections ended, with the consciousness of the proletariat as a class": "We have already seen that a *social* revolution is found to have the point of view of the *whole* because—even if it were to occur in only *one* factory district—it represents man's protest against a dehumanized life, because it starts out from the *point of view of a separate real individual*, because the *community*, against the separation of which from himself the individual reacts, is man's *true* community, *human* nature."[23]

What sets off one age from another—the birthtime of history or the birthtime of a new total philosophy—cannot be grasped by singling out "influences" but by seeing that the breaking point, the point of departure from the old, becomes the translucent direction forward; which is why Marx, the year before, as he was breaking with bourgeois society and bourgeois thought, said that the principle of their projected new organ must be: "Ruthless criticism of all that exists, ruthless in the sense that the critique is neither afraid of its own results nor of conflicting with the powers that be." (Letter to Ruge, September 1843.)

Whether the creative drama of human liberation, as it came to be expressed in the *enragés* in the French Revolution or the early workers' revolts in Marx's day, was romanticized by the young revolutionary philosopher, Marx, the point is that he lived, wrote, organized on this planet, and this planet meant a total uprooting of the old. Marx's world was on the planet of freedom, the planet of new beginnings. And those new beginnings are the ones that point both to the totality of the uprooting needed and the *permanence* of revolution.

I am not skipping to the 1850 Address, where Marx first *developed* the idea; much less am I going to the last years of his life. No. It was in the very essay "On the Jewish Question," which preceded the *Economic-Philosophic Manuscripts*, that Marx, in trying to spell out the totality of his concept of revolution, stressed the fact that political emancipation, necessary as that was in the freeing of the Jews from discrimination, was insufficient since it would only bring them to the level of the Christians and of civil society as a whole. What was needed for the one and the other was "a human revolution." And that could be achieved "only by declaring the revolution to be *permanent*."[24]

Having worked out this phenomenal view, Marx met Engels at the end of August, talked for ten days, and found sufficient affinity of ideas to decide to collaborate on a critique of the Young Hegelians, when, as Marx put it, Engels, too, "settled in Brussels in the Spring of 1845." Before then, however, Marx had not only completed the 1844 Manuscripts, but also had sharply separated himself from Feuerbachian materialism in his magnificent eleven *Theses on Feuerbach*. In the first Thesis, Marx said:

The chief defect of all hitherto existing materialism—that of Feuerbach included—is that the thing (*Gegenstand*), reality, sensuousness, is conceived only in the form of the object (*Objekt*) or of *contemplation (Anschauung)*, but not as *human sensuous activity, practice*, not subjectively. Hence it happened that the *active* side, in contradistinction to materialism, was developed by idealism—but only abstractly . . . Hence, he does not grasp the significance of "revolutionary," of "practical-critical" activity.[25]

In the tenth Thesis, he wrote: "The standpoint of the old materialism is '*civil*' society; the standpoint of the new is *human* society, or socialised humanity."

Engels was not to discover these Theses until 1888, and though he at once designated them as "the first document in which is posited the brilliant germ of a new world outlook"—even as, in the 1885 Preface to the *Communist Manifesto* he rightly credited Marx with sole authorship of the theory of Historical Materialism—the very fact that he appended Marx's *Theses on Feuerbach* to his own "comprehensive" 1888 work on Feuerbach, shows that the gap between the two was very broad indeed.

In any case, the first two great works in which they collaborated—*The Holy Family* and *The German Ideology*, recognized by "orthodox" post-Marx Marxists as the first statement of Historical Materialism—were suddenly left to the "gnawing criticism of the mice." The preoccupation of Marx and Engels at that point was the "practical project," as they set about organizing Correspondence Committees—in Brussels, Paris, and London—and Marx projected the establishment of International Communist Correspondence Committees.

When Marx invited Proudhon to join, Proudhon answered that the educational aspects interested him quite a bit but that he objected to the concept of revolution. The next encounter between them marked the end of the relationship. Proudhon published his *Philosophy of Poverty*, and Marx at once answered with his *Poverty of Philosophy*. That work was not only published at once for its polemical interest but was finally recognized, and remains so to this day, as the first comprehensive statement of what the *new* materialism—historical, dialectical, humanist—was all about.

The practical work on organizing committees continued. In July 1845, Marx and Engels traveled to England and met with George Julian Harney, editor of the most influential working-class paper, *The Morning Star*. Marx, further, got a chance to address the Chartists (Fraternal Democrats) in September 1845. On his return to Brussels, Marx delivered a series of talks on *Wage-Labor and Capital* to the Correspondence Committees. These lectures were later published directly in the *Neue Rheinische Zeitung* in 1849.

The Correspondence Committees, the Chartists, and some other workers' educational societies, as well as the oldest of the emigré groups, then called the League of the Just, had by 1847 decided to merge, called themselves the

Communist League, and assigned Marx to write their manifesto.

The challenging first sentence read: "A spectre is haunting Europe—the spectre of communism." The story of all civilization was told: "The history of all hitherto existing society is the history of class struggles." Nor was the gauntlet that Marx threw down to the bourgeoisie only theoretical: " . . . not only has the bourgeoisie forged the weapons that bring death to itself; it has also called into existence the men who are to wield those weapons—the modern working class, the proletarians."

Marx made clear how total the uprooting of capitalism must be—abolition of private property, abolition of the state, the bourgeois family, the whole "class culture": "In place of the old bourgeois society, with its classes and class antagonism, we shall have an association in which the free development of each is the precondition for the free development of all."

Marx ended the *Manifesto* with: "Let the ruling classes tremble at a communist revolution. The proletarians have nothing to lose but their chains. They have a world to win. Workingmen of all countries, unite!"

Neither the League, which had authorized the writing of the *Manifesto*, nor the author had any idea that the *Manifesto* would be hardly off the printing presses before spontaneous outbursts of the masses would cover Europe. Marx and Engels returned at once to Germany, established the *Neue Rheinische Zeitung*, and became active in both the German and the French revolutions. It is the great experience of those two revolutionary years, as Marx presented it in *The Class Struggles in France, 1848–1850* that has ever since become the ground for post-Marx Marxist revolutionaries. As we saw, in the 1905–07 Russian-Polish Revolutions, it was the 1848 Revolutions—as Marx analyzed them—that were the ground for the great turning point in Rosa Luxemburg's revolutionary activity and theory. Yet she stopped short of considering Marx's 1850 Address with its appeal for a "revolution in permanence," as a forecasting of twentieth-century revolutions.

NOTES

1. This section of Lenin's Abstract of Hegel's *Science of Logic* can be found in Lenin, *Collected Works*, 38:180. I am using my own translation, however, which was included as Appendix B to my *Marxism and Freedom* in 1958 and was the first published English translation.
2. Ibid., p. 277.
3. Ibid., p. 363.
4. Ibid., p. 231.
5. These essays had not been published anywhere until they were obtained by the famous scholar, Ryazanov, for the Marx–Engels Institute in Moscow and published under his editorship, as vol. 3 of the *Archiv Marksa–Engelsa* (Moscow: 1927). They were republished in the *Complete Works of Marx and Engels*, 1932, in the original German and in Russian translation.
6. Luxemburg's reviews of the three volumes of Marx's works that had been edited by Franz Mehring were entitled "From the Legacy of Our Masters," and can be found in *Gesammelte Werke*, 1(2):130–41 and 291–303.
7. There has been confusion over the word "Introduction," since it was obviously written

after Marx had completed the essay. Marx had intended to rewrite this draft and his introduction was meant for the *rewritten* essay. By that time, however, Marx was no longer interested in that subject and proceeded to the *Critique of the Hegelian Dialectic*, instead, centering it on the *Phenomenology of Mind*.

8. This essay was originally published in *Vorwärts*, 14 March 1903. See *Gesammelte Werke*, 1(2):363–68.

9. The great economist Joseph A. Schumpeter, who far preferred economics to philosophy and was especially hostile to Hegelian-Marxian dialectics, nevertheless caught in Marx not only that indivisible whole which he called Marx's "conceptual schema" but wrote a profound analysis of the *Communist Manifesto* on its one hundredth anniversary: "The Communist Manifesto in Sociology and Economics," in *Journal of Political Economy*, June 1949, pp. 199–212. It was he who, in his last, massive, and yet-unfinished nine-hundred-page *History of Economic Analysis*, used the expression, "transformation of historic narrative into historic reason."

10. However, in this letter to Engels of 24 April 1867, Marx rejected the praise of Feuerbach, adding: " . . . although the cult of Feuerbach produces a very humorous effect upon one now."

11. Some original studies have been done in England by Terrell Carver, including such articles as "Marx—and Hegel's *Logic*", *Political Studies*, vol. 24, no. 1 (1976); "Marx's Commodity Fetishism," *Inquiry*, vol. 18 (1975); and especially "Marx, Engels and Dialectics," *Political Studies*, vol. 28, no. 3 (1980), where Carver develops the fact that Engels is not Marx. See also his *Karl Marx, Texts on Method* (Oxford: Basil Blackwell, 1975), which contains new translations of and commentary on Marx's *Introduction to the Grundrisse*, and his *Notes on Adolph Wagner*.

12. See Marx–Engels, *Collected Works*, vol. 1 (New York: International Pub., 1975), which includes the entire thesis and appendix (pp. 25–106), as well as Marx's "Notebooks on Epicurean Philosophy" which they call "From the Preparatory Materials" (pp. 403–514). Page citations in the text refer to this edition. See also the earlier, first English translation by Norman Livergood, *Activity in Marx's Philosophy* (The Hague: Martinus Nijhoff, 1967), pp. 60–109.

13. For a discussion of this, see Cyril Bailey's review, "Karl Marx on Greek Atomism," *Classical Quarterly*, July–October, 1928, pp. 205–6.

14. This is a misnomer, often used by those (like Loyd Easton and Kurt Guddat) who have reproduced only brief sections. Actually there are seven notebooks which cover 111 pages—and even these are not the entire notes, but only those that were found.

15. Marx–Engels, *Collected Works*, 1:492.

16. Marx–Engels, *Collected Works*, 1:155—but I am using my own translation here. This excerpt is from the "Debates on Freedom of the Press," in *Rheinische Zeitung*, 12 May 1842.

17. It becomes necessary to expose the convenient myths which have been created to confine Marx's originality to "materialism" and to credit Feuerbach with what was, instead, most uniquely Marxian. Loyd Easton and Kurt Guddat have gone so far as to place the historic 1844 Manuscripts in a section called "Feuerbachian Critique of Hegel," in their *Writings of the Young Marx on Philosophy and Society* (New York: Doubleday & Co., 1967), p. viii. As early as 1842, when all Left Hegelians, including Marx and Engels, were supposedly Feuerbachians, Marx wrote that, although he agreed with Feuerbach on his ideas in the *Essence of Christianity* on the nature of religion, he disagreed on the "form" ("*Fassung*"). (See Marx–Engels, *Collected Works*, 1:272.) Again, on Feuerbach's *Preliminary Thesis on the Reformation of Philosophy*, Marx wrote that Feuerbach "refers to nature too often and neglects politics. . . " Marx's sharpest criticism occurred in *Critique of the Hegelian Dialectic*, precisely where he praised Feuerbach as having contributed the most serious criticism of Hegel. He nevertheless argued that Feuerbach did not understand the "negation of the negation," stressing that this was Hegel's greatest achievement, as it represented the actual movement of history. It was at this point that Marx departed so far from Feuerbach that he created his own total philosophy, calling it "a new Humanism." These 1844 Manuscripts were followed the next year by the magnificent, brief thesis on Feuerbach in which Marx criticized all of materialism and made a clear break with Feuerbach.

In 1893 Engels balked at showing the early, unknown manuscripts to Alexei Voden, a young Russian scholar who was a protegé of Plekhanov. Voden reports Engels as having asked whether "the fragment on Feuerbach [i.e., the 1845 Thesis] was not sufficient," saying that Engels considered it the most meaty of those "old works." After further insistence by Voden, Engels did stress that Marx "had not displayed any one-sided preference for the materialist systems, but had dwelt particularly on the dialectics. . . " See A. Voden's "Talks with Engels," in *Reminiscences of Marx and Engels* (Moscow: n.d.), pp. 325–34.

18. Included in *Karl Marx's Critique of Hegel's Philosophy of Right*, trans. Annette Jolin and Joseph O'Malley (Cambridge: Cambridge Univ. Press, 1970), p. 142. This work is the first English translation of Marx's *Critique* to be published; it is painstakingly footnoted, with a comprehensive introduction by O'Malley.

19. "The aims of the state transform themselves into the aims of the bureaux, or the aims of the bureaux into those of the state," Marx wrote in the *Critique of Hegel's Philosophy of Right*, during the summer of 1843. "The bureaucracy is a circle from which no one can escape. Its hierarchy is a hierarchy of knowledge . . . The *examination* is nothing other than the *bureaucratic baptism* of knowledge, the official recognition of the trans-substantiation of profane knowledge into sacred (it goes without saying that for every examination the examiner knows all)." Marx–Engels, *Collected Works*, 3:51.

20. The relevance of this book for today is two-fold. First is the recognition of the significance of the Hegelian dialectic that Marx developed throughout his life. Second is the contrast between Lifshitz and Lukacs in their relationship to Stalin. This book was written in 1933 when Stalin had total power; but there is not a single reference to Stalin, as "philosopher" or otherwise. On the other hand, Lukacs' *The Young Hegel* (Cambridge, Mass.: MIT Press, 1976) was published after Stalin's death; and yet it manifests so great a kowtowing to Stalin that Lukacs links Stalin and Lenin as "philosophers of the age of imperialism," thereby creating total confusion not only on the relationship of Lenin to Stalin, but on Lenin's historic break with his own philosophic past as set forth in his *Philosophic Notebooks*.

21. In the quotations that follow in the text I am using my own translation. See chap. 6, n. 8 for other sources.

22. Marx, *Capital*, 3:954.

23. Marx–Engels, *Collected Works*, 3:205.

24. Ibid., p. 156.

25. Marx–Engels, *Selected Works*, 1:13–15. The Theses are published here as Marx wrote them. What Engels published in 1888 as an appendix to his own work, *Ludwig Feuerbach and the End of Classical German Philosophy*, was an edited version.

X

A Decade of Historic Transformation:
From the *Grundrisse* to *Capital*

1. "ECONOMICS," 1857–58: ONLY CLASS STRUGGLES OR "EPOCHS OF SOCIAL REVOLUTION"?

The concrete is concrete, because it is a combination of many objects with different destinations, i.e., a unity of diverse elements. In our thought, it therefore appears as a process of synthesis, as a result, and not as a starting point, although it is the real starting point . . .

Karl Marx, *Introduction to the* Grundrisse[1]

The 1857 crisis, which was the direct impulse to "finish" *Economics* (posthumously entitled the *Grundrisse* by the Marx–Engels Institute), was the focus of Marx's studies throughout the decade. This by no means curtailed him from following the historic and theoretic developments of the decade. Thus, directly after the 1850 Address signed by him and Engels, he was busy encouraging Engels to finish his study of the Peasant Wars, which he published in the final issue of the *NRZ-Revue* (29 November 1850). Thus, he was reporting on the 1850 Taiping Revolution in China for the *Tribune*; and this became a new point of theoretical departure for consideration of the "Asiatic Mode of Production." Thus, in 1855 he offered Lassalle notes he had accumulated for a study of the repealed Corn Laws, saying: "The period of crisis in England is simultaneously that of theoretical investigations." (Letter of 23 January 1855.)

Besides his most profound and brilliant historic work, which has remained a model to this day—*The 18th Brumaire of Louis Bonaparte*—there were continuing relations with individual revolutionaries as well as organizations like the Chartists, whom he addressed in English on the anniversary of the *People's Paper*, 14 April 1856. Here, once again, it is impossible to miss the dialectical approach: "In our days everything seems pregnant with its contrary. Machinery, gifted with the wonderful power of shortening and fructifying human labor, we behold starving and overworking it. The new-fangled sources of wealth, by some strange weird spell, are turned into sources of want . . . All our invention and progress seem to result in endowing material forces with intellectual life and in stultifying human life into a material force."[2]

In a word, far from the focus on *Economics* having in any way transformed Marx into an "economist," he first now elaborated and developed the integrality of philosophy and economics in a way that became known the world over as Marxism. It was no simple question of turning from "idealism" to "materialism." From the very beginning of his break with bourgeois society in the early 1840s, Marx named his philosophy "a new Humanism," a unity of idealism and materialism. By the 1850s he was far enough into the new continent of thought and so far removed from the Left Hegelians that he had developed the economic laws of capitalism in a most original way. Yet it is at exactly this high point—when what we now know as the *Grundrisse* became the determinant turning point—that Marx judged the Hegelian dialectic, the development through contradiction, to be "the source of . . . all dialectic." It was this, *just this*, which quickened the pace of synthesizing his studies of the past fifteen years. In August–September 1857, he wrote the Introduction, which cast so great an illumination on all his studies and so quickened the pace of his work that he finished the whole of this work in seven short months; the *Grundrisse* numbered nine hundred pages.

But when he started preparing it for actual publication, he put away the Introduction altogether. Here is how he explained the reason for so doing in his Preface to *Critique of Political Economy*: "on second thought any anticipation of results that are still to be proven, seemed to me objectionable, and the reader who wishes to follow me at all must make up his mind to pass from the special to the general."[3]

Furthermore, the whole nine hundred pages had not yielded a chapter that he now decided must become Chapter One—"Commodities." That he first had to write anew for the *Critique of Political Economy*. The second chapter, "Money," is all that he published from the *Grundrisse* itself. It took another decade before the *Grundrisse*, as a first draft, was transformed into what we know as *Capital*. As he, himself, had articulated it in the Introduction (which he did not publish): "The method of advancing from the abstract to the concrete is but the way of thinking, by which the concrete is grasped and reproduced in our minds as concrete" (pp. 293–94).

He had already finished the Introduction and was into the *Grundrisse* when, on 8 December 1857, he wrote to Engels: "I am working madly through the night on a synthesis of my economic studies, so that I at least will have the main outline clear before the deluge." As he was working out the form for the *Grundrisse*, he summed up the first section of the Introduction, "Production in

General": "All the stages of production have certain destinations in common, which we generalize in thought; but the so-called general conditions of all production are nothing but abstract conceptions which do not go to make up any real stage in the history of production" (p. 274).

Marx continued his critique of "abstract conceptions" by warning his readers not to get lost in the sphere of distribution "since the definite manner of participation in production determines the particular form of distribution, the form under which participation and distribution takes place" (p. 284). The point to remember in all this is that what dominates over everything is capital: "Capital is the all-dominating economic power of bourgeois society. It must form the starting point as well as the end . . . " (p. 303).

Knowing that, says Marx, removed the danger of forgetting that the real point of departure is actuality, since in our thought the concrete, as a "unity of diverse elements . . . appears as a process of synthesis, as a result, and not as a starting point, although it is the real starting point, and therefore, also the starting point of observation and conception" (p. 293). The titanic development of the eight hundred pages that followed, the rapidity with which the accumulation of fifteen years of research found formulation, was certainly not due alone either to the day-by-day diary that Marx kept of the 1857 crisis, to the historic works that he wrote (be they as brilliant as *The 18th Brumaire of Louis Bonaparte*, which profoundly focused on the difference between bourgeois and proletarian revolutions), or to his contact with the workers. Overriding everything was the dialectical methodology as Marx was articulating it for himself.

As against what has been called "the miracle of compression" in which Marx summarized capitalism's development in the *Communist Manifesto*, we see here in the Introduction the explicitness of the form of presentation—that is, the methodological innovations, whether relating to the interrelationship of economic categories like labor/capital, value/money, commodity/exchange value, or to capital's dominance over everything. Methodologically, the innovation in presentation, "advancing from the abstract to the concrete," creates ground for Marx's historic sweep of humanity's development through the ages, from the primitive commune to capitalism.

Any reader who, at this stage of Marx's achievement, has to depend on Marx's letter to Engels (14 January 1858)—to the effect that the "mere accident" of glancing through Hegel's *Logic* "has been a great service to me as regards the *method* of dealing with the material"—to show that Marx was a dialectician, will certainly not be able to grasp the magnificence of the gigantic work on *Economics*. Not only has Marx here achieved the most brilliant and profound diversion with the writing of "Pre-Capitalist Formations," but, at one and the same time, he has extended his magnificent, unifying vision to Greek art, and viewed humanity's development through the ages as "an absolute movement of becoming." The *Grundrisse* is both more *and* less than

Capital, volume 1. It contains sections which later became parts of volumes 2, 3, and 4 (*Theories of Surplus Value*), but it is less than *Capital*, because it does not have *Capital's* precision, incisiveness, and concentrativeness.

This is not the place to attempt a summary of such an all-encompassing work as the *Grundrisse*. For our purposes, it is the section "Pre-Capitalist Formations" which is the most relevant and urgent because it illuminates the problematic that arose both with the age of Automation and with the emergence of the Third World. It is something that would have shed great illumination, as well, on Rosa Luxemburg's preoccupation with imperialism, had she known about it. It is our age that has made this work live a full century after its first conception.

For one thing, we see that what pulled at Marx was not only the 1857 economic crisis but colonialism, to which the Taiping Revolution in China was contrasted sharply and hailed as opening a new era of revolution. As far back as 14 June 1853 Marx had written to the *New York Daily Tribune* about "the chronic rebellions subsisting in China for about ten years past, and now gathered in one formidable revolution": "Do these order-mongering powers [England, France and America], which would attempt to support the wavering Manchu dynasty, forget that the hatred against foreigners . . . [has] become a political system only since the conquest of the country by the race of the Manchu Tatars?"[4]

Between 1853, when Marx wrote those articles, and 1857, when he wrote the "Economic Notebooks" later called the *Grundrisse*, Marx had worked out his original analysis of capitalism's law of motion; that is to say, he fleshed out the mere skeletal ideas of Historical Materialism with the economic laws of development. Instead of describing the three epochs of social development—slavery, feudalism, capitalism—as if they encompassed the whole of humanity, he now spoke of a fourth, the "archaic form," which in turn was subdivided into the Oriental, the Greco–Roman, the German. Furthermore, whereas in 1847 the *Communist Manifesto* was still sufficiently Euro-centered to refer to China as "vegetating in the teeth of barbarism," in the mid-1850s Marx hailed the Taiping Revolution as an advance, and by 1867, in *Capital*, considered it "encouragement" to the European masses who had become quiescent after the defeat of the 1848–49 Revolutions. And, whereas in 1844 Marx had concentrated on the inhumanity of Alienated Labor under capitalism, in 1857–58 he extended the concept of inhumanity to include Western capitalism's intrusion into Asia. At the same time, he saw positive features in Asian resistance. This despite the fact that he by no means glorified Oriental society. Here is how he put it in the *New York Daily Tribune* on 25 June 1853: "There have been in Asia, generally . . . but three departments of government: that of Finance, or the plunder of the interior; that of War, or the plunder of the exterior; and, finally, the department of Public Works . . . " (p. 95).

Marx was developing some ideas that Engels had first suggested, adding:

> The vast tracts of desert extending from the Sahara through Arabia, Persia, India, Tartary, to the most elevated Asiatic highlands, constituted artificial irrigation by canals and waterworks the basis of Oriental agriculture . . . This prime necessity of an economical and common use of water . . . necessitated in the Orient, where civilization was too low and the territorial extent too vast . . . the interference of the centralizing power of government. Hence an economical function developed upon all Asiatic governments, the function of providing public works [pp. 95–96].

In following through the social division of labor corresponding to different forms of property—beginning with the communal form because humanity first appeared as part of a primitive collective—Marx again was far from glorifying the state: "The first prerequisite of this earliest form of landed property appears as a human community . . . [Man is] *a generic being, a tribal being, a herd animal* . . . In the Asiatic form there is no property, but only individual possession; the community is properly speaking the real proprietor . . . Originally *property* means no more than man's attitude to his natural conditions of production as belonging to him, as the *prerequisites of his own existence* . . . "[5]

Far from glorifying the primitive commune, Marx was showing that the dispersion of the population "in small centers by the domestic union of agricultural and manufacturing pursuits" resulted in the type of self-governing villages that "inoffensive though they may appear, had always been the solid foundation of Oriental despotism." Thus, what Marx calls "undifferentiated unity" is definitely no praise of the so-called self-governing village: "Asian history is a kind of undifferentiated unity of town and country" (pp. 177–78).

As he traced the newly discovered routes out of the primitive communal system, Marx was concluding that there was no Oriental feudalism. It is this which produced all the disputes both in the 1920s and, even more, in the 1950s,[6] when the whole of the *Grundrisse* first became known, and it certainly put an end to the vulgarization that there was only one way of human development. Marx never held a view of unilateral development. We will see that in an especially revolutionary form in the last period of his life, when he dealt with the "semi-Asiatic" commune still existing in Russia. By the time the *Grundrisse* was published in our age, there were a growing number of debates in Russia and in Western academia, which concentrated totally on the question of feudalism.

We cannot possibly sum up these developments in a single phrase like "Oriental despotism." What Marx—and Engels, in this case—were tracing, ever since 1845–46 in the *German Ideology*, was the fact that underlying the development of humanity into classes was the division between mental and manual labor, and with it the division between town and country. By the time Marx and Engels reached the 1850s they designated the "undifferentiated unity of town and country" as responsible for "Oriental despotism." To fully grasp the significance of that in Marx, as against what Wittfogel twisted it to be, we must go deeper dialectically into the whole question of the relationships of the production of material life to history. In Marx's day, China comprised one-third of humanity. Marx had no intention whatever of making a phrase like "Oriental despotism" cover that mass of humanity, much less make a fetish out of it. On the contrary, what Marx was stressing was that the presence of primitive communism in Oriental society shows how complex that society was and how many "advanced" features were inherent in it.

The conclusion that there were four different epochs of human development did not mean that Asiatic was all backward and the slave society of the Greco–Roman was all advanced. Tribal society disappeared in both. Slavery was latent within the family, within the tribal society, reaching its apex in Roman society, where, Marx stresses, "slavery remains the basis of the entire production." Where Marx speaks of "the general slavery of the Orient" as distinct from the personal slavery of Greco–Roman society, he also insists, historically–dialectically, that humanity yearns not to "remain something formed by the past but is in the absolute movement of becoming." What therefore becomes pivotal, decisive, is that in all these stages of development, the contradictions between the productive forces and the production relations reach the explosive point and become "epochs of social revolution."

Thus Marx wrote that the creation of "free" labor meant, " . . . above all, that the worker must be separated from the land, which functions as his natural laboratory. This means the dissolution both of free petty land ownership and of the communal landed property, based on the Oriental commune" (p. 67).

In a letter to Lassalle, 22 February 1858, Marx outlined the *Grundrisse* this way: "The whole thing is divided into six books : (1) Capital (contains introductory chapters). (2) Landed property. (3) Wage labour. (4) The State. (5) International Trade. (6) The World Market."

It took another full decade before Marx completed *Capital*, volume 1. If even to that we add volumes 2, 3, and 4, published posthumously, it is still a fact that there are certain substantive principles that he pointed to in the *Grundrisse* which are not in the completed work—not because they are invalid, but because they posed still more questions that he could not deal with in that incisive work. It is this which makes the *Grundrisse* so very pivotal to our day. The reason we have limited ourselves to the single chapter on "Pre-Capitalist Formations" (which is among those key parts not included in *Capital*) is to bring out a problematic still challenging our age.

On the other hand, in asking the question, what preceded capitalism, and in seeing in those societies a certain "grandeur and historical energies," he was asking: Can humanity fulfill its destiny without the fundamental revolution in the social state of Asia? It is precisely because he was relating all development to epochs of revolution that he could see how some elements of primitive communism had been conserved "in the midst of Oriental despotism." Far from making a fetish of it, as the modern Wittfogels would have it, Marx was tracing the actual historical development, the forward movement from humanity's origin as a "herd animal" to its individualization in the process of history.

Far from seeing capitalism carve up the world only in its origin, however, as Luxemburg thought "Primitive Accumulation of Capital" in volume 1 of *Capital* limited itself to doing, Marx—exactly when he was studying primitive society—saw capitalism's imperial tentacles continue onward to a degree that his hostility to capitalism became all the sharper. Indeed, we see in the *Grundrisse* what was to develop in the last years of his life on the basis not only of Morgan's then-new *Ancient Society*, but also the actual revolutionary movement developing in Russia—the vision of a possible revolution coming first in a backward country like Russia. For the 1860s, a new epoch began for Marx with John Brown's attack on Harper's Ferry. The events that followed led Marx to restructure his greatest theoretical work.[7]

2. CAPITAL: SIGNIFICANCE OF THE 1875 FRENCH EDITION OF VOLUME 1*

The best points in my book are: 1—the double character of labor, according to whether it is expressed in use value or exchange value. (All understanding of the facts depends on this. It is emphasized immediately in the first chapter.); 2—the treatment of surplus value independently of its particular forms as profit, interest, ground rent, etc.

Karl Marx, 24 August 1867

Mr. Wagner forgets that my subject is not "value" and not "exchange value," but a commodity... Secondly, the vir obscurus, *not having understood a word in* Capital... *has glossed over the fact that already in the analysis of the commodity, I have not stopped at the dual form in which it appears, but go straight on to*

*To this day we still do not have a full English translation of the French edition of *Capital* as it was edited by Marx. The recent translation by Ben Fowkes (Middlesex: Penguin Books, 1976) reestablished some of Marx's philosophic language. But the translator did not follow Marx in the sequence of the Parts. He explained it as follows: "For reasons of convenience to English readers, we have held to Engels' arrangement. We have also followed Engels in presenting the chapters on 'So-called Primitive Accumulation' as a separate Part VIII, which is certainly justifiable in view of its special subject matter" (p. 110, n.). Marx, however, far from considering a separate Part 8 "justifiable," held that the real logic of "so-called Primitive Accumulation" was that it was not merely the historic origin, but the logical continuation of the process of capitalist accumulation—which is why he left no doubt in anyone's mind that Part 8 was integral to Part 7.

Kevin Anderson has written a profound critique of Ben Fowkes's translation. He traces the distinction between the original French edition and Ben Fowkes's translation which "follows Engels slavishly," as if Engels had scrupulously followed Marx's instructions. (See "The French Edition of *Capital*, 100 Years After," paper presented by Kevin Anderson to the Conference of the Eastern Sociological Society, Philadelphia, 19 March 1982.)

> *the fact that in this dual being of the commodity is expressed the*
> *dual character of the labor whose product it is . . .*
>   Karl Marx, "Notes on Adolph Wagner," 1881

> *Just as the simple form of value, the individual act of exchange of*
> *one given commodity for another, already includes in an un-*
> *developed form all the main contradictions of capitalism—so the*
> *simplest* generalization, *the first and simplest formation of*
> *notions (judgments, syllogisms, etc.) already denotes man's ever*
> *deeper cognition of the* objective *connection of the world. Here is*
> *where one should look for the true meaning, significance and role*
> *of Hegel's* Logic. *This N.B.*
>   Lenin, Abstract of Hegel's Science of Logic, 14 December 1914

Capital, not the *Grundrisse*, is the *differentia specifica* of Marx's Marxism, its apex. Marx's greatest theoretical work, in fusing economics, history, dialectics, discloses ever new aspects of each along with new-won forces of revolt. Thus, history is not so much a history of theories as of class struggles, civil wars, and battles at the point of production. Economics is a matter not only of the economic laws of the breakdown of capitalism, but of the strife between the worker and the machine against dead labor's domination over living labor, beginning with *hearing* the worker's voice, which had been stifled "in the storm and stress of the process of production." This voice will never be still. In the last part of the work, "Accumulation of Capital," as we approach the most "economist" and "scientific" development—"the organic composition of capital"—Marx reminds us all over again that this organic composition cannot be considered outside of its effects "on the lot of the laboring class." Dialectics, of course, is the method of development of each and of all, objective and subjective, whether that new-won force came out of the actual struggle for the shortening of the working day, or in discerning the law of motion of capitalism, with both a look back to precapitalist formations—from the communal form through slavery and feudalism—and a look forward at what will follow capitalism: "freely associated labor" taking destiny into its own hands.[8]

No doubt a gap in the knowledge of Marxists resulted from the failure to know the *Grundrisse*. The gap was enormous on the question of the *process* of Marx's thought, seen in the multidimensionality of the *Grundrisse*; in the fact that some of the sections, like the "Pre-Capitalist Formations," would become important to the post–World War II generation—not to mention the Hegelian "language." Nevertheless, it is not *Grundrisse* but *Capital*, especially volume 1—which he, himself, prepared for the printer—which is Marx's legacy. And it was *Capital*, not the *Grundrisse* (about which Lenin, like all other Marxists in that period, knew nothing), that Lenin held in hand when he grappled with Hegel's *Science of Logic*.

Whatever illumination Marx's heavy use of Hegelian "language" cast on the fact that Marx did not abandon his Hegelian roots when he worked out in full all of his original economic categories, no one could miss seeing the predominant law of motion of capitalism to its downfall. And certainly Rosa Luxemburg did not miss a beat of it, both insofar as the class struggle was concerned, and insofar as her profound knowledge of the economic laws of capitalism's development: she built her theory of the breakdown of capitalism on it. It even gave her the illusion that, though she deviated from volume 2 of *Capital* (which, in any case, not Marx but Engels prepared for the press), she was the revolutionary Marxist who comprehended Marx most totally and creatively. Yet, at the same time, "suddenly" in the process of writing the *Anti-Critique* she also complained of the "rococo" in volume 1 of Marx's *Capital*.

In a word, it was not only the reformists who demanded the removal of Marx's "dialectical scaffolding," with or without knowledge of the *Grundrisse*. Until World War I had brought down the Second International, revolutionaries felt no sort of compulsion to study seriously the inner relationship of the Marxian dialectic to the Hegelian—and even then it was Lenin alone who returned to Marx's origins in the Hegelian dialectic.

Although Marx found Hegel's *Logic* of "great service, as regards the *method* of dealing with the material,"[9] at the very end of nearly nine hundred pages of the *Grundrisse* Marx decided that he should have started, not with Money or with Value, but with Commodities. Therefore, in preparing to publish the *Critique of Political Economy* Marx wrote a totally new chapter, "Commodities," and used the chapter "Money" in a much abbreviated form. He did follow Hegel's procedure in *Science of Logic*, where Hegel no sooner mentions Being, Nothing, and Becoming than he writes twenty-two pages of "Observations." Marx followed each of his two chapters with "Notes on the History of the Theory of Value." These "Notes," which had grown to three full volumes by the mid-1860s, he not only relegated to the final volume of *Capital* but explained why it must be so, since the dialectic emerging out of the Subject would make it an altogether different book, which indeed we know as *Capital*.

Elsewhere,[10] I have detailed Marx's break with the very concept of theory. Here what concerns us is that, far from the procedure of presenting the ascent from the abstract to the concrete—or even the fact that, as he notes in his Preface to the *Critique of Political Economy*, the reason for omitting the general introduction was that, as we have seen, "any anticipation of results that are still to be proven, seems to me objectionable"—Marx unequivocally declared that "the reader who wishes to follow me at all, must make up his mind to pass from the special to the general."

The decade it took Marx to transform *Critique of Political Economy* into *Capital*, retaining the first as his subtitle, should, but seldom does, make us remember what critique had always meant to Marx: the *practice* of philosophy, or, as he expressed it early, "the *practice* (praxis) of philosophy, however, is itself *theoretical*. It is *criticism* which measures individual existence against essence, particular actuality against the idea." All of this is especially crucial to the understanding of Chapter One, which becomes, *at one and the same time*, the Great Divide between the Marxian and the Hegelian dialectic, *and* reappears in the modern world, at the simultaneous outbreak of World War I and the collapse of *established* Marxism. Lenin did not take it lightly when he wrote in his Abstract of Hegel's *Science of Logic*: "It is impossible fully to grasp Marx's *Capital*, and especially its first chapter, if you have not studied through and understood the *whole* of Hegel's *Logic*. Consequently, none of the Marxists for the past ½ century have understood Marx!!"[11]

In *Philosophy and Revolution*[12] I have detailed what had dawned on Lenin so sharply concerning the dialectics of thought and the dialectics of revolution. Here it is necessary only to point to the fact that—whether you see those categories, Universal, Particular, and Individual in Hegel's Doctrine of the Notion as what reminded Lenin that Marx, in his first chapter of *Capital*, was "imitating" Hegel; or whether you think that there is any parallelism in economics and in dialectics, especially on the syllogism about the objective and subjective path to freedom—*for Lenin*, in the midst of the world holocaust, this shed such great illumination that he decided none of the Marxists had understood *Capital*, and he spelled it out *for himself* in all the writings on *Imperialism* and *State and Revolution*.

Chapter One of *Capital* seems never to stop reappearing on the historic stage. We see the exact opposite to the illumination it shed for Lenin in World War I (or perhaps more precisely because it did shed that illumination) when we see that Stalin, in the midst of World War II, ordered that Chapter One not be taught. Thus, at one and the same time, Stalin broke the dialectical structure of Marx's greatest theoretical work, and perverted Marx's concept of history as something humanity shapes. Instead, he invented an alleged "historic principle" which reduced history from the class struggle in the specifically capitalistic world of commodity production to a Law of Value that supposedly existed before capitalism and will continue to exist under socialism.[13]

Coming even closer to our age, in the period of the turbulent 1960s, the French Communist philosopher, Louis Althusser, after having written *Reading Capital* (which should have been called *How Not to Read Capital*), spelled it out in four short pages directed to "the workers," who are advised *not* to begin reading *Capital* with Chapter One: "It is a recommendation, one which I regard as imperative." This essay, which appeared in *L'Humanité*, 21 April 1969, was actually written as a preface to a new edition of *Capital.*[14]

And, finally, Sartre, at the very time when he considered himself a Marxist trying to fuse Existentialism with Marxism and praising Marx's theory of fetishism—and, of course, we are back in Chapter One—considered that Marx had only posed the question which "had never been developed."[15]

The fact that Chapter One has appeared so often on the historic stage—and one feels that it will surely reappear—is by no means past history, much less an academic exercise. It lives today, not because of all the criticisms, but because of what Marx, himself, wrote. He had caught both the truth of the capitalist age and its absolute opposite—"freely associated men" who would strip the veil from the fetishism of commodities and establish a totally new, classless society.

Capital is a very, very different book than either *Grundrisse* or *Critique of Political Economy*, and it is a very different book from the first chapter to the last. *It* is the Great Divide from Hegel, and not just because the subject is economics rather than philosophy. The other two also were economics, and the "first draft" (if that is what one wishes to call the *Grundrisse*) had a great deal more *obviously* philosophic language than *Capital*. No, it is that Great Divide because, *just because*, the Subject—not subject matter, but Subject—was neither economics nor philosophy but the human being, the masses. Because dead labor (capital) dominates over living labor, and the labor*er* is the "gravedigger of capitalism," all of human existence is involved. *This* dialectic is therefore totally new, totally internal, deeper than ever was the Hegelian dialectic which had *de*humanized the self-development of humanity in the dialectic of Consciousness, Self-Consciousness, and Reason. Marx could transcend the Hegelian dialectic not by denying that it was "the source of all dialectic"; rather, it was precisely because he began with that source that he could make the leap to the live Subject who is the one who transforms reality. *Capital* is the work in which—as Marx works out the economic laws of capitalism, not apart from the actual history of class struggles—historic narrative becomes historic reason. Let us follow Marx, beginning with Chapter One.

It will reveal the whole structure of *Capital*, although in Chapter One we are dealing only with a commodity—that is to say, we are in the phenomenal sphere only, in the market, in exchange. But so distinctive is the Marxian dialectic from the Hegelian that, even when we have not yet reached the Subject, the labor*er*—directly after being told that the commodity is the unit of capitalist wealth that is characterized by two factors—use-value and exchange-value—we are informed that this is only appearance, that in fact this is a manifestation of the dual character of labor itself, and that this is so crucial that though we will not meet labor until we get to the process of production, we must know about it before. In a word, we have now moved from Appearance to Essence.

In both, we have been made aware of their contradictory nature, even as we become oppressively aware throughout the third section on the value-form, on the polar opposites of the nature of all relationships, that, in fact: "The general value-form, which represents all products of labor as mere congelations of undifferentiated human labor, shows by its very structure that it is the social resumé of the world of commodities."[16]

Thus, as we enter the fetishism of commodities, it is clear that it is neither just appearance that we are dealing with, nor even just essence, though the latter remains quintessential for understanding appearance, for knowing what "lies behind." But to get to the totality we cannot leave it at objectivity. The objective may outweigh the subjective, but, unless we see the unity of the two and grapple with the truth of both, we will never be free. And freedom is what all the striving is about.

In a word, we have entered the Doctrine of the Notion, the objective and subjective paths to the realm of freedom. How simplistic it would be—and that, unfortunately, is exactly how established Marxism had taught the "application" of dialectics to political economy—to say that Marx was simply standing Hegel right side up and paralleling the Doctrine of Being to Commodities, Money and the Market, and the Doctrine of Essence to the sphere of production, *when what Marx confronts us with in the very first chapter is not only Appearance and Essence but Notion*.

When Marx gets to fetishism, he starts with what the commodity appears to be: "at first sight, a very trivial thing, and easily understood" (p. 81). He then contrasts that to how analysis shows it to be: "abounding in metaphysical subtleties and theological niceties." For example, a table as something to use is very easy to understand, but the minute it is seen as a commodity: "It not only stands with its feet on the ground, but, in relation to all other commodities, it stands on its head, and evolves out of its wooden brain grotesque ideas, far more wonderful than 'table turning' ever was." At this point, Marx has a footnote reference to China—that is, to the Taiping Revolution, contrasting it to the quiescent Europeans after the defeat of the 1848 Revolutions, as if the Chinese had made their revolution *"pour encourager les autres."*[17]

In asking how it could possibly be that a simple thing like a commodity could become a fetish, Marx answers: "Clearly, from this form itself . . . A commodity is therefore a mysterious thing, simply because in it the social character of man's labor appears to them as an objective character stamped upon the product of that labor; . . . as a social relation, existing not between themselves, but between the products of their labor . . . This Fetishism of commodities has its origin . . . in the peculiar social character of the labor that produces them" (p. 83).

Marx stresses that the fetish persists despite the fact that classical political economy had discovered that labor is the source of all value. The fact is that such a scientific discovery "by no means dissipates the mist through which the social character of labor appears to us to be an objective character of the products themselves" (p. 85), because "material relations between persons and social relations between things" is what production relations *"really are"* (p. 84, my emphasis) in our perverse capitalist society.

In his further analysis of the fetishism of commodities, Marx stresses that: "The categories of bourgeois economy consist of such like forms. They are forms of thought expressing with social validity the conditions and relations of a definite, historically determined mode of production, viz., the production of commodities. The whole mystery of commodities, all the magic and necromancy that surrounds the products of labor as long as they take the form of commodities, vanishes therefore, so soon as we come to other forms of production" (p. 87).

Marx then proceeds to consider everything from the "Asiatic and other modes of production" to the myth of Robinson Crusoe and the question of slavery and feudalism, and concludes that we can find a parallel in the religious world, where the fathers of the church treated their own religion as natural and all pre-Christian religions as "artificial." Whether it is religion or Proudhon, for all these " . . . there has been history but there is no longer any."[18]

Lest anyone be under the illusion that surely Marx by now had no use for the so-called pre-Marxist writings like his doctoral thesis on Epicurus, let us take a second look at this section. At the very moment when he speaks of Christianity "with its *cultus* of abstract man," he writes: "Trading nations, properly so-called, exist in the ancient world only in its interstices, like the gods of Epicurus in the Intermundia" (p. 91).

It is the crucial transition point, from man still being tied to "the umbilical cord that still unites man with his fellow man in a primitive tribal community, or upon direct relations of subjection," to when man enters the realm of freedom after the overthrow of capitalism when "freely associated men" take destiny into their own hands, and it is not only the fetishism of commodities which vanishes but the whole perverse system. Having leaped into that absolute opposite of capitalist society—that is to say, having projected a society of new human relations—it is clear that though we are in the market, we are, indeed, dealing with notional concepts. That path to freedom both separates the Marxian dialectic from the Hegelian and transforms Hegel's revolution *in philosophy* into a philosophy *of revolution*, so that even in economics, i.e., in the production sphere, with Marx's guidance we follow actual forms of the proletarian revolt. Whether that form be questioning "When does my day begin and when does it end?" or going on strike, Marx calls it a century-old "civil war."

One thing, however, we must take with us from the sphere of exchange is the obvious and necessary buying and selling of labor power, which ends with: "He, who before was the money owner, now strides in front as capitalist; the possessor of labour-power follows as his labourer. The one with an air of importance, smirking, intent on business; the other, timid and holding back, like one who is bringing his own hide to market and has nothing to expect but—a hiding" (p. 196).

Parts 3, 4, and 5 on the production of "Absolute Surplus Value" and "Relative Surplus Value," considered separately and as a whole, constitute the greater part of *Capital*, some three hundred pages. It will disclose how the capitalistic labor process transforms living labor into materialized labor and becomes "value big with value, a live monster that is fruitful and multiplies" (p. 217).

At the same time, Marx devotes no less than seventy-five pages to the struggle for the shortening of the working day. Far from it being a "sob story," it is the proof that Marx has moved from a concept of theory as only debate between theoreticians and the idea that it is that history that is important, to a concept of theory as the history of production relations and the idea that the strife between the machine and the worker is really the strife between capital and labor: "In place of the pompous catalogue of the 'inalienable rights of man' comes the modest Magna Charta of a legally limited working day which shall make clear 'when the time which the worker sells is ended, and his own begins' " (p. 330). For with that struggle, labor has put a limit to capitalism's "were-wolf's hunger for surplus labor": "Capital is dead labor, that, vampire-like, only lives by sucking living labor, and lives the more, the more labor it sucks" (p. 257). As Marx puts it a little further on as he specifies the concrete struggles and the Factory Acts, while "capital celebrated its orgies," labor won its struggles.

It is undisputed by Marxists that this struggle for the shortening of the working day, which includes the struggle for different working conditions, is the central core of Marx's *Capital*—and not only in Parts 3 and 4, but in Parts 6 and 7—and of Marxist activities. And, since Marx declared that struggle to be nothing short of "a protracted civil war, more or less dissembled, between the capitalist class and the working class" (p. 327), how does it happen that the publication of volume 2, which is an "extension" of this Part 7, has created a whole century of dispute? How does it happen that Rosa Luxemburg, who believed so totally that the class struggle was, indeed, a civil war between labor and capital from which none must depart, was in the forefront, if not the originator, among Marxists of this dissidence? And, above all, since that final Part[19] is strictly "Economics," how does it happen that this is also where philosophy is most imperative? That is to say, whether it was Lenin during World War I, or Stalin for opposite reasons during World War II, or the French Communist philosopher Althusser in the turbulent 1960s and early 1970s, Chapter One came alive for each and became the *contemporary* Great Divide.

The whole question of the relationship, not only between economics and dialectics, but between dialectics and liberation, has "suddenly" so intensely impinged on the idea of philosophy—and centrally on philosophy of revolution— that it becomes necessary all over again to study *Capital* in a new light, specifically Chapter One, which we have examined, and Part 7, to which we now turn.

Marx had informed us in the Afterword to the French edition of *Capital* (28 April 1875) that it "possesses a scientific value independent of the original and should be consulted even by readers familiar with German." The most fundamental and greatest changes were introduced into "The Accumulation of Capital." We must keep in mind that the very thought of such a Part as that which ended the original edition of *Capital* meant (1) that it was a substitute for the draft ending, "Results of the Immediate Process of Production"[20]; and (2) that the new title for the ending, "Accumulation of Capital," is the centerpoint of volume 2, though it is entitled "The Process of Circulation." (It must not be forgotten that what we know as volume 2 was considered by Marx to be book 2 of volume 1.)

The Part begins with "Simple Reproduction" and, of course, the centerpoint here remains what was described as the foundation for the whole process of capitalist production: "The separation of labor from its product, of subjective labor power from the objective conditions of labor, was therefore the real foundation in fact, and the starting point of capitalist production" (pp. 624–25).

So much of the section on "Erroneous Conception by Political Economy of Reproduction on a Progressively Increased Scale" answers Rosa Luxemburg, that it is almost impossible to understand how she could have failed to see that the problems in volume 2 are answered in volume 1, including even the reference to the fact that "the general change of places in the circulation of wealth of society . . . dazes the sight and propounds very complicated problems for a solution." While Marx refers us to volume 2 for the more comprehensive answer, there is hardly a fundamental point in this critique of classical political economy about expanded reproduction that isn't already anticipated here, including Marx's expression, "incredible aberration," in referring to Adam Smith's "spiriting away" constant capital.

Even the question, the *pons asini*, of all debates about Marx's exclusion of foreign trade is already projected here in volume 1: "We here take no account of export trade by means of which a nation can change articles of luxury either into means of production or means of subsistence, and *vice versa*. In order to examine the object of our investigation in its integrity, free from all disturbing subsidiary circumstances, we must treat the whole world as one nation, and assume that capitalist production is everywhere established and has possessed itself of every branch of industry" (p. 636).

The special additions to "Accumulation of Capital" center around, first, the fact that what is central is that "the separation of property from labor has become the necessary consequence of a law that apparently originated in their identity" (p. 640), while the addition to that section stresses, "So long as the laws of exchange are maintained in every act of exchange, individually considered, the mode of appropriation may be completely revolutionized without in the least affecting the property right bestowed by the production of commodities" (p. 643).

Second, and more important, to this emphasis on the fact that the distribution sphere can be changed without affecting the sphere of production (and, since that is so, the exploitative relations remain) is added the fact that the law of centralization and concentration of capital could reach its limit: "This limit would not be reached in any particular society until the entire social capital would be united, either in the hands of one single capitalist, or in those of one single corporation" (p. 688).

And still exploitative capitalism would remain. Following this foreseeing of what we now call a state-capitalist society, Marx added, further, a section that Engels left out of the English translation. He had called the additions to the French edition of "scientific value."[21] These were pivotal views as to how further mechanization, far from allowing "The So-Called Primitive Accumulation" to remain as a past stage, would give new life to capitalism. Thus, before going into primitive accumulation, Marx had discussed the whole question of how effects can become causes, and introduced into the French edition the question of the ramifications of the extension of capitalism into the world market once the mechanization reaches a certain point and capitalism "successively annexed extensive areas of the New World, Asia and Australia."

Here is what was left out of Engels's English edition:

> But it is only in the epoch where mechanical industry, having sunk roots deeply enough, exercised a preponderant influence on the whole national production; where, thanks to it, foreign trade began to take precedence over internal trade; where the world market annexed for itself vast lands in the New World, in Asia and in Australia; where finally the industrial nations entering the lists become numerous enough: it is from this epoch only that date the renascent cycles whose successive phases embrace years and which converge in a general crisis, the end of one cycle and the point of departure for another. Up to now the average duration of these cycles is ten or eleven years, but there is no reason to think of this figure as constant. On the contrary, we should infer from these laws of capitalist production, as we have just developed them, that it is variable and that the length of the cycles will grow shorter gradually.[22]

What had become a divisive question in Luxemburg's world with the appearance of imperialism, and a burning question for our day, was all introduced, as we see, into Part 7 on "The General Law of Capitalist Accumulation." All this should have been clear from the original section on the primitive accumulation, which began with the "Secret": "The starting-point of the development that gave rise to the wage-labourer as well as to the capitalist, was the servitude of the labourer" (p. 787). It continued with "The Expropriation of the Agricultural Population from the Land," and ended with "The Modern Theory of Colonization." The most famous of all sections is the penultimate one—"The Historical Tendency of Capitalist Accumulation."

But just as the Second International considered that Marx's analysis about the "turning of Africa into a warren for the commercial hunting of black-skins" (p. 823) applied only to the "primitive" stage and disregarded "the negation of the negation" (p. 837), so the omitted paragraph on advanced industrialized capitalism's annexing of the "New World, Asia and Australia" hardly opened new eyes that would be able to grapple with imperialism.

In volume 2 as in volume 1, Marx hardly departs from the central question of the dual character of labor, attributing Adam Smith's aberration to the fact that it "rests on another error in his fundamental conception: he does not distinguish the two-fold nature of labor itself. . . "[23] Whereupon Marx concludes that it is not the saleability of labor that is unusual; it is the form, the fact that the ability to labor takes the form of a commodity.

Above all, the fetishism of commodities, the dialectic of thing-ifying (*dinglich*) the living Subject, the laborer, transforming him into but an appendage of a machine, so revolted Marx that once again, in volume 2, he declared his indebtedness to the Hegelian dialectic. In a footnote (which Engels had left out, in his reorganization of the manuscripts for volume 2) Marx wrote:

> In a review of the first volume of *Capital*, Mr. Dühring notes that, in my zealous devotion to the schema of Hegelian logic, I even discovered the Hegelian forms of the syllogism in the process of circulation. My relationship with Hegel is very simple. I am a disciple of Hegel, and the presumptuous chattering of the epigones who think they have buried this great thinker appear frankly ridiculous to me. Nevertheless, I have taken the liberty of adopting towards my master a critical attitude, disencumbering his dialectic of its mysticism and thus putting it through a profound change, etc.[24]

We must not forget that Marx wrote this after volume 1 had already been published. Contrast this to the empty methodology of Roman Rosdolsky who concluded, after his forced identification of the *Grundrisse* and *Capital*, that one "no longer has to bite into the sour apple and 'thoroughly study the whole of Hegel's *Logic*' in order to understand Marx's *Capital*—one can arrive at the same end, directly, by studying the *Rough Draft*."[25]

Naturally, Marx's reference to Hegel as "master" was not meant in any schoolboy sense. Even when the young Marx had considered himself a Left Hegelian and belonged to the Doctors' Club of the Young Hegelians, he was neither imitative nor arbitrary in his attitude to Hegel. Rather, as we saw at the time he was working on his doctoral thesis, he was approaching the threshold of his own new continent of thought and revolution, recreating the revolutionary essence lodged in the Hegelian dialectic. This is why the mature Marx kept repeating that Hegel's dialectic was the source "of all dialectic."[26]

Instead of using the dialectic as a tool to be "applied," Marx recreated it on the objective-subjective basis of historical developments that emerged *out of* the production relations of labor and capital, with labor as the "grave-digger." Clearly, the unifying whole of Marx's world view was the new Subject—the proletariat. Marx's idea of history was not only as that of the past but as that which live working men and women achieve in transforming reality, here and now—transforming themselves, as well, through the process of revolution into new, all-rounded individuals of a classless society. He would not let the Dührings treat Hegel as a "dead dog"; he wanted to confront them with the fact that the long, arduous, twenty-five-hundred-year trek of human development that Hegel had dialectically traced was, indeed, the basis of new developments for their day.

The question of fetishism reappears in volume 3, after Marx has analyzed the concrete that concerns capitalists—profit, rent, interest and prices. In his letter to Engels of 30 April 1868, Marx dismisses all these phenomena in volume 3: " . . . we have, in conclusion, the *class struggle*, into which the movement of the whole *Scheisse* is resolved."* The necessity for this is further stressed as Marx returns once more to describe just how, under capitalism, human relations are reified, turned into things:

> In Capital-Profit, or better Capital-Interest, Land-Rent, Labor-Wages of Labor, in this economic trinity expressing professedly the connection of value and of wealth in general with their sources, we have the complete mystification of the capitalist mode of production, the transformation of social conditions into things, the indiscriminate amalgamation of the material conditions of production with their historical and social forms. It is an enchanted, perverted, topsy-turvy world, in which Mister Capital and Mistress Land carry on their goblin tricks as social characters and at the same time as mere things. It is the great merit of classic economy to have dissolved this false appearance and illusion, this self-isolation and ossification of the different social elements of wealth by themselves, this personification of things and conversion of conditions of production into entities, this religion of everyday life.[27]

The overriding truth—be it in volume 1, *The Process of Production*; volume 2, *The Process of Circulation*; or volume 3, *The Process of Production as a Whole*—is that the only thing that could possibly uproot capitalism, the revolt of the workers, destroys what is "*the absolute general law of capitalist accumulation*," the endless growth of constant capital at the expense of variable, and with it the unemployed army. Marx concludes: "From that moment new forces and new passions spring up in the bosom of society; but the old social organization fetters them and keeps them down. It must be annihilated; it is annihilated . . . capitalist production begets, with the inexorability of a law of Nature, its own negation. It is the negation of negation" (p. 835–37).

In a word, when Marx reaches the end, having traced "The Historical Tendency of Capitalist Accumulation," the conclusion about negation of the negation, far from being rhetoric, is the actual summation of the whole history

---

*The latest editions of Marx's letters have tried to "clean up" his expression, "*Scheisse*," translating it as "business." I prefer the Dona Torr translation. See Karl Marx and Frederick Engels, *Correspondence, 1846–1895* (N.Y.: International Pubs., n.d.), p. 245.

of capitalism. Marx, being the revolutionary that he was, decided, in the continuing discussion over volume 1 after its publication, that this historical tendency summed up Western, not universal, development, and that the revolution could, in fact, come first in an underdeveloped country like Russia—provided that it was not separated from revolution in the advanced capitalist countries.

NOTES

1. Marx, *A Contribution to the Critique of Political Economy*, (Chicago: Charles H. Kerr & Co., 1904) p. 293. When found in his posthumous papers, this was believed to be Marx's introduction to his *Critique of Political Economy* and was published in this edition as an appendix. Compare this passage to the same section as translated by Nicolaus in Karl Marx, *Grundrisse* (Middlesex: Penguin Books, 1973), p. 101. A still newer translation with a quite significant commentary by Terrell Carver is included in *Karl Marx: Texts on Method* (Oxford: Basil Blackwell, 1975).

2. Marx-Engels, *Selected Works*, 1:500.

3. Marx, *Critique of Political Economy*, p. 9. Page citations here and in the text following refer to the 1904 Kerr edition. See n. 1.

4. See *The American Journalism of Marx and Engels* (New York: New American Library, 1966), p. 90. Page citations in the text following are to this edition.

5. Eric J. Hobsbawm, ed. *Pre-Capitalist Economic Formations* (New York: International Pub., 1965), pp. 68, 96, 79, 89. Page citations in text following refer to this edition.

6. The disputes in 1950 over the Asiatic mode of production were far reaching. For the Russian discussions, see *Voprosi Istorii*, No. 6 (1953); No. 2 (1954); Nos. 2, 4 and 5 (1955). For the discussions in the West, see P.M. Sweezy, et al., *The Transition from Feudalism to Capitalism* (London, n.d.). See also George Lichtheim's "Marx and 'the Asiatic Mode of Production,' " in *St. Antony's Papers*, No. 14 (Carbondale, Ill.: Southern Illinois Univ. Press); and *Marx on China*, ed. Dona Torr (London: Lawrence & Wishart, 1968).

By 1968 Roman Rosdolsky's *Entstehungsgeschichte des Marxschen 'Kapital'* appeared, published as *The Making of Marx's 'Capital'* (London: Pluto Press, 1977). It claimed very nearly an identity between *Grundrisse* and *Capital*. That claim was quite demolished by John Mepham in his article, "From the *Grundrisse* to *Capital*: the Making of Marx's Method," *Issues in Marxist Philosophy*, eds. John Mepham and D-H. Ruben (Atlantic Highlands: Humanities Press, 1979; Sussex: Harvester Press, 1979). I develop this in the next section of this chapter.

7. Marx wrote to Engels from London on 11 January 1860: "In my opinion, the biggest things that are happening in the world today are on the one hand the movement of the slaves in America, started by the death of John Brown, and on the other the movement of the serfs in Russia. . . ." In my *Marxism and Freedom* I have dealt at length with the impact of the Civil War in the United States on the structure of *Capital*.

8. Marx, *Capital*, 1:173. Because Ernest Mandel, in his introduction to the new translation of vol. 1 published in 1976 (Middlesex: Penguin Books), leaves out the word "freely" and misrepresents Marx's concept of "freely associated man" as if that meant the forced association in state-capitalist Russia, I have devoted an entire essay to this question. See "Today's Epigones Who Try to Truncate Marx's *Capital*", in my *Marx's Capital and Today's Global Crisis* (Detroit: News & Letters, 1978).

9. One point must be kept in mind here: Marx's specific reference—"I have overthrown the whole doctrine of profit as it has existed up to now."

10. See part 3, "Marxism: The Unity of Theory and Practice" in *Marxism and Freedom*, which deals with the structure of *Capital*.

11. Lenin, *Collected Works*, 38:180. I am using my own translation. See chap. 9, n. 1.

12. See chap. 3, "The Shock of Recognition and the Philosophic Ambivalence of Lenin," in my *Philosophy and Revolution* (New York: Dell Pub. Co., 1973).

13. My translation into English of "Teaching Economics in the Soviet Union" from *Pod Znamenem Marxizma* ("*Under the Banner of Marxism*"), which issue failed to arrive in United States libraries, was published in the *American Economic Review* (September 1944) and touched off an international debate that lasted an entire year. My rebuttal was published in the *American Economic Review* (September 1945).

14. The rigorous Althusser did not inform the reader that, after a twenty-six-year delay, he was repeating Stalin's 1943 *order* that this is exactly what should be done. See Althusser's preface to vol. 1 of *Capital* in his *Lenin and Philosophy and Other Essays* (London: New Left Books, 1971). Prof. Althusser never stopped trying to eliminate Hegel from Marx, stressing: "One phantom is more especially crucial than any other today; the shade of Hegel. To drive this phantom back into the night. . . ."

15. Jean-Paul Sartre, *Search For a Method* (New York: Alfred A. Knopf, 1965). See also my critique of Sartre in chap. 6, "Outsider Looking In", of my *Philosophy and Revolution*, especially the section on "The Dialectic and the Fetish", pp. 197–210.

16. *Capital*, 1:77. All paginations in the following text refer to the Kerr 1906 edition.

17. This footnote was left out of the Kerr edition. It appears in the Pelican edition (Middlesex: 1976), p. 164, n. 27.

18. Marx, *The Poverty of Philosophy*, p. 131.

19. We are following Marx's division, in which there is no part 8.

20. The Pelican edition of *Capital* includes as an appendix this complete original ending. I had translated parts of this "chapter 6" during the 1940s as part of my preparation for a book on State-Capitalism and Marxism; the translation is included in the documents on deposit with the Wayne State University, Labor History Archives. See chap. 3. n. 33.

21. We must not forget that Marx had put in the afterword to the French edition that "it possesses a scientific value independent of the original and should be consulted even by readers familiar with German." At the start of this section, we called attention to the fact that the translator, Ben Fowkes, had followed Engels's part divisions for the English edition and thus "The So-called Primitive Accumulation" was listed as a part 8, whereas Marx had included it, ever since the French edition, as a separate chapter under part 7, "The General Accumulation of Capital." But there is no reason to put all the blame on the translator's shoulders. It would not have happened without the approval of the editor, Ernest Mandel, who committed many perversions in his pretentious seventy-five page introduction to the Pelican edition. See my critique, "Today's Epigones Who Try to Truncate Marx's *Capital*," in *Marx's Capital and Today's Global Crisis* (Detroit: News & Letters, 1978).

22. This section from the original 1875 French edition appears on p. 1150 of *Oeuvres de Karl Marx, Economie I* (Paris: Editions Gallimard, 1963), which was edited by Maximilien Rubel. It should come immediately after the words "of periodicity," in the middle of line 12 of page 695 of the Kerr edition. The Pelican edition includes their translation as a footnote on page 786.

23. *Capital*, 2:435.

24. See *Oeuvres de Karl Marx, Economie II*, edited by Maximilien Rubel, p. 528.

25. Rosdolsky, *The Making of Marx's 'Capital'*, p. 570.

26. See "The Philosophy of Mind: A Movement from Practice?" in my *Philosophy and Revolution*, pp. 33–46, for an analysis of what our age could see at the point where Marx's "Critique of the Hegelian Dialectic" ended with a sentence from the *Philosophy of Mind* (para. 384): *"The Absolute is Mind*—this is the supreme definition of the Absolute."

27. *Capital*, 3:966-67.

XI

The Philosopher of
Permanent Revolution
Creates New Ground for Organization

1. CRITIQUE OF THE GOTHA PROGRAM[1]

> *The international activity of the working classes does not in any way depend on the existence of the International Working Men's Association. This was only the first attempt to create a central organ for that activity; an attempt which was a lasting success on account of the impulse which it gave but which was no longer realisable in its* first historical form *after the fall of the Paris Commune.*
>
> *Karl Marx,* Critique of the Gotha Program, *1875*

Luxemburg herself may not have seen the great contradiction in the manner in which she projected, even hallowed, spontaneity, and at the same time clung to the party even though she was always calling for (and was convinced that the leadership needed a hefty push from) spontaneous mass actions to move forward. She did not attribute the breakup of her passionate and complex relationship with Jogiches to the strains of organization in a period of open revolution. Yet a serious look back to that highest point of her activity in the 1905–06 Russian Revolution will disclose the sharp dualism in the two aspects of organization and spontaneity, not to mention the other silent feature—the Man/Woman relationship for one as independent as Luxemburg. Yet it became ground for the heart–breaking separation, though they never separated for a single instance as revolutionaries, as Marxist activists. They had the same perspective of world revolution, and Jogiches met his death shortly after hers in the struggle to find her murderer and to continue with the revolutionary work.

In the 1905–06 Revolution, too, the exultation that came with their joint activity never wavered. The fact that she was also with her lover, who was an organization man par excellence, in those 24-hours-a-day whirlwind activities, seemed to have reached the highest point of all. Yet another fact is likewise indisputable. Becoming witness to the overnight transformation of a small organization into a mass party in the midst of masses in motion, modified Luxemburg's appreciation for what Jogiches never left out of his view in this activity—the need also for secrecy, oppressive awareness of the strength of the powers-that-be working night and day to achieve a counterrevolution.

In our search for illumination on this burning question of the relationship of spontaneity to organization, three very different dates and one totally different subject—a philosophy of revolution—are needed: (1) Luxemburg's analysis of Lassalle written in 1904 as celebration of the March 1848 Revolution; (2) Marx's 1875 *Critique of the Gotha Program*, which was a critique of Lassalle's doctrines; and (3) Lenin's transforming that *Critique* as well as *The Civil War in France* into *State and Revolution* as ground for 1917.

Long after his death, Lassalle remained a pervasive force and not only for reformists but for revolutionaries, and specifically on the point of organization. It was in an entirely different period, the eve of the 1917 Revolution, before a single Marxist, Lenin, took Marx's *Critique* so seriously as to build his whole *State and Revolution* on it. On the eve of the first Russian Revolution that was not the case, and everyone from Luxemburg to Trotsky extolled Lassalle, not only very nearly on the same level as Marx, but in fact "when it comes to organization," admitted or otherwise, he stood on a higher, that is, more concrete level. Thus, in the year 1904 Luxemburg wrote of "Lassalle and the Revolution."[2] Its center point was that, though Lassalle had committed many errors, and though Marx's criticism of him was valid, nevertheless, he enters into history because "it was Lassalle who transformed into deed the *most important historical consequence* of the March revolution in finally liberating the German working class, fifteen years later, from the political *Heerbann** of the bourgeoisie and organizing it into an independent class party."

As if that were not clear enough praise, it is further called "immortal work" and that remark is made though it is followed by a reference to Marx's 1868 critique of Lassalle.[3] In a word, the critique is made subordinate to Lassalle's great deed, which does "not diminish but grows more and more with the historical perspective from which we view it."

Why did it grow "more and more with the historical perspective" of forty years? Was this not due to the fact that Marx's *Critique of the Gotha Program* was never fully internalized? Could a duality between the concept of organization and a philosophy of revolution have arisen without awareness if one had not separated Marx's concept of revolution from his concept of organization? Is it not a fact that the need for and the building of organization so preoccupied all Marxists except Marx that a fetish was made of it? It is a fact

*There is no precise English translation for this German term. It hearkens back to the feudal summons for vassals to present themselves for military service.

that this fetish was at the innards of the SPD. From its very birth, that fetish was so overwhelming a factor that although the SPD was preparing to replace the Gotha Program of its predecessor with a new one, the Erfurt Program, its leaders balked at publishing Marx's *Critique*, even fifteen years after the event.[4] Not only that. They seemed to have disregarded the fact that it was Marx, not Lassalle, who founded the First International Working Men's Association. What is starkly evident in this disregard is that they considered *national* organization, the German party, to be more important than the International.

The innumerable articles written about the fact that Marx had no theory of organization obscured, if they did not totally cover up, the fact that Marx was indeed conscious of organization, helped found organizations—from the International Communist Correspondence Committees to the First International. Because that mediation—proletarian organization, an independent proletarian organization, and one that would be both international and have the goal of revolution and a new society—was so central to his views, Marx kept referring to "the Party" when all that was involved was himself and Engels.

What Marx called "party in the eminent historical sense" (Letter to Freiligrath, 29 February 1860) was alive to Marx throughout the entire decade when no organization existed in the 1850s with which he could associate. Once a mass movement emerged, he left the British Museum to help establish the International Working Men's Association. And when at its height—the Paris Commune—the International was disintegrating, he did not consider that its end. On the contrary, he sent it away to make sure, however, that it would not "suddenly" get a totally new philosophy—in this case, anarchism—which was waiting in the wings. But he also was ready to hail the slimmest possibility of another organization which he was sure would result from a new mass movement. This was the case in the United States, when the great class struggles of the mid-1870s in railroads and in the mines, culminating in the first General Strike in the United States, in St. Louis, would result, he hoped, "in an independent working class party."

To underline its significance, Marx said that the First International was but a form of organization suited to the time, and that the creativity of the masses would discover another form. Marx at no time made a fetish of organization, which is why, in the covering letter of the *Critique*, he wrote: "Every step of real movement is more important than a dozen programmes. If, therefore, it was not possible—and the conditions of the time did not permit it—to go *beyond* the Eisenach programme, one should simply have concluded an agreement for action against the common enemy."[5] How inseparable were theory and organization is not only present throughout the modestly entitled "critical marginal notes" but even in his covering note, which includes the fact that he is sending "in the near future the last parts of the French edition of *Capital*." And there were also references to a new edition of the 1852

Revelations Concerning the Communist Trial in Cologne.[6] In a word, 1875 was a most active year politically, philosophically, and organizationally, none of which was separable from both a philosophy of revolution and the perspectives for the future.

The *Critique* itself, is, of course, not just a criticism of a program, but a comprehensive analysis of Lassalle's doctrines. It contains a theory of the state and, more importantly, of the non-state-to-be (as he called the Paris Commune), which was to be the model for the future breakup of the capitalist state and establishment of a commune form of nonstate. Furthermore, not only was capitalism a transient stage, but so was "the revolutionary dictatorship of the proletariat" (p. 28), which was to replace it. These two fundamental principles were to become the basis for the 1917 Revolution and Lenin's *State and Revolution*.

Unfortunately, the great transformation in Lenin, both on philosophy and the revolutionary dictatorship of the proletariat, did not extend to Lenin's concept of the party, which, despite all modifications in actual revolutions, remained essentially what it was in 1903. And since by now his *What Is To Be Done?*, considered by Lenin a tactical work, had been made into a fetish—a universal fetish at the very time that the first workers' state was transformed into its opposite, a state-capitalist society—the relevance of Marx's *Critique of the Gotha Program* gains a special urgency for our age.

Paragraph by paragraph,* beginning with the first paragraph of the program, Marx analyzes how totally wrong (and when not wrong quite imprecise) is the program's analysis of labor and its subordination to what Marx had called "the monopoly of the means of labor." Where, for the First International, the class of monopolists included both capitalists and landowners, Lassalle had spoken as if it were only "the monopoly of the capitalist class" (p. 7), thus letting the Prussian landowners, by no accident, off scot-free.

Along with this came the point that was most objectionable to Marx; this was that "the working-class strives for its emancipation first of all *within the framework of the present day national state* . . . " (p. 18), to which Marx asks: how could socialists "conceive the workers' movement from the narrowest national standpoint . . . after the work of the International!" (p. 21). Marx naturally considered it the greatest retrogression to move back from the international to a national standpoint.

What must tower above all struggles against exploitation, nationally and internationally, is the perspective of a totally classless society; the vision of its ground would be "from each according to his ability, to each according to his needs" (p. 14).

To this day, this remains the perspective for the future, and yet the Marxists who keep quoting it never bother to study just how concretely that arose from the *Critique* of the supposedly socialist program, and what would be required

---

*When it came to the political demands, Marx combined all five points and dismissed them as "a mere echo of the bourgeois People's Party . . . "

to make that real. The revolution that would overthrow capitalism would have to be a great deal more total in its uprooting of the old than just fighting against what is. Thus Marx says that to reach the communist stage, there would have to be an end to the "enslaving subordination of the individual to the division of labor and therewith also the antithesis between mental and physical labor . . . " (p. 14).

This is not the young Marx speaking. This is the mature author of *Capital*, the revolutionary who has experienced both the exciting 1860s and the climax in the historic Paris Commune and the Commune's defeat, and he is projecting so totally new a concept of labor as the creative self-activity of humanity that he is now saying that we will reach communism only when "labor from a mere means of life, has itself become the prime necessity of life . . . " (p. 14).[7]

Now then, what had happened between the transfer of the First International to the United States and the attempts at unity between two different tendencies of the German workers movement, and why was it that Lassalle, who founded the General Association of German Workers in the early 1860s as the first independent mass political organization, should still tower above Marx after he founded the International Working Men's Association? Was there a national strain from the start? How could Rosa Luxemburg, who was the greatest internationalist, not have seen any of this? It could not have been *national* vs *international*. It could have only been *activism* vs *philosophy*. That Marx's *Critique of the Gotha Program* could not win adherents among the new German Social-Democracy may be understandable if the only question at issue was who had the "mass party," Marx or Lassalle? What is not understandable—in fact is very nearly fantastic—is that no revolutionary studied these notes as not just a critique of a particular tendency, but as actual perspective for the whole movement. Let's remember that not only was it Bernstein, the reformist, who tried to revise Marx's principles; it was also Kautsky, then the "orthodox" Marxist. And not only that. No revolutionary took it as a point of departure for working out a theory of organization that would be inseparable from the theory of revolution. Any "orthodox" Leninist who tries to say that Lenin's statement that there could be no revolution without a revolutionary theory meant that his concept of organization was in any way related to Marx's theory in the *Critique of the Gotha Program*, rather than the immediate concrete of having to function under tsarism, would have to contend with both Lenin's own statement in the midst of the 1905 Revolution, when he moved far, far away from his own narrow position,[8] and the position Lenin had on the eve of the 1917 Revolution as he completed his *State and Revolution*. Unfortunately, Lenin's philosophic reorganization dealt with the concept of the revolutionary *smashing* of the bourgeois state, not with the other crucial factor in Marx's *Critique of the Gotha Program*: the inseparable relationship of philosophy to organization itself.

That means that Lenin's philosophic reorganization remained in a separate compartment from the concept of the party and the practice of vanguardism.

Clearly, there is no substitute for the totality that was Marx as organization man, as political theorist, as visionary of a future social order; this idea is exactly the warp and woof of his theory of permanent revolution. The covering letter that Marx wrote with the *Critique of the Gotha Program*, which showed that he had just completed the 1875 French edition of *Capital*, also referred to the reissuance of the 1852 *Revelations of the Cologne Communist Trial*. What is significant about this is that this was the edition which reproduced the 1850 *Address to the Communist League*. In turning to that projection of the permanent revolution, we should also keep in mind the fact that the 1848–49 revolutions had led to a restudy of the peasantry and its great revolts. Marx kept reminding us that the Peasant War in Germany was the only revolutionary moment in German history, and held that its betrayal by Luther and feudalism accounted for Germany's backwardness. Indeed, not only was Engels's *The Peasant War in Germany* important in relation to the 1848 revolutions and the theory of permanent revolution for that period, but for future perspectives.

Once Marx finished with the *Critique of the Gotha Program* and returned to work on volumes 2 and 3 of *Capital*,[9] he became interested, at one and the same time, in Russian agriculture and the study of the primitive commune— elements of which still existed in Russia—and in the possibility of a new independent workers' party in the United States as a result of the new heightened class struggles on the railroads. All of these will reconnect with the theory of the permanent revolution in a totally new, never-before-thought-of way, both in the letters to Zasulich and in the Russian Preface to the 1882 edition of the *Communist Manifesto*.

2. MARX'S THEORY OF PERMANENT REVOLUTION, 1843–83

Revolution is never practical until the hour of revolution strikes. Then it alone is practical, and all the efforts of the conservatives and compromisers become the most futile and visionary of human language.

James Connolly, Workshop Talks

The relationship of the revolutionary workers' party to the petty-bourgeois democrats is this: it marches together with them against the faction which it aims at overthrowing, it opposes them in everything whereby they seek to consolidate their position in their own interests . . . Their battle cry must be: The Revolution in Permanence.

Karl Marx, Address to the Communist League, *1850*

Luxemburg's internationalism was second to none in her thought, in her actions, indeed her whole life. Clearly, her luminous mind, when it came to the question of revolution, was likewise second to none. The 1905 Revolution, which led to her exclamation that the revolution was "everything" and all else was "bilge," was the red thread that permeated all her political writings. Yet when it came to philosophy, even when that was a philosophy of revolution, that was not the dominant factor. Quite the contrary.[10]

To the extent that Marx's 1850 Address on the permanent revolution was a point of reference, it was most often a reference to the "mistake" of thinking after the defeat of 1848–49 that a revolution was still in the offing in 1850, as if the dating was the pivotal point rather than the philosophy of revolution and all that flowed from it, beginning with the fact of taking the highest point of any revolution as the point of departure for the next revolution. Even when, in her 1902 review of Mehring's publication of some of Marx's early works, Luxemburg recognized "the original *conception* . . . the hopes for the so-called 'revolution in permanence'," the emphasis was on the "so-called" as she spelled out Marx's "anticipation that the bourgeois revolution would be only a first act, immediately followed by the petty-bourgeois and finally the proletarian revolution."[11]

The truth, however, is that, in the very first year that he broke with bourgeois society, 1843, and even when he was writing on a "mere" individual subject like the "Jewish Question," Marx refused to leave it at merely "being for" civil rights for Jews. Rather, he insisted that the question revolved around the inadequacy of any bourgeois rights. And because his vision from the start was for totally new human relations, he there, for the first time, projected the concept of permanent revolution:

> At times of heightened self-confidence, political life seeks to suppress its own presumption, [namely] the civil society and its elements, and to set itself up as the real species-life of man without any contradictions. But it can do this only in *violent* contradiction with its own conditions of existence, only by declaring the revolution to be *permanent*, and hence the political drama ends with the restoration of religion, private property and all the elements of the civil society just as inevitably as war ends with peace.[12]

It is true that there were elements of the concept of permanent revolution once Luxemburg was in the actual 1905 Revolution and judged that revolution to be no mere extension of 1848 but rather initiation of twentieth-century European revolutions. But she had not worked it out as a theory, as Trotsky had, in what later became known as the theory of Permanent Revolution.* What Luxemburg singled out was the general strike, which did combine politics and economics, but she not only had no philosophy of revolution emerging out of it, even the totally new form of organization which had emerged spontaneously—soviets—was mentioned only in passing. It would remain so until the very eve of the 1919 Revolution, when Luxemburg rejected the reactionary call for a Constituent Assembly and called for the creation of Workers Councils.

*See Afterword to this Chapter.

To put it even more sharply, even when finally the Spartacus League did decide to transform itself into a separate and independent communist party, the fetish of "unity of party" persisted, as was seen once again by the fact that even then she instructed the German delegation to oppose the immediate establishment of a new Third International.

Karl Marx on the other hand, as we have seen, was grounded in a philosophy of permanent revolution as far back as 1843, and kept developing the concept and the activities in revolutionary struggles culminating in the 1848–49 Revolution, after which he worked it out, not just in passing, but in full in his March 1850 *Address to the Communist League.*

In reviewing "the two revolutionary years, 1848–1849" and the activities of the League "in the movement, in all places, in the press, on the barricades, and on the battlefields," Marx's report to the League stresses in the very next sentence that it was rooted in "the conception of the movement as laid down in circulars of the congresses and of the Central Committee of 1847 as well as in the *Communist Manifesto . . .*" In a word, not a single element of this Address to the League—whether it concerned the need for "reorganization" in a centralized way because "a new revolution is impending, when the workers' party, therefore, must act in the most organized, most unanimous and most independent fashion," or whether it concerned the outright declaration "Revolution in Permanence"—is in any way separated from the total conception of philosophy *and* revolution. The most important conclusion for the movement then and now was that never again will a workers' movement be tied to the bourgeois democratic movement, even when they fight together against feudalism: "The relation of the revolutionary workers' party to the petty-bourgeois democrats is this: it marches together with them against the faction which it aims at overthrowing, it opposes them in everything whereby they seek to consolidate their position in their own interests."[13]

He kept stressing the fact that "far from desiring to revolutionize all society," the democratic petty-bourgeois were striving to work within the bourgeois framework and in fact showed themselves to be a more deadly enemy than the liberals. The search for revolutionary allies, therefore, must include the "rural proletariat." The stress on achieving the workers' own class interests was made the center point of everything, even as the international outlook would mean that the German workers look upon not only their country but "the direct victory of their own class in France." In developing the strategy and tactics for a continuous revolution, this Address, that was actually distributed in illegal leaflet form, ended as follows:

> But they themselves must do the utmost for their final victory by clarifying their minds as to what their class interests are, by taking up their position as an independent party as soon as possible and by not allowing themselves to be seduced for a single moment by the hypocritical phrases of the democratic petty bourgeois into refraining from the independent organization of the party of the proletariat. Their battle cry must be: The Revolution in Permanence [p. 185].

Far from that Address being something "Blanquist" that Marx discarded afterwards, it was followed with another Address in June, in which Marx reviewed the concrete activities in five of the countries—Belgium, Germany, Switzerland, France, and England. And the Minutes of the Central Committee meeting of 15 September 1850 pointed to the possibility of defeats. There was no letting go of what was needed for total uprooting of this society, even if it needed "15, 20, 50 years of civil war to go through in order to change society." In a word, what remained in the statutes of the Communist League was: "The aim of the Communist League is to bring about the destruction of the old order of society and the downfall of the bourgeoisie—the intellectual, political and economic emancipation of the proletariat, and the communist revolution, using all the resources of propaganda and political struggle towards this goal."[14]

For that matter, it wasn't the phrase "Permanent Revolution" that was the proof of the concept, but the fact that in the constant search for revolutionary allies the vision of the revolutions to come was in no way changed. Thus— whether it was a question of the organization itself, i.e., the Communist League which was in fact disbanded in 1852 (and Marx kept referring to the party "in the eminent historical sense"); or whether it was the search for historic roots and with it, the projection of a revolutionary role for the peasantry (and Engels in that very same period wrote the magnificent work *The Peasant War in Germany*, which was published in the *NRZ Revue*)—Marx was concluding: "The whole matter in Germany will depend upon the possibility of supporting the proletarian revolution with a sort of second edition of the peasant war. Then the thing will be excellent" (Letter to Engels, 16 April 1856).

It should not need to be said that this philosophy of revolution, far from diminishing in the mid 1850s, was intensified with his original study of "Economics." But, since the fact that Marx was "closeted" in the British Museum has been interpreted as "a scientific period," it does need to be stressed that it is precisely his work on the *Grundrisse* and its relationship to what Marx called "epochs of social revolution" that gave him a new appreciation of the Asiatic mode of production and the Oriental society's resistance to British imperialism. In a word, the dialectics of economic development and the dialectics of liberation led to a further development of the concept of permanent revolution, world revolution, under no matter what name. The establishment of the First International, on the one hand, and the final structuring of *Capital* on the other hand, in the 1860s revealed, at one and the same time, not only the break with the concept of theory as a debate with theoreticians, and the development of the concept of theory as a history of class struggles, but a concept also of a new revolutionary force—Black.[15] The culmination of all these theories and activities was, of course, the historic appearance of the Paris Commune of 1871, and there, too, we saw—along with the great discovery of a historic form for working out the economic emancipation of the proletariat—a new force of revolution, women.

The greatest concretization of the philosophy of revolution, and its reconnection with the deep roots of the concept of permanent revolution first developed in the 1850 Address, came in the last years of Marx's life and the study of the prehistory, as well as the history, of humanity.

It is that March Address which is to this day still a point of debate. The first revisionists began not only attacking it but trying to attribute the thought to Blanqui rather than Marx.[16] Whether it was the Mensheviks' slanders, that the concept of permanent revolution was Blanquist; or revolutionaries like Trotsky, who had developed the theory of permanent revolution but one that was hardly rooted in Marx's; or even Lenin, who certainly did ground the whole theory of *State and Revolution* in Marx's *Critique of the Gotha Program*—none seemed to have made a special category of Marx's 1882 Preface to the Russian edition of the *Communist Manifesto*. There the concept was worked out anew as the relationship between advanced and underdeveloped countries, where the latter rather than the former might spark the revolution. No doubt part of this was due to the fact that the *Ethnological Notebooks* were unknown and so was the letter to Zasulich, all of which would have shown how deep were the roots of a seemingly wild statement for 1882. But we do have that advantage.

NOTES

1. All page citations in the text of this chapter are to Karl Marx, *Critique of the Gotha Program* (London: Lawrence & Wishart), an undated, revised translation of an earlier edition published by Martin Lawrence, London, in 1933. It was first published by the Cooperative Publishing Society of Foreign Workers in the U.S.S.R., and was reprinted by Lawrence and Wishart to correspond to the Russian edition of the Marx–Engels–Lenin Institute, Moscow, 1932. There are many editions of the *Critique of the Gotha Program*, but I am using this one because this edition was the first to have as appendix 4, the original "Draft Programme of the German Workers' Party," which Marx is criticizing; and because it also includes, as appendix 2, "Lenin on the *Critique*," from his notebook "Marxism on the State." Appendix 3 reprints "Extracts from Lenin's *The State and Revolution*," and appendix 1 includes the 1875 "Correspondence of Marx and Engels Concerning the Gotha Programme," as well as Engels's 1891 foreword and letter to Karl Kautsky on that foreword.
2. *Gesammelte Werke*, 1(2):417–21, March 1904.
3. See Marx's critique of Lassalle in his letter to Schweitzer, 13 October 1868.
4. See Engels's letter to Kautsky, 23 February 1891, reproduced in appendix 1 of *Critique*, pp. 58–63.
5. Letter to W. Bracke, 5 May 1875 in *Critique*, appendix 1, p. 48.
6. Included in *The Cologne Communist Trial*, trans. Rodney Livingstone (London: Lawrence & Wishart, 1971).
7. See also my discussion with Marcuse referred to in my "In Memoriam", *News & Letters*, August–September 1979, reprinted in *Newsletter of International Society for the Sociology of Knowledge*, ed. Kurt Wolff, December 1979.
8. See Lenin, *Collected Works*, vol. 13. In preface to his *12 Years*.
9. In a letter to Schott, 3 November 1877, Marx wrote: "Confidentially speaking, I in fact began 'Capital' in just the reverse (starting with the third, the historic part) of the order in which it is

presented to the public, except that the first volume, the one begun last, was immediately prepared for publication while the two others remained in that primitive state characteristic of all research at the outset."

10. See chapter 9.

11. See *Gesammelte Werke*, 1(2):130–41.

12. Marx–Engels, *Collected Works*, 3:156.

13. Marx–Engels, *Selected Works*, 1:177–78. Page citations in the text following are to this edition.

14. *The Cologne Communist Trial*, pp. 251–257.

15. Marx wrote in *Capital*, vol. 1: "Labor cannot emancipate itself in the white skin where in the black it is branded." This oft-quoted sentence, far from being rhetoric, was the actual reality *and* the perspective for overcoming that reality.

16. Hal Draper must be thanked for digging out and including in vol. 2 of his *Karl Marx's Theory of Revolution*, all of Marx's references to permanent revolution. He also exposed as total myth the claims of Nicolayevsky that neither the expression nor the concept of permanent revolution were Marx's, but Blanqui's. See esp. pp. 591–95. Unfortunately, Draper is good only at "excavation," and remains confined within his own narrow Trotskyist framework when it comes to analysis.

Afterword to Chapter XI

Trotsky's Theory of Permanent Revolution

The Revolutions of 1905 and 1917 have forever enshrined Trotsky's great historical role. The same two revolutions, however, tell a very contradictory story about the theory with which Trotsky's name will likewise always be connected, as he is the creator of the twentieth century version of the theory of the Permanent Revolution. The expression "contradictory story" is not a reference to the critiques of that theory. Rather, the phrase refers both to Trotsky's own claims and to the development of the theory as it related, on the one hand, to Lenin's analysis of and participation in these revolutions; and, on the other hand, to Rosa Luxemburg. It is these three revolutionary leaders who have put their unique stamp on history not only as past, but as present, and this is sure to extend into the future.

As we saw, the 1905–07 Revolution, as a turning point in Rosa Luxemburg's life, became crucial, not just in regard to her views, but to those of Lenin and Trotsky at the 1907 London Congress of the Russian Social-Democratic Labor Party, since it was the united Congress of Bolsheviks and Mensheviks that all tendencies attended; Leon Trotsky was there as an independent. In 1922, in reproducing his book, *1905*,[1] to be included in the Moscow publication of his *Collected Works*, Trotsky included among the appendices (1) an article entitled "Our Differences," in which he had attacked the Bolsheviks as well as the Mensheviks, and which had been published in Luxemburg's Polish journal in 1909; and (2) his main speech on "The Relationship of the Social-Democracy to Bourgeois Parties," delivered to the 1907 RSDLP London Congress. These two essays, especially the first, became the springboard for the Stalinist attack on Trotsky, which has never abated. In 1930–32, he likewise returned to both points again, this time in the

Appendices to nothing less important than his monumental *History of the Russian Revolution.*[2]

What was not included in the appendices to either work, although it was a continuation of the 1909 article on "Our Differences," was his 1910 article in the *Neue Zeit,* entitled "The Development of the Tendencies of Russian Social-Democracy."[3] It has not been translated into English, to my knowledge, to this day. Yet this is *the* undercurrent of all the disputes. Lenin's article "The Historical Meaning of the Internal Party Struggle in Russia"[4] was in answer to, and was a critique of, this 1910 article by Trotsky.

It poses the question at issue: What *is* theory? What is the relationship of theory to practice? And how do both relate to the objective situation? To get to that nub, it is necessary to begin at the beginning, with Trotsky's participation in the 1907 Congress, which revolved around the 1905 Revolution.

Keep in mind that this Congress occurred after Trotsky had reached the highest point of activity, the General Strike led by the St. Petersburg Soviet, which he headed. Not only was that a highpoint of revolution. It became the highest point of Trotsky's theoretical development, as he drew from it what "later" (as he put it in the 1922 Preface to *1905*) "received the name, 'the theory' of Permanent Revolution." Absolutely no one, including Lenin and Luxemburg, matched the leap in cognition which proclaimed that backward Russia, involved in a bourgeois revolution, could be the one not only to have the revolution before the advanced countries, but—in absolutist Russia—to reach for socialism "in an unbroken chain." That expression, "unbroken chain," which referred concretely to the 1905 Russian Revolution—and not the *concept* of permanent revolution which Marx had developed in his 1850 *Address to the Communist League*—was the issue in dispute.

Trotsky's original projection, which later became known as the theory of Permanent Revolution, was *not,* however, on the agenda of that 1907 Congress, because Lenin's proposal to discuss "The Present Moment of Revolution" was defeated by the Mensheviks—with Trotsky's help.[5]

When the Congress got down to discussing the one "general," i.e., theoretical, question—the relationship of Social-Democracy (as Marxism was then called) to bourgeois parties—and Luxemburg spoke quite eloquently on her concept of the Russian Revolution and its relation to practice—Trotsky said: "I can testify with pleasure that the point of view that Luxemburg developed in the name of the Polish delegation is very close to mine, which I have defended and continue to defend. If between us there is a difference, it's a difference of shading, and not of political direction. Our thought moves along one and the same materialistic analysis."[6]

But Luxemburg did not speak on the theory of permanent revolution and neither did Trotsky, as he continued with his own speech on the question of the relationship of Social-Democracy to bourgeois parties. He did develop his opposition to the Menshevik position, which had maintained that, since this was a bourgeois revolution, it "has to be carried out by the democratic bourgeoisie." Trotsky said:

> As materialists, we must first of all ask ourselves the question of the social foundation of a bourgeois democracy. In what classes, what strata of the population, can it find support? . . . It is true that we have enormous masses of revolutionary peasantry . . . the peasantry, however revolutionary it may be, is not capable of playing an independent, still less a leading political role . . . [p. 276].
>
> I have not had an answer to my central question, though I have asked it many times. You have no prognosis for revolution. Your policy lacks perspective [p. 283].

Trotsky did not present a resolution different from the one the Bolsheviks presented, though he tried to amend that one. Indeed, he reproduced his speech in the 1922 edition of *1905* precisely to show that he opposed the Mensheviks and voted with the Bolsheviks. Yet in the years immediately following the Congress, he wrote a whole series of articles attacking the Bolsheviks as well as the Mensheviks. The major one (and the one he was proud enough to reproduce in both the 1922 edition of *1905* and in the 1930 pamphlet, *The Permanent Revolution*, as well as in *The History of the Russian Revolution*) was the article that had been published in Luxemburg's paper in 1909. Here is how it concluded: " . . . while the anti-revolutionary aspects of Menshevism have already become fully apparent, those of Bolshevism are likely to become a serious threat only in the event of victory" (p. 316).

As if that were not a fantastic enough statement to make in 1909 in "predicting" the future revolution, Trotsky in 1922—that is to say, nearly five years after Lenin had led the greatest revolution in history—superciliously footnoted the 1909 statement as follows:

> *Note to the present edition.* This threat, as we know, never materialized because, under the leadership of Comrade Lenin, the Bolsheviks changed their policy line on this most important matter (not without inner struggle) in the spring of 1917, that is, before the seizure of power (Author) [p. 317, n.].

Trotsky evidently did not think it supercilious because the aim he had in mind, as is clear from the 1922 Preface to the whole volume, was to reiterate sole authorship of the theory of permanent revolution and claim it as the reason for the success of the 1917 Revolution. Here is what he wrote:

> It was precisely in the interval between 9 January and the October strike of 1905 that those views which came to be called the theory of "permanent revolution" were formed in the author's mind. This rather high-flown expression defines the thought that the Russian Revolution, although directly concerned with bourgeois aims, could not stop short at those aims . . . Despite an interruption of 12 years, this analysis has been entirely confirmed [pp. vi-vii].

The point is what *did* happen in those intervening twelve years? As we already saw, in 1907 Trotsky did not wish to discuss the nature of the present moment of the revolution. In 1909 he published the above cited criticism of Mensheviks *and* Bolsheviks. In 1910 he followed it up with the article in *Neue Zeit* (referred to at the beginning of this Afterword), where the first point Trotsky made was, "Theory cannot replace experience."[7]

As if 1905 meant, not the greatest experience ever—be it for him or the Russian proletariat and peasantry, as well as for the world working class—but only factional disputes between "Economists," Mensheviks and Bolsheviks; as if Russian Marxism arose merely out of fighting a "primitive ideological viewpoint" (i.e., the Narodniks), Trotsky reached the following conclusion regarding those factional disputes between Mensheviks and Bolsheviks: the differences arise out of "the process of adaptation of Marxist intellectuals to the class struggle, i.e., the political immaturity of the Russian proletariat." What such argumentation betrays, I would say, is that it was not only the "nature" of the peasantry about which Leon Trotsky had a low opinion; it was also the proletariat, which he considered backward—"politically immature." Trotsky's logic, however, led him to accuse the Bolsheviks, Lenin especially, of "ideological fetishism," "sectarianism," and "intellectual individualism."

Far from returning to his theory of Permanent Revolution, much less to the Luxemburgian view of the advanced nature of the Russian proletariat, Trotsky veered off to psychology, talk against "lack of morality" and "piracy" (a reference to expropriations), not to mention "sexual anarchy."

It all sounds as if somebody were writing a farcical caricature about Trotsky. But unfortunately, it is not a caricature. It is not somebody writing about Trotsky. It is Trotsky's own writing only a few years after he had projected nothing short of a theory of Permanent Revolution; after he had separated from both Mensheviks and Bolsheviks and declared he was out to unite all factions into one Social-Democratic Party. And that was, indeed, the grand climax of the 1910 article: "What is needed is a party united and capable of action." Further separating both action and organization from theory, not to mention reducing the concept of organization to "apparatus," he added that, of course, to achieve unity of disparate tendencies: "what is needed is the re-organization of the Party apparatus."

Those who say—since that was the period climaxed by the infamous "August Bloc" which Trotsky acknowledged was a "fundamental error," and since he accepted Lenin's characterization of him as "conciliationist"—that Trotsky's joining of the Bolshevik Party, like his revolutionary activities in 1917, "eliminated all differences," *show they understand nothing of either theory or organization*. The whole point of Marxist theory, and organization to correspond, is that they are inseparable from the goal—the revolutionary road to a classless society. If one creates a theory of revolution but thinks a

"Party" can reach the end of that long trek without that theory, he is, indeed, underestimating what theory is. That is the only reason Trotsky could have written that "theory cannot replace experience." It is the only reason he could have failed to put his theory on the 1907 Agenda and refused to discuss *any* theory of the "nature of the present moment of revolution"—and could then proceed to try to unite all tendencies, not by forging a theoretical basis for a revolutionary party, but by proposing the "re-organization of the Party apparatus."

It is not true that Lenin criticized Trotsky only for organizational conciliationism. Quite the contrary. He took issue with the specific 1910 article because of Trotsky's "utter lack of theoretical understanding," and because Trotsky was arguing not about the objective nature of the Russian Revolution, but subjectively reducing even his own "philosophy of history" to "the struggle for influence over the politically immature proletariat."[8]

The point here is not so much whether Lenin or Trotsky was right in this or that dispute. Rather, the amazing fact is that Trotsky, the creator of the theory of Permanent Revolution, was practicing not just organizational but *theoretical* conciliationism—*and the theoretical conciliationism was not only toward "others" but toward himself.* In a word, not a single serious point Trotsky made in *1905* was either developed or related to anything he did in those twelve long years between 1905 and 1917.

How, then, did the question of Trotsky's theory mature when, finally, in 1917 a proletarian revolution did indeed succeed and was led by Lenin and himself? The November 1917 Revolution remains the highest point of proletarian revolution and is magnificently retold in Trotsky's *The History of the Russian Revolution*. This book is a landmark of historical writing by one who was both a leader of a revolution and an historian of it. All the Appendices in the history of 1917 are expressions of Trotsky's view of his theory of the Permanent Revolution. That is natural enough. What is not natural is some rewriting of history in the Appendices, especially as it related to Lenin and *the* theoretic division between the two on Lenin's slogan, "the revolutionary-democratic dictatorship of the proletariat and the peasantry," which is almost always abbreviated by Trotsky as just "bourgeois-democratic dictatorship of the proletariat and peasantry." To prove how that kept the Bolsheviks from understanding the course of 1917, he shows how hard Lenin had to work "to rearm the Party."

That, in part, is true. The whole truth, however, is that it was not the theory of Permanent Revolution that "rearmed the Party," but Lenin's famous April Thesis. To try to claim that the April Thesis somehow implied Lenin's conversion to Trotsky's theory is to skip entirely Lenin's philosophic-dialectic reorganization which, far from bringing him closer to Trotsky, led to the most fundamental dispute between them over Lenin's slogans—

"Defeat of your own country is the lesser evil" and *"Transform the imperialist war into civil war."* *It was not Leon Trotsky's theory of Permanent Revolution, but the dialectics of revolution that led Lenin both to the April Thesis and to the writing of* State and Revolution, *as well as to putting conquest of power on the agenda of the Bolshevik Party. And it was then that Trotsky joined Lenin, not Lenin Trotsky.*

In *The History of the Russian Revolution* there is, finally, a quite serious development of the theory of Permanent Revolution. As against *1905*, which has not a single word to say of Marx's 1850 Address—which first projected the slogan "revolution in permanence" for the German proletariat who had fought and lost the 1848 revolution—in the 1932 Appendix to the *History*, Trotsky tries to root his theory in Marx's. Trotsky introduces a concretization of his theory by his analysis of the law of combined and uneven development, which relates to Marx's statement about the industrially more advanced country's showing the less developed country the image of its own future. Methodologically, Trotsky shows that Marx there had in mind, not the world economy, but the single country as a type. He proceeds to show the differences between England's industrial development's revealing the future of France "but not in the least of Russia and not of India." And he concludes that because the Mensheviks "took this conditional statement of Marx unconditionally," they refused to see where the Russian Revolution was moving and ended up agreeing with the liberals.

On the other hand, another statement of Marx, that no social formation disappears until all productive forces have developed, has a different point of departure. This time Marx is talking not about individual countries, but about "the sequence of universal social structures (slavery, medievalism, capitalism)." The Mensheviks, however, applied this to a single country, thus acting as if productive forces develop in a vacuum. By disregarding both the class struggle and the world context, they, instead of confronting the actual Russian capitalists, produced nothing but "abstract economic possibilities."[9]

Such is the analysis of Menshevism. But what about what Trotsky called "ideological restoration"? (p. 381). Here once again we see the inner contradiction within Trotsky. By shifting the debate to the context of the post-Lenin Stalinist slanders against Trotsky, and to Stalin's revisionist concept which confined the world revolution to the nationalistic "socialism in one country," the "ideological restoration," insofar as Lenin's position in 1905 and 1917 is concerned, gets quite lost. He quotes (for the first time, I should add, as he had disregarded the writings when they were written in 1905)[10] some very beautiful passages from Lenin which referred to the "beginning of a decisive struggle for the socialist revolution . . . it will be the beginning of the real struggle of the proletariat." And he also quotes Lenin's statement of September 1905: "From the democratic revolution we will immediately begin to pass over, and in the exact measure of our strength, the strength of a conscious and organized proletariat, we will begin to pass over to the socialist revolution. We stand for a continuous revolution. We will not stop half-way" (p. 382). This was written *before* Trotsky's *1905* (published in 1906) and *before* the November 1905 Revolution itself.

But Trotsky quotes Lenin not so much to prove that the theories of the two, irrespective of the slogans, were not as far apart as factional debates made them appear, but in order to maintain that the difference that compelled a "rearming" would have been unnecessary had Lenin himself been armed with Trotsky's theory! Thus, Trotsky explains away the *affinity* of ideas by quoting another passage from Lenin on another occasion, when Lenin wrote of the fact that revolutionists have the right "to dream," as if Lenin had said it only as "a dream."

Since Lenin's article did relate to the fact that the workers in Europe would also rise up "and show us 'how it is done'," Trotsky correctly extends this international aspect to his whole struggle against Stalin's "theory" of socialism in one country vs the Marxian concept of world revolution. But, though the Appendix is, as a totality, directed against Stalin, and profoundly presents Lenin's internationalism, Trotsky does a great deal less justice to Lenin's position on the peasantry, very nearly attributing to Lenin his own view that the peasantry is "an unreliable and treacherous ally" (p. 385).[11]

Above all, what stands out is Trotsky's failure to grasp the totally new theoretical point of departure on that question which Lenin introduced in his "Theses on the National and Colonial Questions," presented at the Second Congress of the Communist International. Trotsky's reference to that thesis is limited to the context of his fight with Stalin—internationalism vs nationalism—and not *the* pivotal point of the revolutionary live force of the peasantry, of the national question, *and* of the perspective that, since world revolution has not come by way of Berlin, "then perhaps" it can come by way of Peking. That new point of departure in theory was not grasped, much less developed, by Trotsky.

His attempt, retrospectively, to credit the 1917 Revolution's success to his theory of Permanent Revolution was not, of course, at the bottom of the Trotsky–Stalin struggle that ensued after the death of Lenin. No. More objective causes are at the root—the new stage of world capitalism, reflected in Stalin's revisionist capitulation to the capitalistic impulse as he moved in the opposite direction of the workers' demands. But, of course, Stalin took advantage of the specific dispute over the appendices to the 1922 edition of Trotsky's *1905*, as he began his usurpation of the mantle of Lenin.

Though that is beyond the shadow of a doubt, there is also no way to evade grappling with what Lenin called Trotsky's "lack of theoretical understanding" in the period of 1907–12. It is that which led Lenin to characterize Trotsky as "conciliationist" in theory as well as in organization. Indeed, because the conciliationism was theoretical, it led Trotsky to a rather checkered organizational alliance with the Mensheviks, and at the same time made it nearly impossible for him to develop even his own theory.

The nodal points of a serious revolutionary theory are rooted in self-activity of the masses who make the revolution, and the leadership's singling out of those live forces of revolution, not only as Force, but as Reason. And that holds true when facing either a concrete revolution or a *counter*-revolution. The 1917 Revolution was certainly a spontaneous outpouring. Its success can hardly be attributed to a single factor. Lenin's contribution was the greatest, but that doesn't mean that it was spotless—least of all in his concept of the party-to-lead, and especially so in the elitist way it was first spelled out in 1902.* That Trotsky bowed to *that* in 1917 only further weighted down Trotsky's own great contribution to that revolution.

Whether the theory of Permanent Revolution was confirmed or unconfirmed in 1917 is not proven, as we showed before, by the mere repetition of the theory of 1905–06 in 1922. The real point at issue by the time of the writing of *The History of the Russian Revolution* in the early 1930s was whether one has a theory to meet the challenge of the new stage of world capitalism—the Great Depression which brought on state-capitalism as a world phenomenon. Although Trotsky by the mid-1930s had fought Stalin's bureaucracy for a solid decade, had written *The Revolution Betrayed*, he denied the transformation of Russia into a state-capitalist society.[12] And he ended up tailending Stalinism, calling for the defense of Russia as a "workers' state, though degenerate" at the very time when the infamous Hitler–Stalin Pact had given the green light to World War II.

Which is why it becomes imperative to see the two revolutions, not weighted down with factional disputes, much less slanted to theoretical conclusions, but with eyes of today turned to future revolutions. Trotsky himself cited that reason for restating his 1905 position. The implication was that had Russia followed Trotsky's theory it would have saved the Chinese Revolution of 1925–27 as against Stalin's nationalistic "socialism in one country," which brought about its defeat. Elsewhere[13] I have analyzed this claim in detail. Here all that is needed is to point to the gulf between that and the reality of Mao's time, when the Chinese Revolution was brought to a successful finish. Nothing was further removed from reality than the last words we have from Trotsky in

---

*Contrast what Lenin wrote in 1902 to what he wrote once the 1905 Revolution broke out: "The working class is instinctively, spontaneously Social-Democratic, and more than ten years of work put in by Social-Democracy has done a great deal to transform this spontaneity into consciousness" ("Reorganization of the Party," in *Collected Works*, 10:32). See also Lenin's "Preface to the Collection *12 Years*," in which he wrote that "*What Is To Be Done?* is a *summary* of *Iskra* tactics and *Iskra* organizational policy in 1901 and 1902. Precisely a '*summary*,' no more and no less . . . Nor at the Second Congress did I have any intention of elevating my own formulations, as given in *What Is To Be Done?*, to 'programmatic' level, constituting special principles . . . " (pp. in ibid., 13:102, 107).

restating the theory of Permanent Revolution in his work on *Stalin*: "I have repeatedly returned to the development and the grounding theory of the permanent revolution . . . the peasantry is utterly incapable of an *independent political role*."[14]

NOTES

1. Leon Trotsky, *1905* (New York and London: Vintage Books; Penguin Press, 1972). Page citations in the text are to this edition. Trotsky had reproduced one of his speeches at the 1907 Congress, as well as that part of the 1922 Preface to *1905* which is under dispute, in *The Permanent Revolution* (New York: Pioneer Pub., 1931).

2. See vol. 1, appendix 2 to "Rearming of the Party"; vol. 3, appendix 2, "Socialism in a Separate Country?"; and vol. 3, appendix 3, "Historic References on the Theory of 'Permanent Revolution,'" in Leon Trotsky, *The History of the Russian Revolution*.

3. Leon Trotsky, "Die Entwicklungstendenzen der russischen Sozialdemokratie" *Neue Zeit*, 9 September 1910.

4. V. I. Lenin, *Selected Works* (New York: International Pub., 1943), 3:499–518.

5. See chap. I.

6. This paragraph was omitted when Trotsky reproduced his speech as an appendix to his *1905* in the 1922 edition.

7. See n. 3.

8. Lenin, *Selected Works*, 3:515.

9. Trotsky, *History of the Russian Revolution*, 3:378. Following page citations in the text are to this work.

10. A much more consistent and thorough series of quotations from all of Lenin's writings of 1905–07 is reproduced by the Menshevik, Solomon M. Schwartz in his *The Russian Revolution of 1905* (Chicago: Univ. of Chicago Press, 1967). Of course he has his ulterior motives—to try to prove how allegedly "dictatorial" both Lenin and Trotsky were. The only way to see what Lenin did stand for is to read his own *Collected Works*—and there are no less than six volumes (vol. 8–13) devoted to the years 1905 07.

11. See also my analysis of Trotsky on the peasantry in "Leon Trotsky as Man and Theoretician," *Studies in Comparative Communism*, Spring/Summer 1977.

12. See part 5, sec. 1 ("Russian State Capitalism vs. Workers' Revolt"; "Stalin"; "The Beginning of the End of Russian Totalitarianism") in my *Marxism and Freedom*.

13. See chap. 4, "Leon Trotsky as Theoretician," and chap. 5, "The Thought of Mao Tse-tung," of my *Philosophy and Revolution*. See also my essay, "Post-Mao China: What Now?" in *New Essays* (Detroit: News & Letters, 1977).

14. Leon Trotsky, *Stalin: An Appraisal of the Man and His Influence* (New York: Harper & Row, 1941), p. 425.

XII

The Last Writings of Marx
Point a Trail to the 1980s

> *I love all men who* dive. *Any fish can swim near the surface, but it takes a great whale to go downstairs five miles or more; and if he don't attain the bottom, why all the lead in Galena can't fashion the plummet that will. I'm not talking about Mr. Emerson now— but that whole corps of thought-divers that have been diving and coming up again with bloodshot eyes since the world began.*
> *Herman Melville, Letter of 3 March 1849*

> *Everything depends upon the historical background in which it finds itself. . . . If the revolution takes place at the right time, if it concentrates all its forces to ensure the free development of the village commune, the latter will soon emerge as the regenerative force in Russian society and as something superior to those countries which are still enslaved by the capitalist regime.*
> *Karl Marx, March 1881*
> *First Draft of Letter to Vera Zasulich*

1. POST-MARX MARXISTS, BEGINNING WITH FREDERICK ENGELS

It has become necessary to draw together all the threads of Marx's life and thought, as well as the threads of this work. A Great Divide in Marxism occurred when the outbreak of World War I brought with it the collapse of the Second International. Since the counter-revolution came *from within* established Marxism, revolutionaries had to do more than shout "betrayal." Or so Lenin thought, and felt compelled to return to the origins of Marx in Hegel. He discovered that Marx's never-ending encounter with the Hegelian dialectic held the key, not only to the mid-nineteenth century but to the twentieth century, and involved both the dialectics of revolution and the dialectics of thought.

Lenin held that Plekhanov, who had been considered "the father of Russian Marxism," comprehended neither Marx's philosophy of revolution, nor the Hegelian dialectic. Lenin was speaking to himself as he was excerpting and commenting on Hegel's *Science of Logic* and wrote: "Plekhanov criticises Kantianism . . . more from the vulgar materialistic than the dialectic materialistic point of view . . . "[1]

Although Lenin was the lone revolutionary Marxist who did turn to a study of Hegel in 1914, the fact that he nevertheless kept his profound Abstract of Hegel's *Science of Logic* to himself bears out the truth of the subordinate position of philosophy in established Marxism. It also points to the fact that Lenin himself was not ready to openly reveal his break with his old mechanistic position in *Materialism and Empirio-Criticism* and thus blunted creative new points of departure for future generations.

Luxemburg felt no such compulsion for a philosophic reorganization of herself. Nor did she question what any other post-Marx Marxists had done in the sphere of philosophic continuity with Marxian dialectics, other than praising what Mehring had done in bringing out what she thought were all the early economic–philosophic essays left by Marx. Nor did she question post-Marx Marxists's lack of achievements in the economic sphere, except for when she disagreed with Marx himself on the central question of accumulation in volume 2 of *Capital*, at which point she questioned what Engels "had made out of" the manuscripts left by Marx for that volume.

It took a series of revolutions, from the 1917 Russian Revolution to the 1949 Chinese Revolution, to lay the ground for digging out, first, the rich early heritage of Marx (the now famous *1844 Economic–Philosophic Manuscripts*) that marked not only a crucial event in the history of Marxist studies, but a new view of Marx's total philosophy. Later, the publication of the 1857 "Economics Notebooks" (the first draft of *Capital*, posthumously entitled the *Grundrisse*) revealed that economics and philosophy were so integrated that it became impossible any longer to claim that it was only the young Marx who was "a philosopher." The *Grundrisse*, by disclosing Marx's analysis of pre-capitalist economic forms, especially "the Asiatic mode of production," made it crystal clear, at one and the same time, how wrong it was to consider that Marx had been concerned only with the West, and how "incomplete" was Marx's greatest work, *Capital*, when compared to the six volumes he had projected for it. Finally, it was only after the birth of a new Third World, as well as the rise of a totally new Women's Liberation Movement, that the transcript of the *Ethnological Notebooks*, Marx's last writings, was published. All of these works were unknown to Luxemburg, Lenin, Trotsky, and the leaders of the Russian and German Revolutions: ours is the first age to have Marx's *oeuvres* as a totality.

The leaders of the Russian Revolution were the first to seriously begin unearthing the entire heritage of Marx—unearth, but not fully publish. With the beheading of the German Revolution, the loathing for the Second International and passion to extend the Russian Revolution to Germany was boundless. With his epoch-making book, *History and Class Consciousness*, Lukacs stressed the indispensability of the Hegelian dialectic for revolutionary Marxian thought, and, very nearly simultaneously, Karl Korsch raised the same subject in his work, *Marxism and Philosophy*. This philosophic probing, however, soon stopped. By the time the independent Frankfurt School arose in the late 1930s and early 1940s, dialectics was discussed more as an academic discipline than what Marcuse was attempting to work out—its relationship to actual revolution—in his *Reason and Revolution*.[2]

The pivotal question that still remains unanswered is why so much balderdash has been spread about the last decade of Marx's life, not only by Stalinists but by revolutionaries. To grasp the reason why, it becomes necessary to clear away what post-Marx Marxists said, in order to get to what Marx said and did. It is true that we would not have had volumes 2 and 3 of *Capital* were it not for Engels. It is also true, unfortunately, that just as he assumed that his *Origin of the Family* was a "bequest" from Marx, so he assumed that Marx would have deeded his documents to the German Social-Democracy as "the heirs," which is what Engels did with both Marx's and his own documents. The "heirs," however, not only never attempted to publish the collected works of Marx, but heavily edited what they did publish.[3]

What is most shocking is the attitude of scholars, revolutionaries of the caliber of Mehring in Germany and Ryazanov in Russia, who, instead of diving into the latest unpublished Notebooks of Marx, felt free to offer their criticism before they had studied them.

At the head of the Marx-Engels Institute stood the well-known scholar, David Ryazanov. He announced a plan to publish two parallel series of documents: one, the "finished" works of Marx; the other, fragmented manuscripts. But Ryazanov—who did so much to bring out Marx's early works, creating an entirely new view of Marx as a total person and not just an economist—had no such appreciation for the works of Marx's last decade. No doubt, Ryazanov was influenced in part by Mehring, who, in his biography of Marx, called the last decade "a slow death."[4] But by what right did Ryazanov allow himself the following quite gratuitous commentary when he announced the rich heritage, the *Ethnological Notebooks* especially, to the Socialist Academy?

> This methodical and systematic way of working Marx retained until the end of his life. If in 1881–82 he lost his ability for intensive, independent intellectual creation he nevertheless never lost the ability for research. Sometimes, in reconsidering these Notebooks, the question arises: Why did he waste so much time on this systematic, fundamental summary, or expend so much labor as he spent as late as the year 1881, on one basic book on geology, summarizing it chapter by chapter. In the 63rd year of his life—that is inexcusable pedantry.

Here is another example: he received, in 1878, a copy of Morgan's work. On 98 pages of his very miniscule handwriting (you should know that a single page of his is the equivalent of a minimum of 2.2 pages of print) he makes a detailed summary of Morgan. In such manner does the old Marx work.[5]

The superficial attitude Ryazanov displayed toward the epoch-making Notebooks which rounded out Marx's life's work, just four months before his death, stands in the sharpest of contrasts not only to the great number of unpublished manuscripts, but to the *historic* continent of thought and revolution which Marx had discovered and for which Marxism was supposed to stand. Ryazanov himself said the unpublished manuscripts were so massive that "to sort out all this heritage" would take thirty to forty years, and it was impossible for any single person to do it—but evidently not impossible for that single person, Ryazanov, to reach conclusions . . . even though he had not read the work. He did stress that he had found no less than fifty notebooks, reaching as far back as the notebooks for Marx's doctoral thesis, 1840–41, those for 1843–45, and others written during the decades of the 1850s, 1860s, 1870s.

That by no means exhausted the heritage, as there were three huge volumes just on the question of a *day-to-day* history of the 1857 crisis, compiled at the time Marx was writing what we now know as the *Grundrisse*, and which in itself totaled some nine hundred pages. Ryazanov calls attention to a four-volume compilation that Marx made—a chronological survey of the world up to the mid-seventeenth century. Ryazanov also continued to emphasize that the fifty notebooks, which comprised some thirty thousand pages, were written in Marx's miniscule handwriting, and therefore printed pages would be more than double that number. Furthermore, there were notebooks on mathematics which Ryazanov confessed Fritz Adler had given him as far back as nine years before, and that just "recently" he had received another one from Bernstein. Above all—and that's what the cornerstone of the whole report was about—were the 1881–82 Notebooks on anthropology, plus one substantial work on geology. It was at that point that Ryazanov interjected his gratuitous commentary about "inexcusable pedantry."

Intellectuals, who in no way measure up to the rare discoverer of a new continent of thought which is also one of revolution, seem to find irresistible the temptation to bring the bigger-than-life founder down to their size.

Here is what had occurred directly after Marx's death: Engels too was overwhelmed by the vast amount of Marx's writing that he knew nothing about—from their first meeting in Paris in 1844 to the very last months of Marx's life. What Engels did know was the uncompleted *Capital* which, Marx had told his daughter Eleanor, Engels was "to make something out of."

What came first from Engels's pen was *The Origin of the Family*, not volume 2 of *Capital*, much less volume 3.

Neither of the books had priority over what Engels considered to be Marx's "bequest" when he found Marx's notebooks on Morgan and realized that Marx had wanted him to read *Ancient Society* several years earlier. Here is how Engels expressed that "bequest" in his Preface to *The Origin of the Family*: "No less a man than Karl Marx had made it one of his future tasks to present the results of Morgan's researches in the light of the conclusions of his own—within certain limits I may say our—materialist examination of history, and thus to make clear their full significance."

It's very doubtful that all Marx meant to do was to expound on the "full significance" of Morgan's work. But at that time, and unfortunately ever since, it was assumed that Engels reproduced, more or less in full, Marx's "Abstract." That Engels thought he was doing just that can be seen also from his 30 August 1883 letter to Bebel, who had been amazed that Engels was unacquainted* with so much of Marx's works: "You ask: How could it happen that I was not even aware of the condition in which Marx left his work? Very simple: if I knew about it I would have given him no rest day or night until the book would be completed and published. Marx knew about this more than anyone else; but he knew also that at the worst, as is true right now, I would publish the manuscripts totally in his spirit, and it's about this that he talked to Tussy."

To what extent is Marx's "spirit" reflected in Engels's own work, *The Origin of the Family*, which he had likewise considered a "bequest" of Marx? Now that we finally have a transcription of Marx's *Ethnological Notebooks*, we can see for ourselves. It is not a quantitative question, though that is vast in itself: Marx's excerpts from and commentaries on Morgan's work alone numbered no less than ninety-eight pages, whereas Engels's quotation from the Abstract numbered but a few paragraphs. Nor is it a matter that Engels ignored other anthropological works that had been summarized: Maine, Phear, and Lubbock. No, the serious, overwhelming, if not bewildering, fact leaps out in the sharp differences between Engels's *The Origin of the Family* and Marx's Notebooks, whether these relate to primitive communism, the Man/Woman relationship, or, for that matter, the attitude to Darwin.[6]

---

*For that matter, we must not forget, Engels first saw volume 1 of *Capital* when it was already in galley form, and some of the questions he then posed show how very far away he was from Marx's profound discoveries.

2. THE UNKNOWN ETHNOLOGICAL NOTEBOOKS, THE UNREAD DRAFTS OF THE LETTER TO ZASULICH, AS WELL AS THE UNDIGESTED 1882 PREFACE TO RUSSIAN EDITION OF THE COMMUNIST MANIFESTO*

Marx's historic originality in internalizing new data, whether in anthropology or in "pure" science, was a never-ending confrontation with what Marx called "history and its process."[7] That was concrete. That was ever-changing. And that ever-changing concrete was inexorably bound to the universal, because, precisely because, the determining concrete was the ever-developing Subject—self-developing men and women.

Nothing less than the vital question of transitions is at stake in the differences between Marx's and Engels's views. Marx was showing that it is *during* the transition period that you see the duality emerging to reveal the beginnings of antagonisms, whereas Engels always seems to have antagonisms only at the end, as if class society came in very nearly full blown *after* the communal form was destroyed and private property was established. *Moreover, for Marx the dialectical development from one stage to another is related to new revolutionary upsurges, whereas Engels sees it as a unilateral progression.*[§]

In the 1850s, for example, what inspired Marx to return to the study of pre-capitalist formations and gave him a new appreciation of ancient society and its craftsmen was the Taiping Revolution. † It opened so many new doors on "history and its process," that materialistically a stage of production wasn't just a stage of production—be it the Western or the Asiatic mode of production—but a question of revolutionary relations. Whether he was studying the communal form or the despotic form of property, to Marx the development of the relationship of the individual to society and to the state was crucial. It was no accident, on the other hand, that Engels, who certainly agreed with Marx's analysis of the Asiatic mode of production, nevertheless skipped over the question of the Oriental commune in *his* analysis of primitive communism in *The Origin of the Family*.

Marx, on the contrary, showed that the elements of oppression in general, and of woman in particular, arose from *within* primitive communism, and not only related to change from "matriarchy," but began with the establishment of

*Marx's *Ethnological Notebooks* include his studies of Lewis Henry Morgan's *Ancient Society*, John Budd Phear's *The Aryan Village*, Henry Sumner Maine's *Lectures on the Early History of Institutions*, and John Lubbock's *The Origin of Civilization*. The Notebooks were written by Marx in English, but include many phrases and full sentences in French, German, Latin and Greek. We still do not have a translation.

The 1970 edition of the three-volume *Selected Works* finally published the first draft of Marx's reply to Zasulich. Excerpts from the second and third drafts of Marx's answer to Vera Zasulich are included in *Pre-Capitalist Economic Formations*. All four drafts, including the last which was sent to her, are included in full in *Arkhiv Marksa y Engelsa*, volume 1. They are also included in the *Sochineniya (Collected Works)*, volume 19. Actually, Marx wrote all the drafts in French.

† It is not clear whether Engels knew Marx's *Grundrisse*, but he did know the articles in *The New York Tribune* on the Taiping Revolution.

§ See "New Thoughts on *Rosa Luxemburg, Women's Liberation, and Marx's Philosophy of Revolution*," p. xxxvi.—Ed.

ranks—relationship of chief to mass—and the economic interests that accompanied it. Indeed, in volume 3 of *Capital*, as Marx probed "The economic conditions at the basis" of class "individuality" in his chapter "Genesis of Capitalist Ground Rent," you can see the actual dialectical foundation for his stress, in the Notebooks on anthropology, on property as the material base for changing social relations. He was not using Morgan's phrase, "career of property," as if it were a synonym for Historical Materialism.

Engels's uncritical acclaim of Morgan notwithstanding, Morgan did not "discover afresh in America the materialist conception of history discovered by Marx 40 years ago."[8]

Far from considering Morgan a fellow "historical materialist," Marx emphasized in his draft letter to Zasulich[9] that Morgan, who "can certainly not be suspected of revolutionary tendencies and whose works are supported by the Washington government," nevertheless spoke of the "archaic system" as "higher" than capitalism.

Marx acknowledged Morgan's great contribution on the theory of the gens and its early egalitarian society, but he certainly did not tie that theory to the precedence of matriarchy over patriarchy alone, as did Engels in the Preface to the Fourth Edition of *The Origin of the Family* in 1891. "This rediscovery of the primitive matriarchal gens as the earlier stage of the patriarchal gens of civilized peoples has the same importance for anthropology as Darwin's theory of evolution has for biology and Marx's theory of surplus value for political economy." Marx rejected biologism in Morgan as he had in Darwin.

Marx did not take issue with Morgan's findings about the Iroquois society and especially singled out the role of women in it. But he did not stop there. He called attention to other societies and other analyses, and brought new illumination to the writings of Plutarch with his own commentaries in his *Ethnological Notebooks*: "The expression by Plutarch, that the lowly and poor readily followed the bidding of Theseus and the statement from Aristotle cited by him, that Theseus 'was inclined toward the people' appear, however, despite Morgan, to indicate that the chiefs of the gentes etc. already entered into conflict of interest with the mass of the gentes, which is inevitably connected with the monogamous family through private property in houses, lands, herds" (p. 21).

Marx demonstrated that, long before the dissolution of the primitive commune, there emerged the question of ranks *within* the egalitarian commune. It was the beginning of a transformation into opposite—gens into caste. That is to say, within the egalitarian communal form arose the elements of its opposite—caste, aristocracy, and different material interests. Moreover, these were not successive stages, but *co-extensive* with the communal form. As Marx scathingly observed of the period when they began changing the names of the children to assure paternal rather than maternal rights (a paragraph Engels did reproduce in *The Origin of the Family*): "Innate casuistry! To change things by changing their names! And to find loopholes for violating tradition while maintaining tradition, when direct interest supplied sufficient impulse."

In a word, though Marx surely connects the monogamous family with private property, what is pivotal to him is the antagonistic relationship between the chief and the masses.

That is why Marx, while singling out how much more freedom the Iroquois women enjoyed than did women in "civilized" societies, also pointed to the limitations of freedom among them: *"The women allowed to express their wishes and opinions through an orator of their own selection. Decision* given by the Council. *Unanimity was a fundamental law of its action among the Iroquois. Military questions* usually left to the *action of the voluntary principle."*[10]

Moreover, and this is the critical point, the Russians took liberties when, in 1941, they did translate the Marx text on Morgan. Engels, naturally, cannot be blamed for this mis-translation. Nor can the Russians excuse themselves on the basis that the inspiration for using the words "private" and "hallowed" came from Engels. Here is how Marx excerpted a part of Morgan:

> When *field culture* bewiesen hatte, dass d(ie) *ganze Oberfläche der Erde could be made the subject of property owned by individuals in severalty* u(nd) (das) *Familienhaupt* became *the natural center of accumulation,* the *new property career of mankind* inaugurated, fully done *before the close of the Later Period of Barbarism,* übte einen grossen *Einfluss auf (the) human mind,* rief *new elements of character* wach . . .

Here is the original Morgan excerpt:

> When field agriculture had demonstrated that the whole surface of the earth could be made the subject of property owned by individuals in severalty, and it was found that the head of the family became the natural center of accumulation, the new property career of mankind was inaugurated. It was fully done before the close of the Later Period of barbarism. A little reflection must convince any one of the powerful influence property would now begin to exercise upon the human mind, and of the great awakening of new elements of character it was calculated to produce . . .

Here is how the Russian translation reads:

> When field agriculture had demonstrated that the whole surface of the earth could be made the *object* of property of separate individuals and the head of the family became the natural center of accumulation of wealth, mankind entered the new *hallowed path of private property.* It was already fully done before the later period of barbarism came to an end. *Private* property exercised a powerful influence on the human mind, awakening new elements of character . . . [12]

Now the Russians have very concrete *class* (state-capitalist class) interests that inspire them to translate "the career of property" as "private property" and repeat the word twice. But why should independent Marxists who are not statist-Communists likewise narrow the subject to collective-vs-private property, when Marx's point is that the "property career," i.e., accumulation of wealth, is that which contains the antagonisms of the development of patriarchy and later class divisions?

If we are to grapple with that seriously, we must, first, appreciate the totality of Marx's philosophy of revolution sufficiently to want to unearth what Marx had said from under all the twaddle that was attributed to him from the time of his death in 1883.

How Marx himself, as world revolutionary, "applied" what he was researching to what he was a participant in and a theorist of (whether in volume 2 or volume 3 of *Capital* on which he was working), can be seen in the letters he was writing to Russian revolutionaries and independent scholars. The first three draft letters to Vera Zasulich (which we will take up in more detail later) were never sent, but there is no mistaking what it is Marx was working out there. It is confirmed by the clearly written and well known—but never digested—Preface to the Russian edition of the *Communist Manifesto*, where he projected the possibility that revolution in backward countries might precede revolution in the West. What he was stressing in those drafts of his answer to Zasulich was, first, the historic determinant; second, the *theoretic* concept which would result *if* that historic determinant were related to a capitalist *world in crisis*, since it is this which creates favorable conditions for transforming primitive communism into a modern collective society: "In order to save the Russian commune there must be a Russian Revolution." In a word, revolution is the indispensable, whether one has to go through capitalism, or can go to the new society "directly" from the commune.

Marx died before he could write up his Notebooks on anthropology either as a separate work or as part of volume 3 of *Capital*. There is no way for us to know what Marx intended to do with this intensive study, much less the concrete manner in which he would have dialectically related the external to the internal factors in the dissolution of the primitive commune. What is clear, however, is that the decline of the primitive commune was not due just to external factors, nor due only to "*the world historic defeat of the female sex.*" That was Engels's phrase, not Marx's.

Just as it was important to keep in mind that Marx never let go of his concept of revolution either in talking of the history of pre-capitalist societies or present needs, so here it is important to remember Marx's concept of Man/Woman relations, whether he was analyzing it in his 1844 Essays or talking about the concrete world of the First International which he headed and which, as far back as 1868, elected a woman, Madame Harriet Law, to its highest body, the General Council. It is true that it took our age to discover just how extensive and concrete were the historic roles of women in the Paris Commune, but it is

Marx who not only described them in *The Civil War in France* as both brave and thinking, but in 1871, before it erupted, had encouraged Elizabeth Dmitrieva to go to Paris where she became active in the Paris Commune and organized the *Union des Femmes Pour la Défense de Paris et les Soins aux Blessés*, the independent women's section of the First International. In a word, it was always a question of not separating theory from practice or vice versa. At no time did Marx consider any defeat, least of all as far back as the move from matrilineal to patrilineal society, as a "world historic defeat." There was always one more revolution to make and the proof was in what one learned from defeat to transform the next battle into a victory.

Now then, more equal as Man/Woman relations were under primitive communism compared to patriarchal society, Marx was not about to glorify the former as "model." Therefore he called attention to the fact of conquests, even when the commune was at its height. Just as there was conquest, even when the commune was at its height, and the beginning of slavery when one tribe defeated another, so there was the beginning of commodity exchange between the communes as well as emergence of conflict within the commune and within the family, and not only between the family and the gens. All these conflicts coalesced during the dissolution, which is why Marx's Notebooks keep stressing the duality in primitive communism.

In the paragraph that Engels did quote in *The Origin of the Family*, Marx emphasized that not only slavery, but also serfdom, was latent in the family; indeed, that all conflicts developing in the transition to class society were present in the family "*in miniature.*"

Finally, what Marx called "the excrescence of the state" in class-divided society—and he uses that expression in his reference to a period during the dissolution of the commune—is introduced into the question of transition from primitive communism to a political society. The point at all times is to stress a differentiation in the family, both when it is part of the gens and as it evolves out of the gens into another social form, at which point Marx again differentiates between the family in a society that already has a state and the family before the state emerged. The point at all times is to have a critical attitude to both biologism and uncritical evolutionism.

It was by no means simple, unitary development, and it cannot under any circumstances be attributed to a single cause like patriarchy winning over matriarchy and establishing thereby nothing less than some sort of "world historic defeat of the female sex." Marx, by taking as the point of departure not the *counter*-revolution but new stages of revolution, was enabled to see even in the Asiatic mode of production the great resistance to Western imperial encroachments, contrasting China to India, where British imperialism won.

Throughout Marx's Notebooks, his attack on colonialism, racism, as well as discrimination against women, is relentless, as he refers to the British historians, jurists, anthropologists, and lawyers as "blockheads" who clearly failed to appreciate what discoveries were being made and therefore often skipped over whole historic periods of humanity. Listen to the criticisms included in Marx's Notebooks on Maine: "Herr Maine als blockheaded Englishman geht nicht von gens aus, sondern von Patriarch, der später Chief wird etc."[13] And a little later: "Nach dem *Ancient Irish Law* women had some power of *dealing with their own property without the consent of their husbands*, and this was one of the institutions *expressly declared by the English blockheaded Judges to be illegal at the beginning of the 17th century.*"[14]

As against Engels, who was so overwhelmed with all the new data on forms of marriage and the development of a family, in and out of the gens, that it very nearly subsumed the question of property (i.e., economics), Marx, in assembling new data, never fails to criticize the major writers he is excerpting. He does this, not just "politically," by calling attention to the fact that they are bourgeois writers, but calling attention to the fact that their method is empiric and nowhere is empiricism as method so vacuous as when gathering new facts. What Marx was doing, instead, was following the empiric facts dialectically, relating them not only to other historic facts, but tracing the development of each fact, its petrifaction and transformation into opposite, caste. That is why he kept his eye on the differences in rank in the gens and on the emergence of conflict within it, in both changing material interests and changing relations between chief and ranks. And yet, Marx drew no such unbridgeable gulf between primitive and civilized as Engels had. As he wrote to Zasulich, the pivotal point was that everything "depends on the historical environment in which it occurs."

Whereas there was no difference between Marx and Engels on such a conclusion—indeed, the expression "Historical Materialism" was Engels's, not Marx's—the relationship of concrete to universal always remains, with Engels, in two totally separate compartments. Put differently, "knowing" Historical Materialism, and having that always at the back of his mind, and recognizing Marx as "genius" whereas he and the others were "at best, talented," did not impart to Engels's writings *after Marx's death*, the totality of Marx's new continent of thought. Engels's *The Origin of the Family*, as his first major work after the death of Marx, proves that fact most glaringly today, because Women's Liberation is an Idea whose time has come, and for that, *The Origin of the Family* provides little direction.

As Marx, in the last years of his life, was turning to anthropology, his reference was neither the philosophic anthropology that ran through his 1844 Essays nor just the latest empiric data of the 1880s. Rather, whether Marx focused on the equality of women during primitive communism or on Morgan's theory of the gens, his point of concentration always remained that revolutionary praxis through which humanity self-developed from primitive communism to the period in which he lived. That is what kept him enthralled as he dug deep into the latest in anthropology, archeology, early history, technology, agriculture, craftsmanship, and primitive human relations. Truly, we see here that *no greater "empiricist" ever lived than the great dialectician, Karl Marx.* Marx was not hurrying to make easy generalizations, such as Engels's characterization of the future being just a "higher stage" of primitive communism. No, Marx envisioned a totally new man, a totally new woman, a totally new life form (and by no means only for marriage)—in a word, a totally new society.

That is why it is so relevant to today's Women's Liberation Movement and why we still have so much to learn from Marx's concept of Man/Woman, not only in the abstract 1844 articulation, but in the empiric 1880 formulation when it was integrated with the need for total uprooting of capitalism and creation of a class-less society.

Today's revolutionaries have as much to learn from Marx's drafts of his answer to Vera Zasulich, and what they reveal of his never–ending search for new paths to revolution. In 1881 he suddenly found it difficult to answer a simple question on the future of the Russian Commune as it was being debated between the Narodniks and those who considered themselves Marxists. They wanted to know if the commune could lead to communism without needing to go through capitalism and evidently without a revolution! He wrote no less than four different versions of his answer, the first of which was fully ten pages long. From that first draft until the very much abbreviated one that he finally sent, what is clear is that his preoccupation is not "the commune" but the "needed Russian Revolution."

The second draft manifests also what he had developed with the Asiatic mode of production: "The archaic or primary formation of our globe contains a number of strata of different ages, one superimposed on the other . . . [isolation] permits the emergence of a central despotism above the communities . . . I now come to the crux of the question. We cannot overlook the fact that the archaic type to which the Russian commune belongs, conceals an internal dualism."

The third draft, quoted in part above on the crucial nature of the historical environment, was a conclusion Marx reached as he emphasized "the dualism within it [the commune] permits of an alternative: either the property element in it will overcome the collective element, or the other way."

This is always the key to the whole. We must remember that just as Marx, in 1844, was not only projecting the overthrow of the old but stressing that a new society must totally change human relationships, actually as well as philosophically, so, once the 1848 Revolutions were defeated, Marx developed a new concept—the "Revolution in Permanence." In a word, it was in the 1850 *Address to the Communist League* that Marx first projected both the deepening of the concrete revolution as well as the world revolution, the interrelatedness of both.

As we saw, the Taiping Revolution in the 1850s led, at one and the same time, to Marx's probing of pre-capitalist forms of society, *and* his seeing the

Chinese Revolution as "encouraging" the West European proletariat, which was quiescent at the moment, to revolt. The *Grundrisse*, which contained that most brilliant chapter on pre-capitalist formations, also contained the projection of so total an uprooting of the old, that the human relationship "does not seek to remain something formed by the past, but is in the absolute movement of becoming."

And here—*after* the great "scientific-economic" work, *Capital* (which, however, likewise projected "human power is its own end"),[15] *after* the defeat of the Paris Commune, and *after* four full decades from the start of Marx's discovery of a whole new continent of thought, first articulated in 1844–we see that Marx returns to probe the origin of humanity, *not* for purposes of discovering new origins, but for perceiving new revolutionary forces, *their* reason, or as Marx called it in emphasizing a sentence of Morgan, "powers of the mind." How total, continuous, global must the concept of revolution be now? One culminating point in this intensive study of primitive communism and in the answer to Vera Zasulich[16] can be seen in the Preface Marx and Engels wrote for the Russian edition of the *Communist Manifesto*, which, without changing a word in the Manifesto itself,[17] projected the idea that Russia could be the first to have a proletarian revolution ahead of the West.

The Preface was dated January 1882. Marx continued his work in ethnological studies for the rest of the year. The last writer he excerpted—Lubbock—was studied but four months before his death. He did not abate his criticism of either the writers or their reports. Thus, in excerpting Lubbock's statement, "Among many of the lower races relationship through females is the prevalent custom . . . " and noting that Lubbock still continues to talk of "a man's heirs," Marx contemptuously noted, "but then they are not the man's heirs; these civilized asses cannot free themselves of their own con-ventionalities."[18] For these British scholars he had nothing but contempt, calling them "rogues," "asses," and "blockheads" who were expounding "silliness," whereas Marx called the Australian aborigine "the intelligent black" who would not accept the talk by the cleric (quoted by Lubbock) about there being a soul without a body.

How could anyone consider the very limited quotations from Marx that Engels used in *The Origin of the Family* as any kind of summation of Marx's views? How can anyone, like Ryazanov, think that those *Ethnological Notebooks* dealt "mainly with landownership and feudalism"? In truth they contain nothing short of both a pre-history of humanity, including the emergence of class distinctions from within communal society, and a history of "civilization" that formed a complement to Marx's famous section in *Capital* on the historical tendency of capitalist accumulation, which was, as he wrote to Zasulich, "only of Western civilization."

There was one scholar, M.A. Vitkin (whose work, *The Orient in the Philosophic-Historic Conception of K. Marx and F. Engels*,[19] was suddenly withdrawn from circulation), who did try to bring the Marx-Engels thesis on the Asiatic Mode of Production, if not on Women's Liberation, into the framework of the 1970s. This original contribution had concluded that "it is as if Marx returned to the radicalism of the 1840s, however, on new ground." And the new ground, far from being any sort of retreat to "old age" and less creativity and less radicalism, revealed "principled new moments of his [Marx's] philosophic–historic conceptions."

3. THE NEW MOMENTS OF THE REVOLUTIONARY PHILOSOPHIC-HISTORIC CONCEPTS DISCOVERED BY MARX IN THE LAST DECADE OF HIS LIFE

With eyes of the 1980s, let us take one more look at the new "moments" discovered by Marx in the last decade of his life. Far from the slander— perpetrated, as we saw, not so much by the bourgeoisie as by the Marxist "heirs"—that the last decade of Marx's life was a "slow death,"[20] the truth is that Marx produced, despite all his illnesses and family tragedies, the type of profound writings that, at one and the same time, summed up his life's work and created new openings. These openings were found to contain a trail for the 1980s by discovering the link of historic continuity to *Marx's* Marxism. Just as intellectuals who wish to narrow Marx to a "single discipline" cannot escape the overpowering fact that Marx was a revolutionary, so Marxists cannot escape what was, for Marx, inseparable from revolution itself: dialectical philosophy, Marx's transformation of Hegel's revolution *in* philosophy into a philosophy *of* revolution.

Let us consider three new moments in the writings of Marx's last decade: One, the impact of the Paris Commune is to be seen here, not only as Marx so profoundly and brilliantly presented it in *The Civil War in France*, but as he deepened his "economic" theories, i.e., his very greatest theoretical work, *Capital*. It is the 1872–75 French edition that remains the most mature and last word by Marx on this, his life's most important work. It is there that he introduced the additions in "Accumulation of Capital" on the concentration and centralization of capital which laid the ground for our monopolistic age, for the theory of state-capitalism; and for colonialism becoming visible not only during "So-called Primitive Accumulation of Capital", but in later capitalist development into what we now call imperialism.

And it was in that edition of *Capital* (the one Marx was so anxious for everyone to read, including those who had already studied the German original) that Marx also expanded the section, "Fetishism of Commodities." Decidedly, Marx was not dealing only with the exchange of commodities. As we know, early in the chapter on commodities, Marx analyzed not only the dual nature of commodities but the dual character of labor, his most original category. Moreover, neither "Appearance" nor even "Essence" summed up all Marx had to say. With "fetishism" Marx recreated "Notion"—the sphere of the Hegelian Absolute that Marx broke in two, for the only way to transcend the Absolute of the fetishism was with its absolute opposite, "freely associated labor." Marx never stopped working out anew the live forces of revolution and Reason, whether it be the freely associated labor here, in Chapter One, volume 1; or whether it be in the very last part of volume 3, where he concluded, "human power is its own end."

Two, the other magnificent 1875 work is *Critique of the Gotha Program*, which Marx modestly named "Marginal Notes," sending them to only a few leaders. It was never published in his lifetime. In it, Marx so integrated philosophy and organizational "programs" and relations that it has not yet been fully digested. Surely, our age has much to learn from it. When the work is studied in the light of the objective situation of our age, it casts a new illumination also on Luxemburg's concept of organization and its relationship both to spontaneity and to consciousness. Luxemburg surely wanted that concept of spontaneity with organization as the centerpoint of a workers' party not only as it was fighting for power, but after it had gained power, as we saw from her critique of Lenin and Trotsky in 1918.

On the other hand, though Lenin had analyzed the section of the *Critique* dealing with the state and non-state, relating it to the Paris Commune and the need to smash the bourgeois state to smithereens so brilliantly that it became the *theoretical* foundation of his *State and Revolution* and the *practical* ground for the actual 1917 Revolution, he nevertheless stopped short of transcending his 1902 concept of the party, despite his modifications at revolutionary turning points both in 1905 and in 1917.

In general, the mid-1870s were so filled with class struggles in the U.S. that despite the fact that the First International had been dissolved—Marx considered that the great 1877 railroad strikes, culminating in the First General Strike in St. Louis,[21] could lead to a new form of Workers International and an independent workers party in the United States. Because Marx never separated theory from practice, nor practice from theory, we also got a "confession" from Marx that year about the order in which he had written the four volumes of *Capital*. (Marx called Book 4, "A History of Theories of Surplus-Value," volume 3.) Here is what he wrote to Sigmund Schott on 3 November 1877: "Confidentially speaking, I in fact began 'Capital' in just the reverse (starting with the 3rd, the historic part) of the order in which it is presented to the public, except that the first volume, the one begun last, was immediately prepared for publication while the two others remained in that primitive state characteristic of all research at the outset."

So much for the academicians who accumulated endless "scholarly" tomes since the publication of volume 3 which "proved" Marx wrote it after all the "errors" in volume 1 had been exposed in order "to correct" his theory of value! Marx, instead, kept up with his practical activities, collaborating with Guesde who was establishing a workers' party in France. Marx articulated a theoretical introduction to the program of that party as: "Considering that the working class, without distinction as to race and sex, can be free only when it is in collective possession of the means of production, the emancipatory endeavor must be undertaken through the action of an independent political party of the working masses, using all means at their disposal."[22]

Three, Marx's last writings—the *Ethnological Notebooks*—are a critical determinant in themselves and in the light they cast on Marx's works as a totality, as he was completing the circle begun in 1844. With his study of works on primitive societies, like Morgan's *Ancient Society*, Marx was diving into the study of human development, both in different historic periods and in the most basic Man/Woman relationship. The concept he held fast was the one he had worked out in his *1844 Economic-Philosophic Manuscripts*. This was not, as anthropologists would have it, simply a move from a philosophic to an empiric, scientific, and anthropological view. Rather, as a revolutionary, Marx's hostility to capitalism's colonialism was intensifying. The question was how total must be the uprooting of existing society and how new the relationship of theory to practice. The studies enabled Marx (*Marx, not Engels*) to see the possibility of new human relations, not as they might come through a mere "updating" of primitive communism's equality of the sexes, as among the Iroquois, but as Marx sensed they would burst forth from a new type of revolution.

It is true the *Ethnological Notebooks* are only Notebooks and not a book polished for publication. A lot of hard work is needed to grasp all that Marx was saying. There is no way for us to know how Marx would have developed all this, but there is no doubt about his magnificent, revolutionary, unifying vision. The point is that—whether it was because Engels's name, after the death of Marx, had become sacrosanct, or because Engels's views reflected their *own* later views—not a single one of the post-Marx Marxists, beginning with Engels and continuing with Luxemburg, Zetkin, Lenin and Trotsky, all the way into our age with Mao, worked on the ground *Marx* had laid out, either on precapitalist societies or on the question of Women's Liberation. That is the ground that our age has dug out, especially since the mid-1970s.

That isn't because we are "smarter" than any of these great revolutionaries. It is because we, who have been struggling under the whip of the many *counter-revolutions*, do have one advantage—the maturity of our age. Ours is the age that has witnessed a movement *from practice*, the emergence of a whole new Third World—Afro-Asian, Latin American, Middle Eastern—as well as Women's Liberation, which has moved from being an Idea to being a *Movement*. Ours is the age that can also finally see the totality of Luxemburg, both as revolutionary theoretician and as Women's Liberationist, the latter more even than she was fully aware of. There is a new reality regarding both the Women's Liberation Movement and the relationship between spontaneity and organization, which likewise impinges on our age. It is because of this, and because we have the advantage, at one and the same time, of seeing the totality of Marx's works and the newness of today's Women's Liberation Movement, that we can grapple with the lacuna also in Luxemburg's views on Women's Liberation. The difference between the Women's Liberation Movement of the early twentieth century and that of the last two decades is that today's movement, by being rooted in *the movement from practice to theory which is itself a form of theory*, calls for a new relationship of theory to practice, from which a new Man/Woman relationship is certainly not excluded. On the contrary, it is integral *in* the revolution and the day *after* power is won.

A new revolutionary force, Women's Liberation, rebelled both against the existing capitalist, exploitative society, and against male chauvinism *within* the New Left. What germinated in the "quiescent" 1970s, as compared to the turbulent 1960s, was a passion for a philosophy of total human liberation that would become real.

In 1882, the very year before his death, when Marx was very ill and had been sent by his doctor to the warmer climate of Algiers, as if all he would do there was relax, Marx "took advantage of his stay in Algiers," as Paul Lafargue put it in his report to Engels on 16 June 1882. "Marx has come back with his head full of Africa and the Arabs," he wrote. Marx had, indeed, become enthusiastic about "Mahomet's sons," both as to their dignity and their hostility to the West. He studied both their oppression and their resistance. To his daughter, Jenny, he wrote: "Their dress—even when ragged—is elegant and graceful . Even the poorest Moor excels the greatest European actor in the *art de se draper* in his cloak and in keeping a natural, graceful and dignified bearing." And in another letter, to his daughter Laura, he wrote, "Moslems in fact recognize no subordination; they are neither subjects nor administrative objects, recognizing no authority." But he didn't fail to also note: "Nevertheless, they will go to the devil without a revolutionary movement."[23]

The intense research Marx had been doing in Russian agriculture for his volume 3 of *Capital*, on the one hand, and on the other his study of the "New World," both as it destroyed the American Indian nations and as it reached the latest monopoly stage in the United States, makes it clear that Marx would not feel himself a stranger in the United States today, with its preoccupation over oil. In 1881, he was busy reading about the Standard Oil Company in Lloyd's "The Story of a Great Monopoly", and about the *Cattle Ranches in the Far West* by Grohmann. He never stopped probing the complexities of historical development, and always his lucid view of the human condition shone forth.

4. A 1980s VIEW

Marx's Marxism, from the very beginning of his break with bourgeois society, disclosed that no concept of his was separate from that of permanent revolution,[24] whether in his 1843 essay on civil rights ("On the Jewish Question") which Marx was already contrasting to "permanent revolution"; in his 1844 Essays on Labor and the Critique of the Hegelian dialectic—"the negation of the negation"; in his 1860 letters on organization when none actually existed but he insisted on using the expression, "party in the eminent historical sense"; or in the last years of his life when he projected the possibility of nothing short of a revolution in technologically backward Russia ahead of one in the technologically advanced Western Europe. Clearly, Marx never stopped working out anew the live forces of revolution and reason. So deep were his concepts of a philosophy of revolution and its live forces that he even disagreed with those who interpreted his "Historical Tendency of Capitalist Accumulation" as if it were a universal. In his critique of Mihailovsky, Marx insisted that his analysis was a generalization only of the development of capitalism in Western Europe, and that Russia had "the best chance history has ever offered to a people" to avoid that same disastrous consequence. After which Marx quoted from the "Historical Tendency of Capitalist Accumulation" the principle, "the negation of the negation"—the inexorability of the downfall of capitalism and the creation of a totally new social order on truly human beginnings.

As against the first discovery of Marx's 1844 Humanist Essays by Ryazanov in the 1920s, their rediscovery in our age had ramifications undreamed of by any of the post-Marx Marxists. This was so because the rediscovery followed the 1950s movement from practice that was itself a form of theory, and that challenged the movement from theory for a totally new relationship of practice to theory. Once the slogan "Bread and Freedom" issued from that first revolt from under totalitarian state-capitalist tyranny calling itself Communism—in East Germany on 17 June 1953—what Marx had called "vulgar communism" could no longer be considered merely rhetorical. Nor could the "new Humanism" Marx had projected be considered as only theory. It had been given concrete historical urgency. The revolts that erupted in East Europe in the 1950s—and that continue to this day—left not an iota of doubt that, in fact and in theory, the masses were rebelling against *existing* Communism, seeing it as the imperialist state-capitalist tyranny that it is. The rebellious men and women thereby made it clear that Marx's designation of his philosophy as "a new Humanism" meant either classless, totally new human relations in life and in philosophy, *or it meant nothing*.

The decisive determinant in Marx's thought was "revolution in permanence." Our age saw this concept in a totally new way when the 1949 Chinese

Revolution led to the republication of the *Grundrisse*,[25] which included both the phenomenal section on "Pre–Capitalist Economic Formations" and a new world concept of the "Asiatic mode of production." Above all, Marx's 1857–58 work was permeated with his new Humanism, now spelled out as "the absolute movement of becoming."

As against the debates around the "Asiatic mode of production" that followed the defeated 1925–27 Chinese Revolution and were hemmed in by the factional debates between Trotsky and Stalin, the debates in the 1950s and 1960s rested on the new ground developed by Marx in the *Grundrisse*. At the same time, the successful 1949 Chinese national Revolution and the Afro-Asian, Middle East and Latin American Revolutions,[26] which signified the rise of a new Third World, disclosed a totally new dimension in philosophy. Frantz Fanon articulated it the most profoundly in *Wretched of the Earth* when he said that the "natives' challenge to the colonial world" was not "a treatise on the universal but the untidy affirmation of an original idea propounded as an absolute." Nor did the international dimension escape him: "This new humanity," he wrote, "cannot do otherwise than define a new humanism both for itself and for others . . . National consciousness, which is not nationalism, is the only thing that will give us an international dimension."

The quest for a new revolutionary humanism—indeed, Gramsci called it an "absolute humanism"—was raised by Gramsci from Mussolini's dungeons in the 1930s: "It has been forgotten that in the case of a very common expression (historical materialism) one should put the accent on the first term—'historical'—and not on the second which is of metaphysical origin. The philosophy of praxis is absolute 'historicism,' the absolute humanism of history. It is along this line that one must trace the thread of the new conception of the world." While that new conception was not heard then, nor paid attention to in the post-World War II world even when Gramsci's *Prison Notebooks* became well–known, it was impossible to disregard Marx's articulation of an "absolute movement of becoming" once a whole new Third World arose.[27]

The fact that a new light could be cast on today's colonial revolutions by a work Marx wrote one hundred years ago—and that this was the mature Marx who could be seen adhering aggressively to Hegelian dialectical language—made it impossible for post-Marx Marxists and non-Marxists alike to dismiss Marx's rootedness in the Hegelian dialectic as a mere matter of style. What confronted both revolutionaries and serious scholars was the need to re-examine Hegel "in and for himself." This became obvious in 1970, when a multitude of conferences—on the one hundredth anniversary of Lenin's birth and the two hundredth of Hegel's—kept criss-crossing. Since then there has been so great a flood of Hegel studies, new critical editions and translations of Hegel's works, and Hegel conferences that the 1970 *Hegeljahre* was clearly but the start of a whole decade of such studies.[28]

In the early 1970s, still other manuscripts that had never before seen the light of day—Marx's *Ethnological Notebooks*—were transcribed. The fact that by then Women's Liberation had developed from an Idea whose time had come to a Movement helped us see other forces of revolution as Reason. What was new in these last writings from Marx's pen is that, on the one hand, he was returning to his first discovery of a new continent of thought when he singled out the Man/Woman relationship as the most revealing of all relationships; and, on the other hand, he was developing so new a concept of "revolution in permanence" that, in 1882, he was projecting something as startling as the possibility of revolution coming in backward lands ahead of the advanced countries.[§]

The two paragraphs that Engels omitted from *Capital*—the one from volume 1 on the extension of the world market and the one from volume 2 on Marx having remained "a disciple of Hegel" but "disencumbering his dialectic of its mysticism and thus putting it through a profound change"—reveal how deeply the newness of imperialism, which Luxemburg thought was missing from *Capital*, was imbedded right there in volume 1. It was there in Marx's analysis of "Capitalist Production on a Progressively Increasing Scale" as well as in "The General Law of Capitalist Accumulation." What was needed to see it, and what was missing in Luxemburg, was Marx's firm, integral, deep relationship between dialectics and economics.

Without such a vision of new revolutions, a new individual, a new universal, a new society, new human relations, we would be forced to tailend one or another form of reformism just when the age of nuclear Titans—the United States and Russia—threatens the very survival of civilization as we have known it. The myriad crises in our age have shown, over and over again, from Russia to China,[29] from Cuba to Iran, from Africa to Pol Pot's Cambodia, that without a philosophy of revolution activism spends itself in mere anti-imperialism and anti-capitalism, without ever revealing what it is *for*. We have been made to see anew that, just as the movement from practice disclosed a break in the Absolute Idea that required both a new relationship of practice to theory, and a new unity of practice and theory, so that new unity is but a *beginning*: Absolute Idea as New Beginning.[30] Clearly, along with the actual struggles for the self-determination of nations, we need what Hegel called "self-determination in which alone the Idea is, is to hear itself speak."

Just as the relationship of dialectics to economics did not exhaust the significance of the dialectics of revolution, neither did the "self-determination of the Idea" exhaust itself by being parallel with the struggle of self-determination of nations. Absolute negativity manifests its pivotal role in the Idea precisely because it is both totality (summation) and new beginning, which each generation must first work out for itself.[31] Marx, after all,

§ See "New Thoughts on *Rosa Luxemburg, Women's Liberation, and Marx's Philosophy of Revolution*," p. xxxvii.—Ed.

throughout his life continuously developed as well as practiced the dialectics of his discovery of a new continent of thought and of revolution. We must repeat:

It isn't because we are any "smarter" that we can see so much more than other post-Marx Marxists. Rather, it is because of the maturity of our age. It is true that other post-Marx Marxists have rested on a truncated Marxism; it is equally true that no other generation could have seen the problematic of our age, much less solve our problems. Only live human beings can recreate the revolutionary dialectic forever anew. And these live human beings must do so in theory as well as in practice. It is not a question only of meeting the challenge from practice, but of being able to meet the challenge from the self-development of the Idea, and of deepening theory to the point where it reaches Marx's concept of the philosophy of "revolution in permanence."[§]

What is needed is a new unifying principle, on Marx's ground of humanism, that truly alters both human thought and human experience. Marx's *Ethnological Notebooks* are a historic happening that proves, one hundred years after he wrote them, that Marx's legacy is no mere heirloom, but a live body of ideas and perspectives that is in need of concretization. Every moment of Marx's development, as well as the totality of his works, spells out the need for "revolution in permanence." This is the absolute challenge to our age.

NOTES

1. I was the first to translate Lenin's Abstract of Hegel's *Science of Logic* into English and it is my translation that I am using here. See appendix B in my *Marxism and Freedom, from 1776 until Today*, first edition (New York: Bookman Associates, 1958). See also chapter 10 in that work, "The Collapse of the Second International and the Break in Lenin's Thought," as well as chapter 3, "The Shock of Recognition and the Philosophic Ambivalence of Lenin," in my *Philosophy and Revolution, from Hegel to Sartre and from Marx to Mao*.

2. By 1960, in a new edition of that work, however, Marcuse added a "Note on the Dialectic," which pointed in a very different, "one-dimensional" direction. As for Adorno's reductionism of the dialectic in *Negative Dialectics*, I dealt with that in my 1974 paper given to the Hegel Society of America. See n. 30

3. Marx called Book 4 of his *Capital, History of the Theory*. When Karl Kautsky published this in 1905–10 as *Theories of Surplus Value* in 3 volumes, he took liberties with Marx's arrangement. We did not see this section, *in toto*, as Marx wrote it, until volume 1 was published in 1963, volume 2 in 1968, and volume 3 in 1971, (Progress Publishers, Moscow). Engels should have paid more attention to Marx's description of Kautsky when he first met him: "A small-minded mediocrity, clever by half (he is only 26), industrious in a certain way, busies himself with statistics but does not derive anything intelligent from them, belonging by nature to the tribe of philistines" (Marx's letter to his daughter, Jenny, 11 April 1881).

4. Bebel gave Mehring a first try at the heritage but Mehring limited himself to a selected few of the early works. When Mehring got around to writing the biography, which is still considered authoritative, he not only showed his own tilt toward Lassalle in his dispute with Marx, but presented Marx's entire last decade as a "slow death." See Franz Mehring, *Karl Marx* (New York: Covici, Friede Pub., 1935).

5. "New data about the literary legacy of Marx and Engels (report of Comrade Ryazanov made to the Socialist Academy on 20 November 1923)," in *Bulletin of Socialist Academy*, book

[§] See "New Thoughts on *Rosa Luxemburg, Women's Liberation, and Marx's Philosophy of Revolution*," pp. xxxvii–xxxviii.—Ed.

6, October–December 1923 (Moscow and Petrograd: State Pub. House, 1923), pp. 368–69. Lawrence Krader, who first made public in English part of Ryazanov's report to the Socialist Academy, stopped his quotation before Ryazanov's presumptuous remark about "inexcusable pedantry."

6. Engels's overestimation of Darwin, like his overestimation of Morgan, led to some fantastic ramifications. See Margaret A. Fay, "Marx and Darwin, a Literary Detective Story," *Monthly Review*, March 1980. She has traced through the 1880 letter, long assumed to have been sent by Darwin to Marx, and found it to have been sent, instead, to Aveling, who had wanted to dedicate his book, *The Students' Darwin*, to him. Darwin's answer, declining "the intended honor," had been addressed only to "Dear Sir," and had been mixed in with Marx's documents when they were in Eleanor and Aveling's possession after Marx's death.

7. *Capital*, 1:406n: "The weak points in the abstract materialism of natural science, a materialism that excludes history and its process, are at once evident from the abstract and ideological conceptions of its spokesmen, whenever they venture beyond the bounds of their own speciality." See also chapter 2, "A New Continent of Thought," in my *Philosophy and Revolution*.

8. See Engels's preface to the first edition of *The Origin of the Family*.

9. The 1970 edition of the three-volume *Karl Marx and Frederick Engels: Selected Works* (Moscow: Progress Publishers) finally published the first draft of Marx's reply, 3:152–63.

10. In the edition of *Ancient Society* I am using, (Chicago: Charles H. Kerr Pub. Co., 1877), this appears on p. 118. Not only is there no underlining in Morgan, but in Marx the role of the women is not limited by "even," nor is the word "decision" limited by a "but" as in Morgan: "Even the women were allowed to express their wishes and opinions through an orator of their own selection. But the decision was made by the council. . . ."

11. Marx, *Ethnological Notebooks*, p. 135.

12. *Arkhiv Marksa y Engelsa*, 9:52. Emphasis is mine to stress what was neither in Morgan nor in Marx's excerpt.

13. Marx, *Ethnological Notebooks*, p. 292: "Mr. Maine, as a blockheaded Englishman, doesn't proceed from *gens*, but rather from Patriarch, which later becomes Chief, etc. Silliness. The same goes for the oldest form of the gens! . . ." Marx's sharpest criticism of Maine is on the question of women, defending even Bachofen's 1861 work, *Mutterrecht* ("Mother-right").

14. Ibid., p. 323.

15. *Capital*, 3:954. One erudite anthropologist, who is certainly no Marxist, Sir Raymond Firth, also focuses on the fact that *Capital* is not so much an economic work as "a dramatic history designed to involve its readers in the events described." (See Raymond Firth, "The Sceptical Anthropologist? Social Anthropology and Marxist Views on Society," in *Marxist Analyses and Social Anthropology* (London: Malaby Press, 1975).

16. Her letter to Marx is included in *The Russian Menace to Europe* (Glencoe, Illinois: The Free Press, 1952), edited by Paul W. Blackstock and Bert F. Hoselitz, but the liberties they take by trying to create a one-page composite of the four drafts of Marx's answer leave a great deal to be desired.

17. In that 1882 introduction, signed by both Marx and Engels, Marx saw no reason for making any changes, although he was then intensively studying primitive communism, something they knew little about in 1847 when the Manifesto was first written. Engels, on the other hand, in the 1888 English edition, felt called upon to offer a demurrer to the epoch-making statement: "All history is a history of class struggles." He claimed, in a footnote, that this meant all *"written"* history but that, since the publication of Morgan's *Ancient Society*, much more had been learned about primitive communism. To this writer, Engels thereby modifed the dialectical structure of Marx's historic call to revolution.

18. *Ethnological Notebooks*, p. 340.

19. Mikhail Vitkin, *Vostok v Philosophico–Historicheskoi Kontseptsii K. Marksa y F. Engelsa* (Moscow: 1972) is available only in Russian. See also "Marx and the Peasant Question" by Teodor Shanin and "Marx and Revolutionary Russia" by Haraki Wada in *History Workshop Journal*, London, Autumn 1981.

20. Franz Mehring's demurrer that the expression "a slow death" greatly exaggerated the situation only helped spread that anonymous assertion far and wide. See Franz Mehring, *Karl Marx*, p. 525.

21. For a discussion of this, see Terry Moon and Ron Brokmeyer, *On the 100th Anniversary of the First General Strike in the U.S.* (Detroit: News & Letters, 1977).

22. Maximilien Rubel and Margaret Manale, *Marx Without Myth*, p. 317.

23. These letters are included in Saul K. Padover, *Karl Marx: An Intimate Biography* (New York: McGraw Hill, 1978). See also, Frederick Engels, Paul and Laura Lafargue, *Correspondence* (3 vols.), (Moscow: Foreign Languages Pub. House, 1959–60).

24. On the surface, it may appear as if Trotsky did develop that concept; but in truth his theory of permanent revolution was an original, in the sense that it *wasn't* related to Marx's concept. (See afterword to chapter 11.)

25. The English translation was not published until 1973.

26. I have analyzed the developing Latin American revolutions elsewhere. See my essay, "The Unfinished Latin American Revolutions," included in the bilingual pamphlet *Latin America's Revolutions, in Reality, in Thought* (Detroit: News & Letters, 1981), pp. 23–30. Includes also "The Peasant Dimension in Latin America: Its Test of the Relation of Theory to Organization," by Mike Connolly, "Latin America: Revolution and Theory," by Eugene Walker, and "El Salvador in Revolution," by Francisco Aquino.

27. Here is how Gramsci expressed his view of praxis: "The philosophy of praxis is consciousness full of contradictions in which the philosopher himself, understood both individually and as an entire social group, not merely grasps the contradictions, but posits himself as an element of the contradictions and elevates this element to a principle of knowledge and therefore of action." For this essay on "Problems of Marxism" as well as his critique of Nikolai Bukharin's address to the Second International Congress of the History of Science in London in 1931, see Part III, "The Philosophy of Praxis," in *Selections from the Prison Notebooks of Antonio Gramsci* (New York: International Pub., 1971).

28. A fairly good summation of this can be found in a three–part study, "Recent Hegel Literature" by James Schmidt, in *Telos*, Winter 1980–81, Summer 1981.

29. Elsewhere I have analyzed Mao the Leader becoming the prototype of the intellectual bureaucrat "come to lead" the revolutions of the Third World, and ending by consigning them to a half-way house between imperialism and capitalism, between capital and labor. See my *Nationalism, Communism, Marxist-Humanism and the Afro-Asian Revolutions*, published by the Left Group, Cambridge University Labour Club in 1961. See also my *Political–Philosophic Letters: Volume II*, on Iran (Detroit: News & Letters, 1980).

30. I have developed this concept more fully both in chapter 1, "Absolute Negativity as New Beginning," in my *Philosophy and Revolution*, and in my paper delivered to the Hegel Society of America in 1974, "Hegel's Absolute Idea as New Beginning," in *Art and Logic in Hegel's Philosophy*. The concept began with two letters on the Absolute Idea written in May 1953. See "The Raya Dunayevskaya Collection," vol. 3, in Wayne State University Labor History Archives.

31. See my pamphlet, *25 Years of Marxist-Humanism in the U.S.* (Detroit: News & Letters, 1980), which relates the anti-nuclear movement to the question of war and revolution from "1962—A Year of Confrontations, to the Brink of Nuclear Holocaust" to the 1979 anti-nuclear protests following the Three Mile Island near-disaster, where the Marxist-Humanist banner carried Marx's principle: "Human Power is its Own End."

Appendix

Rosa Luxemburg's Address* to the Fifth Congress of the Russian Social-Democratic Labor Party, London, 1907

**SEVENTH EVENING SESSION, 16 MAY,†
3–6 P.M. CHAIRMAN: LENIN**

Comrades! The Central Committee of the German Social-Democratic Party, having known about my intention to participate in your Congress, decided to take advantage of this opportunity and delegated me to bring you fraternal greetings and wishes for the greatest success. The multimillions of class-conscious German proletariat have followed with lively sympathy and the closest attentiveness the revolutionary struggle of their Russian brothers, and have already demonstrated in deed that they are ready to draw for themselves fruitful lessons from the rich treasures of the experiences of the Russian Social-Democracy. At the very beginning of 1905, when the first thunderstorm of the revolution erupted in Petersburg with the emergence of the proletariat on 9 January, a revival stirred in the ranks of the German Social-Democracy. From it flowed heated debates on the question of tactics, and the Resolution on the general strike at the Jena Congress was the first important result which our Party drew from the struggle of the Russian proletariat. It is true that thus far this decision has had no practical application, and it will hardly become a reality in the near future. Nevertheless, its principal significance is beyond doubt.

*Translated from the Russian *Pyatyi Londonskii S'ezd RSDRP, April–May 1907 goda. Protokoly*. Moscow, Institute of Marxism–Leninism, 1963, pp. 97–104.
†The 1907 Congress took place 13 May–1 June (1–20 May by the old Russian calendar).

Up until 1905 a very negative attitude to the general strike prevailed in the ranks of the German Social-Democratic Party; it was thought to be a purely anarchistic, which meant reactionary slogan, a harmful utopia. But as soon as the German proletariat saw in the general strike of the Russian proletariat a new form of struggle, not in opposition to the political struggle, but as a weapon in that struggle, not as a miraculous remedy to achieve a sudden leap to a socialist order, but rather as a weapon of class struggle for the winning of the most elementary freedoms from the modern class state, it hastened fundamentally to change its attitude to the general strike, acknowledging its possible application in Germany under certain conditions.

Comrades! I consider it necessary to turn your attention to the fact—to the great honor of the German proletariat—that it did change its attitude to the general strike, not at all influenced by the marks of any formal successes of this method of struggle, which impressed even bourgeois politicians. The Resolution at the Jena Congress was passed more than a month before the first, and, at the time, only great victory of the revolution, before the memorable October Days* that wrested from absolutism the first constitutional concessions in the form of the October 17th Manifesto. Still, Russia suffered only defeat, and already the German proletariat, with true class instinct, felt that in these outward defeats lies hidden a never-before-seen proletarian strength, a genuine ground for future victories. The fact remains that the German proletariat, before the Russian proletariat achieved any formal victories, hurried to pay tribute to this experience. They incorporated this new tactical slogan into earlier forms of their struggles, aimed not at parliamentary action, but at involvement of the broadest proletarian masses.

Further events in Russia—the October and November days and especially the high point the revolutionary storm reached in Russia, the December crisis in Moscow—were reflected in Germany in a great awakening of spirit in Social-Democratic ranks. In December and January—after the massive demonstrations in Austria for general electoral rights—there began in Germany a new spirited debate on the question of whether it wasn't time to apply some form of a general strike in connection with the electoral struggle in Prussia, in Saxony, and in Hamburg. The question was decided negatively: the idea of artificially creating a mass movement was rejected. However, on January 17, 1906, it was tested for the first time with a brilliantly executed half-day general work stoppage in Hamburg. This further enhanced the daring and consciousness-of-power of the working masses in the major center of the German Social-Democracy.

At first glance, last year, 1906, appears one of defeat for the Russian Revolution. In Germany, too, it ended with an apparent defeat of the German Social-Democracy. You are acquainted with the fact that the first democratic

*The Jena Congress that met 17–23 September 1905 passed the Luxemburg resolution, "On the Political Mass Strike and the Social-Democracy."—Trans.

general elections in January (January 25), the German Social-Democracy lost nearly half of their delegates. But this electoral defeat comes at the very time when it is in closest connection to the Russian Revolution. For those who understand the interdependence of the position of the Party in the last election, there was no doubt that the Russian Revolution was for it the most important point, the determining factor in the results of the electoral campaign. There is no doubt whatever that the stamp of the revolutionary events in Russia, and the fear with which this filled the bourgeois classes in Germany, was one of the factors that united and rallied all layers of bourgeois society and the bourgeois parties, with the exception of the center, under one reactionary slogan: Down with the class representatives of the class-conscious German proletariat, down with Social-Democracy! Never before was Lassalle's formulation that the bourgeoisie was "one reactionary mass" realized in so palpable a manner as in this election. But for that very reason the result of the election compelled the German proletariat to turn, with redoubled attention, to the revolutionary struggle of their Russian brothers.

If one could, in a few words, sum up the political and historical results of the last elections to the Reichstag, then it would be necessary to say that, after January 25 and February 5, 1907, Germany showed itself to be the only modern country in which not a trace of bourgeois liberalism and bourgeois democracy remained in the strict sense of the word. Bourgeois liberalism and democracy definitively and irrevocably took their stand on the side of reaction in the struggle against the revolutionary proletariat. It is, precisely, the treason of liberalism, above all, which delivered us directly into the hands of Junker reaction in the last elections. And, although presently the liberals in the Reichstag increased their representation, they nevertheless are nothing but the liberal cover-up for the pathetic toadies of reaction.

A question arose in our ranks in relation to this situation which, to an ever greater degree, concerns you, our Russian comrades. To the extent to which I am aware, one of the circumstances which is playing a fundamental role in the determination of tactics of the Russian comrades is the view that the proletariat in Russia faces a very special task wrought with great inner contradiction: to create, at one and the same time, the first political conditions of the bourgeois order and yet to carry on the class struggle against the bourgeoisie. This struggle appears fundamentally different from that of the proletariat in Germany and all of West Europe.

Comrades! I think that such a conception is a purely formalistic expression of the question. We, too, to a certain degree, are finding ourselves in just such a difficult position. To us in Germany this became graphically clear in the last elections—the proletariat is the only true fighter and defender even of bourgeois democratic rights in a bourgeois state.

Even were we not to speak of the fact that there is no universal suffrage in the majority of the electoral districts in Germany, it is still a fact that we suffer from many leftovers of medieval feudalism; even the few freedoms we do enjoy, like general electoral rights for election to the Reichstag, the right to strike, to form trade unions, freedom of assembly—these are not seriously guaranteed and are subject to constant attack from the side of reaction. And in all these instances bourgeois liberalism has definitely proven to be a treacherous ally. Under all these circumstances, the class-conscious proletariat is the only durable bulwark for democratic development in Germany.

The question that surfaced in connection with the last electoral defeat was the relationship to bourgeois liberalism. Voices—true, not many—were heard bewailing the premature death of liberalism. In connection with this also came advice from France to take into consideration in one's tactics the weak position of bourgeois liberalism, in order to spare its remains so that we could use it as an ally in the struggle against reaction and for the defense of the general foundation of democratic development.

Comrades! I can testify to the fact that these voices that lamented the political development of Germany were sharply rejected by the class-conscious German proletariat. (Applause from the Bolsheviks and part of the Center.) I can gladly testify to the fact that in this case there were no differences in the Party between the various factions, and the whole Party with a single voice declared: "We may be saddened by the electoral results of this historic development, but we will not take a single step backward toward liberalism, nor by a single iota retreat from our principled political tactics." The conscious German proletariat drew very different conclusions from these last elections to the Reichstag: if bourgeois liberalism and bourgeois democracy are proving themselves so brittle and shaky that with each energetic gesture of the class struggle of the proletariat, they are willing to sink into the abyss of reaction, then they get what they deserve! (Applause from the Bolsheviks and part of the Center.)

Under the impact of the elections of January 25, it has become clear to ever broader layers of the German proletariat that, in view of the disintegration of liberalism, it is necessary for the proletariat to free itself of all illusions and hopes of any help from liberalism in the struggle against reaction, and at the present time more than at any other time, to count only on itself in the struggle for its class interests as well as in the struggle against reactionary attacks upon the democratic development. (Applause from the Bolsheviks and part of the Center.) In the light of these electoral defeats, a greater clarity than even before was achieved regarding class antagonisms. The internal development of Germany has reached a point of maturity that the most optimistic could not have dreamed before. Marx's analysis of the development of bourgeois society had, once again, reached its highest and most brilliant confirmation. But along with this it is clear to all that this development, this sharpening of class contradictions, not just sooner or later, but inevitably, would lead to the period of the stormiest political struggle also in Germany. And, in connection with this, questions of different forms and phases of the class struggle are followed by us with very special interest.

For that very reason, the German workers presently fix their gaze with redoubled attention on the struggle of their Russian brothers as the more advanced fighters, the vanguard of the international working class. From my limited experience in the electoral campaign, I can testify that in all electoral meetings—and I had the opportunity to appear in meetings of two to three thousand people—the workers resounded in a single voice: "Tell us about the Russian Revolution!" And in this is reflected not only their natural sympathy flowing from instinctive class solidarity with their struggling brothers. It also reflects their recognition that the interests of the Russian Revolution are indeed their cause as well. What the German proletariat expects most from the Russian is the deepening and enrichment of proletarian tactics, the application of the principles of class struggle under totally new historic conditions. Indeed, that Social-Democracy tactic which is being applied in the present time by the proletarian class in Germany and to which we owe our victories is primarily adapted to parliamentary struggles, a struggle within the framework of bourgeois parliamentarism.

The Russian Social-Democracy is the first to whom has fallen the difficult but honorable task of applying the principles of Marx's teaching not in a period of quiet parliamentary course in the life of the state, but in a stormy revolutionary period. The only experience that scientific socialism had previously in practical politics during a revolutionary period was the activity of Marx himself in the 1848 revolution. The course itself of the 1848 revolution, however, cannot be a model for the present revolution in Russia. From it we can only learn how not to act in a revolution. Here was the schema of this revolution: the proletariat fights with its usual heroism but is unable to utilize its victories; the bourgeoisie drives the proletariat back in order to usurp the fruits of its struggle; finally, absolutism pushes the bourgeoisie aside in order to crush the proletariat as well as defeat the revolution.

The class independence of the proletariat was still in a most embryonic state. It is true that it already had the *Communist Manifesto*—that great charter of class struggle. It is true that Karl Marx participated in the revolution as a practical fighter. But precisely as a result of the particular historic conditions, he had to express, not socialist politics, but that of the extreme left position of bourgeois democracy. The *Neue Rheinische Zeitung** was not so much an organ of class struggle as the organ of the extreme left wing of the bourgeois revolutionary camp. True, there was not in Germany the kind of

---

Neue Rheinische Zeitung, Organ der Demokratie, with Karl Marx the editor and Frederick Engels a member of the editorial board, appeared daily from June 1848, until 19 May 1849. Its international scope, its concentration on revolutions, left no doubt in readers' minds of the focus on the proletarian nature of revolutionary militancy. Long before Karl Marx's 1850 Address, with its resounding conclusion about "revolution in permanence," the *Organ der Demokratie* not only articulated the historic dimension of the ongoing revolutions but also the integrality, the unity, of theory and practice between economics and politics. Thus, the 4 April 1849 issue started a new series of articles, which has since become famous as the pamphlet *Wage-Labor and Capital*. (In the following text, I am abbreviating *Neue Rheinische Zeitung* as *NRZ*.)—Trans.

democracy for which the *NRZ* could have become ideological spokesman. But this is precisely the politics that Marx had to carry out with indefatigable consistency during the first year of the revolution. Doubtless, his politics consisted in this, that Marx had to support with all means the struggle of the bourgeois democracy against absolutism.

But in what did the support consist? In this, that from the first to the last he mercilessly, relentlessly, lashed out against the half-way measures, inconsistency, weakness, cowardice of bourgeois politics. (Applause from the Bolsheviks and part of the Center.) Without the slightest vacillation he supported and defended every action of the proletarian masses—not only the eruption which was the first fleeting sign of victory—March 18—but also the memorable storming of the Berlin Armory on June 14, which then and later the bourgeoisie obstinately claimed was a trap reaction laid for the proletariat, and the September and October uprisings in Vienna—these last attempts of the proletariat to save the revolution from perishing from the wobbliness and treachery of the bourgeoisie.

Marx supported the national struggles of 1848, holding that they were allies of the revolution. The politics of Marx consisted in this, that he pushed the bourgeoisie every moment to the limits of the revolutionary situation. Yes, Marx supported the bourgeoisie in the struggle against absolutism, but he supported it with whips and kicks. Marx considered it an inexcusable mistake that the proletariat allowed, after its first short-lived victory of March 18, the formation of a responsible bourgeois ministry of Camphausen–Hansemann. But once the bourgeoisie got power, Marx ·demanded from the very first moment that it should actualize the revolutionary dictatorship. He categorically demanded, in the *NRZ*, that the transitional period after each revolution demanded the most energetic dictatorship. Marx very clearly understood the total impotence of the German "Duma," the Frankfurt National Assembly. But he saw this, not as a mitigating circumstance, but the contrary. He showed that the only way out of the impotent situation was through winning actual power in open battle against the old power, and in this, depending on the revolutionary national masses.

But, comrades, how did the politics of Marx end? The following year Marx had to abandon this position of extreme bourgeois democracy—a position completely isolated and hopeless—and go over to pure class-struggle politics. In the autumn of 1849, Marx with his cothinkers left the bourgeois democratic union and decided to establish an independent organization of the proletariat. They also wished to participate in a projected all-German workers' congress, an idea which emerged from the ranks of the proletariat of East Prussia. But when Marx wanted to change the course of his politics, the revolution was living out its last days and before he succeeded in carrying out the new, pure proletarian tactics, the *NRZ* became the first victim of triumphant reaction.

Clearly comrades, you in Russia at the present time have to begin, not where Marx began, but where Marx ended in 1849, with a clearly expressed, independent proletarian class policy. Presently the Russian proletariat finds itself, not in the position of the embryonic state that characterized the German proletariat in 1848, but representing a cohesive and conscious political proletarian force. The Russian workers need not feel themselves isolated, but rather part of the all-world international army of the proletariat. They cannot forget that the present revolutionary struggle is not an isolated skirmish, but one of the greatest battles in the entire course of the international class struggle.

It is clear that in Germany, sooner or later, in accordance with the maturing class relations, the proletarian struggle will inescapably flow out into mass collisions with the ruling classes, and the German proletariat will need to utilize the experience, not of the 1848 bourgeois revolution, but of the Russian proletariat in the current revolution. Therefore, comrades, you are carrying responsibility to the whole international proletariat. And the Russian proletariat will attain its height in this task only if, in the range of the tactics in its own struggles, it shows the decisiveness, the clear consciousness of its goal, and that it has learned the results of the international development in its entirety, has achieved the degree of maturity that the whole capitalistic society has reached.

The Russian proletariat, in its actions, must show that between 1848 and 1907, in the more than half-century of capitalist development, and from the point of this development taken as a whole, we are not at the beginning but at the end of this development. It must show that the Russian Revolution is not just the last act in a series of bourgeois revolutions of the nineteenth century, but rather the forerunner of a new series of future proletarian revolutions in which the conscious proletariat and its vanguard, the Social-Democracy, are destined for the historic role of leader. (Applause.) The German worker expects from you not only victory over absolutism, not only a new foothold for the liberation movement in Europe, but also the widening and deepening of the perspectives of the proletarian tactic: he wishes to learn from you how to step into this period of open revolutionary struggle.

However, in order to carry out this role, it is necessary for the Russian Social-Democracy to learn one important condition. This condition is the *unity* of the Party, not just a formal, purely mechanical unity, but an inner cohesion, an inner strength which genuinely will result from clear, correct tactics corresponding to this inner unity of the class struggle of the proletariat. The extent to which the German Social-Democracy counts on the unity of the Russian Party you can see from the letter which the Central Committee of the German Social-Democracy has authorized me to deliver to you. At the start of my talk I delivered the fraternal greetings which the Central Committee sent to all the representatives of the Social-Democracy. The rest of this letter reads:

The German Social-Democracy has fervently followed the struggle of the Russian brothers against absolutism and against plutocracy striving to share power with it.

The victory which you have achieved in the elections to the Duma, despite the rigged electoral system, has delighted us. It showed that, no matter what the obstacles, the spontaneous triumphant force of socialism is irresistible.

As the bourgeoisie tries everywhere, so the Russian bourgeoisie is attempting to conclude peace with its rulers. It wants to stop the victorious forward march of the Russian proletariat. It tries also in Russia to steal the fruit of the proletariat's unyielding struggle. Therefore the role of leader in the liberation movement falls to the Russian Social-Democracy.

The necessary condition for carrying out this emancipation struggle is unity and cohesion of the Russian Social-Democratic Party. What we expect to hear from the representatives of our Russian brothers is that the deliberations and decisions of their Congress have fulfilled our expectations and wishes for the realization of the unity and cohesion of the Russian Social-Democracy.

In this spirit we are sending our fraternal greetings to your Congress.

Central Committee of the Social-Democracy of Germany, Berlin, April 30, 1907.

SELECTED BIBLIOGRAPHY

To this day, there are no English editions of the complete works of Marx, and there are not even any Selected Works of Luxemburg. I have used, mainly, the Russian edition of the Collected Works of Marx (*Sochineniya*, 46 volumes) and the German edition of the Collected Works of Luxemburg (*Gesammelte Werke*, 5 volumes). With the sole exception of the writings of Lenin, whose Complete Works are available in English, I have used my own translations. I wish to call attention, especially, to the fact that the Minutes of the crucial 1907 Congress of the Russian Social-Democratic Labor Party have not appeared in English to this day. I have translated from the Russian (*Pyati S'ezd RSDRP, Aprel'-mai 1907 goda, Protokoly*) one of Luxemburg's speeches at that Congress, which appears here as an Appendix, as well as the excerpts from the speeches of Trotsky and Plekhanov which appear in the text. I would like to thank David Wolff, the translator of Luxemburg's *Theory and Practice,* for his assistance in the German translations, and Urszula Wislanka, the editor and translator of *Today's Polish Fight For Freedom*, for her assistance with the Polish translations.

What are called Luxemburg's "Selected Writings" are non-representative of her massive works. They are listed in the bibliography that follows. As for the correspondence—whether the letters are by Luxemburg, or by Marx—I have referred to the date of the letters, rather than to any single source, as this is the easiest way to find them in any language.

The explosion of books, journals and newspapers that accompanied the growth of the Women's Liberation Movement over the last decade makes it impossible to list all the works that are important to a study like this. What follows is, therefore, a Selected Bibliography only. The listings for Part Two have been divided into three sections. The first section, on the Black Dimension, does not divide that dimension in America from its expression in Africa. Nor does it mean that the Black Dimension is not also present in the works listed in the other two sections. It should also be noted that, because many studies of the earlier women's movement were inspired by today's movement and written by today's women's liberationists, some works truly belong in both of those sections.

Insofar as Part Three is concerned, it is necessary to stress that even the *Sochineniya* (Collected Works) and *Arkhivy* (Archives) have not brought out all of the works of Marx, especially from the final decade of his life. I wish to call attention to the fact that I have used Lawrence Krader's transcription of *The Ethnological Notebooks of Karl Marx*; and, for the two paragraphs that were in the original French edition of *Capital* which Marx edited, but which Engels omitted when he worked on the English and new German editions, I have used Maximilien Rubel's *Oeuvres de Karl Marx, Economie II*.

Attention also must be called to the fact that the many works of Marx, Luxemburg, Lenin, Trotsky, Engels, and Hegel, that are important to this work, are singled out separately as primary sources and thus are not included with the supplementary works listed for the individual Parts One, Two and Three of this book.

–Raya Dunayevskaya

ROSA LUXEMBURG

Luxemburg, Rosa, *Gesammelte Werke* (Collected Works), vols. 1–5 (Berlin: Dietz Verlag, 1974).
Accumulation of Capital (London: Routledge & Kegan Paul, Ltd., 1951; New York: Monthly Review Press, 1968).
The Accumulation of Capital—An Anti-Critique (includes also *Imperialism and the Accumulation of Capital* by Bukharin), ed. and with an Introduction by Kenneth J. Tarbuck (New York and London: Monthly Review Press, 1972).
Briefe an Freunde (Letters to Friends), ed. by Benedikt Kautsky (Hamburg: Europäische Verlagsanstalt, 1950).
Comrade and Lover: Rosa Luxemburg's Letters to Leo Jogiches, ed. by Elzbieta Ettinger (Cambridge, Mass. and London: MIT Press, 1979).
Lettres de la Prison (Paris: Librarie du Travail, 1933).
Letters from Prison (London: Socialist Book Centre, 1946).
The Letters of Rosa Luxemburg, ed. and with an Introduction by Stephen Bronner (Boulder, Colo.: Westview Press, 1978).
Letters to Karl and Luise Kautsky from 1896 to 1918, ed. by Luise Kautsky (New York: Robert McBride, 1925; New York: Gordon Press, 1975).
The National Question: Selected Writings by Rosa Luxemburg, ed. and with an Introduction by Horace B. Davis (New York: Monthly Review Press, 1976).
Prison Letters to Sophie Liebknecht (London: Independent Labour Party, 1972).
Reform or Revolution (New York: Three Arrows Press, 1937; New York: Pathfinder Press, 1973).
Rosa Luxemburg: Selected Political Writings, ed. by Robert Looker (New York: Grove Press, 1974).
Rosa Luxemburg: Le Socialisme en France, ed. and with an Introduction by Daniel Guérin (Paris: Editions Pierre Belfond, 1971).
Rosa Luxemburg Speaks, ed. by Mary-Alice Waters (New York: Pathfinder Press, 1970). This collection includes more of Luxemburg's work than other collections of Selected Writings—for example, both *The Russian Revolution* and her Speech to the Founding Convention of the German Communist Party; both *The Mass Strike, the Political Party and the Trade Unions* and "The Spirit of Russian Literature: Life of

Korolenko"; both the *Junius* pamphlet and "What is Economics." But nothing on women.

Róza Luksemburg Listy do Leona Jogichesa-Tyszki, ed. by Feliks Tych (Warsaw: Ksiazka i Wiedza, 1968).

The Russian Revolution (New York: Workers Age Publishers, 1940; London: Socialist Review Publishing Co., 1959).

Selected Political Writings of Rosa Luxemburg, ed. by Dick Howard (New York: Monthly Review Press, 1971).

Theory and Practice, first English translation by David Wolff (Detroit: News & Letters, 1980). Includes also excerpt from "Attrition or Collision."

KARL MARX

Marx, Karl, *Sochineniya* (Collected Works), vols. 1–46 (Moscow: Marx-Lenin Institute, 1955–69). Also, *Arkhivy* (Archives), vols. I–VII, ed. by D. Ryazanov, Adoratsky, *et al.*

Karl Marx–Frederick Engels, Collected Works, vols. 1–17, incomplete (New York: International Publishers, 1975–81). Vol. 15 has not been printed.

Karl Marx and Frederich Engels, Selected Works, 3 vols. (Moscow: Progress Publishers, 1978). These volumes contain, among others, the following fundamental shorter works: *Manifesto of the Communist Party; Wage-Labour and Capital; Value, Price and Profit; Germany: Revolution and Counter-Revolution; Address of the Central Council to the Communist League; Class Struggles in France, 1848–50; Eighteenth Brumaire of Louis Bonaparte; Civil War in France; Address to the General Council of the International Working Men's Association; Critique of the Gotha Programme; Socialism: Utopian and Scientific;* and the drafts of *Marx's Letter to Vera Zasulich*

The American Journalism of Marx and Engels, ed. by Henry Christman (New York: New American Library, 1966).

Capital, 3 vols., Moore-Aveling trans. v. 1; Untermann, v. 2,3 (Chicago: Charles H. Kerr, 1909; reprinted by International Publishers, New York, 1967). A completely new translation of vol. 1 by Ben Fowkes, which re-established Marx's philosophic language was published in 1976 (Middlesex: Penguin Books; New York: Vintage Books, 1977); vol. 2, trans. by David Fernbach, was published by Penguin in 1978.

The Civil War in the United States (New York: International Publishers, 1940, 1961).

A Contribution to the Critique of Political Economy, trans. by N.I. Stone (Chicago: Charles H. Kerr, 1904).

_____and Friedrich Engels, *Correspondence*, 1846–1895 (New York: International Publishers, 1934). An enlarged collection was published in 1955 (Moscow: Progress Publishers); a third revised edition came out in 1975.

Critique of the Gotha Program (London: Lawrence and Wishart, n.d.). This edition includes the original "Draft Programme of the German Workers' Party" as well as Lenin's notebook on the *Critique*. It was republished in that same form by International Publishers in 1938; reprinted in 1966.

Economic-Philosophic Manuscripts, 1844, trans. and ed. by Raya Dunayevskaya as Appendix to *Marxism and Freedom* (New York: Bookman, 1958). See also trans. by Martin Milligan (London: Lawrence and Wishart, 1959); trans. by T.B. Bottomore in *Marx's Concept of Man* by Erich Fromm, 2nd ed. (New York: Frederick Ungar, 1963); and the Easton and Guddat translation in *The Writings of the Young Marx on Philosophy and Society* (New York: Doubleday, 1967).

The Ethnological Notebooks of Karl Marx, transcribed and with an Introduction by Lawrence Krader (Assen: Van Gorcum, 1972).

_____and Friedrich Engels, *The German Ideology* (Moscow: Progress Publishers, 1964; New York: International Publishers, 1972).

The Grundrisse, trans. with Foreword by Martin Nicolaus (London: Penguin Books, 1973; New York: Vintage Books, 1973).

_____and Friedrich Engels, *The Holy Family* (Moscow: Foreign Languages Publishing House, 1956).

Karl Marx and Frederick Engels: Ireland and the Irish Question (Moscow: Progress Publishers, 1971).

Karl Marx's Critique of Hegel's Philosophy of Right, trans. by Annette Jolin and Joseph O'Malley (Cambridge: Cambridge University Press, 1970). In the *Collected Works*, this is called *Contribution to the Critique of Hegel's Philosophy of Law*.

Letters to Americans (New York: International Publishers, 1953).

Letters to Dr. Kugelmann (New York: International Publishers, 1934; Westport, Conn.: Greenwood Press, 1973).

Manuscrits de 1861–1863 (Contribution à la Critique de l'Économie Politique) (Paris: Editions Sociales, 1979).

Marx on China, with Introduction and Notes by Dona Torr (London: Lawrence and Wishart, 1968; New York: Gordon Press, 1975).

Oeuvres de Karl Marx, Economie I, ed. by Maximilien Rubel (Paris: Editions Gallimard, 1963). *Economie II* published in 1968.

The Poverty of Philosophy, trans. by H. Quelch (New York: International Publishers, 1963).

Pre-Capitalist Economic Formations (excerpted from *The Grundrisse*), ed. by Eric Hobsbawm, trans. by Jack Cohen (London: Lawrence and Wishart, 1964).

Texts on Method, a new translation with commentary by Terrell Carver (Oxford: Basil Blackwell, 1975).

Theories of Surplus-Value, 3 vols. (Moscow: Progress Publishers, 1963, vol. 1; 1968, vol. 2; 1971, vol. 3).

FREDERICK ENGELS

Engels, Frederick, *The Condition of the Working Class in England, in 1844* (London: George Allen & Unwin, 1926; Stanford: Stanford University Press, 1958).
_____, Paul and Laura Lafargue, *Correspondence* (3 vols.), (Moscow: Foreign Languages Pub. House, 1959–60).
The Dialectics of Nature (New York: International Publishers, 1940; Moscow: Progress Publishers, 1978).
Herr Eugen Dühring's Revolution in Science (Anti-Dühring) (Chicago: Charles H. Kerr, 1935; New York: International Publishers, 1966).
Feuerbach (Chicago: Charles H. Kerr, 1903; New York: AMS Press, 1977).
The Origin of the Family, Private Property and the State (New York: International Publishers, 1942); published in 1972 with a new Introduction by Eleanor Burke Leacock.
The Peasant War in Germany (New York: International Publishers, 1966).

V. I. LENIN

Lenin, Vladimir Ilyich, *Sochineniya* (Collected Works), vols. 1–46 (Moscow: Marx-Engels-Lenin Institute).
Collected Works, vols. 1–45 (Moscow: Foreign Languages Publishing House, 1960, vol. 1; 1970, vol. 45).

LEON TROTSKY

Trotsky, Leon, *The Chinese Revolution: Problems and Perspectives* (New York: Pathfinder Press, 1970).
The Death Agony of Capitalism and the Tasks of the Fourth International: The Transitional Program (New York: Pathfinder Press, 1970).
The First Five Years of the Communist International, 2 vols. (New York: Pioneer, 1945; New York: Monad, 1972).
The History of the Russian Revolution, 3 vols., trans. by Max Eastman (New York: Simon and Schuster, 1937; Ann Arbor: University of Michigan Press, 1959).
My Life (New York: Scribner's, 1931; New York: Pathfinder Press, 1970).
1905 (New York: Vintage Books, 1972; London: Penguin Books, 1972).
Permanent Revolution (New York: Pioneer, 1931; New York: Pathfinder Press, 1970).
Problems of the Chinese Revolution (New York: Pioneer, 1932; New York: Paragon Book Reprint Corp., 1966).
Stalin: An Appraisal of the Man and His Influence, trans. and ed. by

Charles Malamuth (New York: Harper & Row, 1941; New York: Stein and Day, 1967).
Trotsky's Diary in Exile, 1935 (Cambridge, Mass.: Harvard University Press, 1958).

G. W. F. HEGEL

Hegel, G. W. F., *Sämtliche Werke: Jubilaeumsausgabe in 20 Bänden,* ed. by Hermann Glockner (Stuttgart, 1927–30). This work is supplemented by the *Hegel-Lexikon*, 4 vols. (1935 and later editions.)
Hegel's Logic, trans. by William Wallace from the *Encyclopaedia of the Philosophical Sciences* (London: Oxford University Press, 1931; new edition, 1975).
Phenomenology of Mind, trans. by A.V. Miller (Oxford: Oxford University Press, 1977); trans. by J.B. Baillie (London and New York: Macmillan, 1931).
Philosophy of Mind, trans. by William Wallace from the *Encyclopaedia of the Philosophical Sciences* (Oxford: Oxford University Press, 1894). A new edition, including the translation of the *Zusatze* by A.V. Miller was published in 1971 (Oxford: Clarendon Press).
Philosophy of Right, trans. with notes by T.M. Knox (Oxford: Oxford University Press, 1945).
Science of Logic, 2 vols., trans. by W.H. Johnston and L.G. Struthers (New York: Macmillan, 1951). See also new translation by A.V. Miller (London: Allen and Unwin, 1969; New York: Humanities Press, 1969).

PART ONE: ROSA LUXEMBURG AS THEORETICIAN, AS ACTIVIST, AS INTERNATIONALIST

Basso, Lelio, *Rosa Luxemburg, a Reappraisal* (New York: Praeger, 1975).

Cliff, Tony, *Rosa Luxemburg* (London: International Socialism, 1959).

Craig, Gordon A., *Germany, 1866–1945* (New York: Oxford University Press, 1978).

Fanon, Frantz, *The Wretched of the Earth* (New York: Grove Press, 1968).

Frölich, Paul, *Rosa Luxemburg: Her Life and Work* (New York and London: Monthly Review Press, 1972).

Gankin, Olga Hess and H.H. Fisher, *The Bolsheviks and the World War* (Stanford: Stanford University Press, 1940).

Geras, Norman, *The Legacy of Rosa Luxemburg* (London: New Left Review, 1976).

The German Spartacists, Their Aims and Objects (London: British Socialist Party, 1919).

Mommsen, Wolfgang J., *Theories of Imperialism*, trans. by P.S. Falla (New York: Random House, 1980).

Nettl, Peter, *Rosa Luxemburg*, 2 vols. (London: Oxford University Press, 1966).

Pyati (Londonskii) S' ezd RSDRP, Aprel'-mai 1907 goda, Protokoly (Minutes of the 1907 Fifth Congress of the Russian Social-Democratic Workers Party) (Moscow: 1963). These minutes are available only in Russian; they were originally published in Paris in 1909.

Roland-Holst, Henriette, *Rosa Luxemburg: ihr Leben und Wirken* (Zurich: Jean Christophe Verlag, 1937).

Rosdolsky, Roman, *The Making of Marx's 'Capital'* (London: Pluto Press, 1977).

Roux, Edward, *Time Longer Than Rope: A History of the Black Man's Struggle for Freedom in South Africa* (Madison: University of Wisconsin Press, 1966).

Schorske, Carl E., *German Social Democracy, 1905–1917* (Cambridge: Harvard University Press, 1955).

Schwarz, Solomon M., *The Russian Revolution of 1905* (Chicago: University of Chicago Press, 1967).

Wolfe, Bertram D., *Three Who Made a Revolution* (New York: Dial Press, 1948).

PART TWO: THE WOMEN'S LIBERATION MOVEMENT AS REVOLUTIONARY FORCE AND REASON

THE BLACK DIMENSION

Angelou, Maya, *I Know Why the Caged Bird Sings* (New York: Random House, 1970).

——————, *The Heart of a Woman* (New York: Random House, 1981).

Bell, Roseann, P., Bettye J. Parker and Beverly Guy-Sheftall, *Sturdy Black Bridges: Visions of Black Women in Literature* (Garden City, N.Y.: Doubleday, 1979).

Bernstein, Hilda, *For Their Triumphs and for Their Tears* (London: International Defense and Aid Fund for Southern Africa, 1975).

Brooks, Gwendolyn, *Annie Allen* (New York: Harper, 1949).

——————, *To Disembark* (Chicago: Third World Press, 1981).

Cade, Toni, ed., *The Black Woman* (New York: New American Library, 1970).

Carson, Josephine, *Silent Voices (The Southern Negro Woman Today)* (New York: Dell, 1969).

Chapman, Abraham, ed., *New Black Voices* (New York: New American Library, 1972).

Coleman, James S., *Nigeria: Background to Nationalism* (Berkeley: University of California Press, 1958).

Conrad, Earl, *Harriet Tubman* (New York: Paul S. Eriksson, 1943, 1969).

Davis, Angela, "Reflections on the Black Woman's Role in the Community of Slaves," *The Black Scholar*, Dec. 1971. The entire issue of *Black Scholar*, March–April 1973, was devoted to "Black Women's Liberation."

Dunayevskaya, Raya, *American Civilization on Trial: Black Masses as Vanguard* (Detroit: News & Letters, 1963, expanded 1970).

——————, "The Black Dimension in Women's Liberation," *News & Letters*, April 1976.

——————, "The Gambia Takes the Hard, Long Road To Independence," *Africa Today*, July 1962.

Hafkin, Nancy J. and Edna G. Bay, eds., *Women in Africa* (Stanford: Stanford University Press, 1976). Includes Judith Van Allen's " 'Aba Riots' or Igbo 'Women's War'?"

Hamilton, Mary, Louise Inghram et al., *Freedom Riders Speak For Themselves* (Detroit: News & Letters, 1961).

Hughes, Langston, ed., *An African Treasury* (New York: Pyramid Books, 1960).

Jordan, June, *Civil Wars* (Boston: Beacon Press, 1981).

Lerner, Gerda, ed., *Black Women in White America* (New York: Vintage Books, 1973).

Loewenberg, Bert James and Ruth Bogin, eds. *Black Women in 19th Century American Life* (University Park, Pa.: Penn State University Press, 1967).

Lorde, Audre, *From a Land Where Other People Live* (Detroit: Broadside Press, 1973).

——————, *Between Ourselves* (Point Reyes, California: Eidolon Editions, 1976).

Morrison, Toni, *Tar Baby* (New York: Knopf, 1981).

"Mozambican Women's Conference," in *People's Power*, no. 6, Jan.–Feb. 1977.

Ntantala, Phyllis, *An African Tragedy* (Detroit: Agascha Productions, 1976).

Shange, Ntozake, *For Colored Girls Who Have Considered Suicide/When the Rainbow Is Enuf* (New York: Macmillan, 1977).

Truth, Sojourner, *Narrative and Book of Life* (Chicago: Johnson Publishers, 1970).

EARLIER MOVEMENTS

Anthony, Katharine, *Susan B. Anthony* (New York: Doubleday, 1954).

Atkinson, Dorothy, Alexander Dallin, and Gail Warshofsky Lapidus, eds., *Women in Russia* (Stanford: Stanford University Press, 1977).

Balabanoff, Angelica, *My Life as a Rebel* (Bloomington: Indiana University Press, 1973).

Beard, Mary R., *Woman as Force in History* (New York: Macmillan, 1946; New York: Collier Books, 1971).

Bebel, August, *Woman Under Socialism*, trans. by Daniel DeLeon (New York: Labor News Co., 1904).

Blackwell, Alice Stone, ed., *The Little Grandmother of the Russian Revolution: Reminiscenses and Letters of Catherine Breshkovsky* (New York: Little, Brown & Co., 1917).

Bridenthal, Renate, "Beyond Kinder, Küche, Kirche: Weimar Women at Work," *Central European History*, vol. 6, no. 2, June 1973.

Chevigny, Bell Gale, *The Woman and the Myth: Margaret Fuller's Life and Writing* (Old Westbury, N.Y.: Feminist Press, 1976).

Clements, Barbara Evans, *Bolshevik Feminist: The Life of Aleksandra Kollontai* (Bloomington: Indiana University Press, 1979).

Desanti, Dominique, *A Woman in Revolt: a Biography of Flora Tristan* (New York: Crown Publishers, 1976).

DuBois, Ellen Carol, *Feminism and Suffrage: 1848–1869* (Ithaca: Cornell University Press, 1978).

_____, *Elizabeth Cady Stanton, Susan B. Anthony* (New York: Schocken Books, 1981).

Engel, Barbara Alpern and Clifford N. Rosenthal, eds., *Five Sisters: Women Against the Tsar* (New York: Schocken Books, 1977).

Farnsworth, Beatrice, *Aleksandra Kollontai* (Stanford: Stanford University Press, 1980).

Figner, Vera, *Memoirs of a Revolutionist* (New York: International Publishers, 1927).

Flexner, Eleanor, *Century of Struggle* (New York: Atheneum, 1972).

Flynn, Elizabeth Gurley, *The Rebel Girl, an Autobiography* (New York: International Publishers, 1973).

Goldman, Emma, *The Traffic in Women* (Albion, Cal.: Times Change Press, 1970).

Heinen, Jacqueline, "Kollontai and the History of Women's Oppression," *New Left Review*, July–Aug. 1978.

Kapp, Yvonne, *Eleanor Marx*, 2 vols. (New York: Pantheon Books, 1972).

Kollontai, Alexandra, *The Autobiography of a Sexually Emancipated Communist Woman* (New York: Schocken Books, 1975).

_____, *Women Workers Struggle for Their Rights* (Bristol: Falling Wall Press, 1971).

_____, *The Workers Opposition* (Reading, England: E. Morse, 1961?).

Lapidus, Gail Warshofsky, *Women in Soviet Society* (Berkeley: University of California Press, 1978).

Lenin, V.I., *The Emancipation of Women*, with an Appendix, "Lenin on the Woman Question" by Clara Zetkin and Preface by Nadezhda Krupskaya (New York: International Publishers, 1934, 1972).

Lib Women: Bluestockings (1844) and Socialist Women (1849), a collection of Daumier lithographs with Preface by Francoise Partivrier and Notes by Jacqueline Armingeat (Paris and New York: Leon Amiel Publishers, 1974).

McNeal, Robert H., *Bride of the Revolution: Krupskaya and Lenin* (Ann Arbor: University of Michigan Press, 1972).

Peltz, William A.P., "The Role of Proletarian Women in the German Revolution, 1918–1919," a paper presented at the Conference on the History of Women, College of St. Catherine, St. Paul, Minn., Oct. 24–25, 1975.

Porter, Cathy, *Alexandra Kollontai* (New York: Dial Press, 1980).

Pruitt, Ida, *A Daughter of Han: The Autobiography of a Chinese Working Woman* (Stanford: Stanford University Press, 1945, 1967).

Quataert, Jean H., *Reluctant Feminists in German Social Democracy, 1885–1917* (Princeton: Princeton University Press, 1979).

Rossi, Alice S., ed., *The Feminist Papers: From Adams to de Beauvoir* (New York and London: Columbia University Press, 1973).

Schneir, Miriam, ed., *Feminism: The Essential Historical Writings* (New York: Vintage Books, 1972).

Smedley, Agnes, *Portraits of Chinese Women in Revolution* (Old Westbury, N.Y.: Feminist Press, 1976).

Stites, Richard, *The Women's Liberation Movement in Russia: Feminism, Nihilism, and Bolshevism, 1860–1930* (Princeton: Princeton University Press, 1978).

Thomas, Edith, *The Women Incendiaries* (New York: George Braziller, 1966).

Thönnessen, Werner, *The Emancipation of Women: The Rise and Decline of the Women's Movement in German Social Democracy, 1863–1933* (London: Pluto Press, 1973).

Tristan, Flora, *Flora Tristan's London Journal, 1840* (Promenades dans Londres) (Charlestown, Mass.: Charles River Books, 1980).

Tsuzuki, Chushichi, *The Life of Eleanor Marx* (Oxford: Clarendon Press, 1967).

Wardle, Ralph M., ed., *Godwin and Mary* (Lincoln: University of Nebraska Press, 1977).

Woolf, Virginia, *A Room of One's Own* (New York: Harcourt, Brace and World, 1929, 1957).

TODAY'S STUDIES

Ashbaugh, Carolyn, *Lucy Parsons: American Revolutionary* (Chicago: Charles H. Kerr, 1976).

Barreno, Maria Isabel, Maria Teresa Horta, and Maria Velho da Costa, *The Three Marias: New Portuguese Letters* (New York: Doubleday, 1975).

Baxandall, Rosalyn, Linda Gordon, Susan Reverby, eds., *America's Working*

Women (New York: Vintage Books, 1976).

De Beauvoir, Simone, *The Second Sex* (New York: Alfred A. Knopf, 1953).

Beck, Lois and Nikki Keddie, eds. *Women in the Muslim World* (Cambridge: Harvard University Press, 1978).

Bond, Edward, *The Woman* (London: Eyre Methuen, 1979).

Ding Ling, "Thoughts on March 8," included in *Ting Ling, Purged Feminist* (Tokyo: Femintern Press, 1974).

Draper, Hal, "Marx and Engels on Women's Liberation," *International Socialism*, July–August 1970.

Dunayevskaya, Raya, *Sexism, Politics and Revolution in Mao's China* (Detroit: Women's Liberation—News & Letters, 1977).

—————, *Woman as Reason and as Force of Revolution* (Detroit: Women's Liberation—News & Letters, 1981). A collection of writings by Dunayevskaya, with an Appendix, "Women in the Iranian Revolution: In Fact and in Theory" by Neda.

Feminist Revolution (New Paltz, N.Y.: Redstockings, 1975).

Feminist Studies, vol. 3, Spring–Summer, 1976. Includes, among others, "Women's History in Transition: The European Case" by Natalie Zemon Davis, and "Clara Zetkin: A Socialist Approach to the Problem of Woman's Oppression" by Karen Honeycutt.

Firestone, Shulamith, *The Dialectic of Sex* (New York: Bantam Books, 1970).

Flug, Mike, *The Maryland Freedom Union: Black Working Women Thinking and Doing* (Detroit: News & Letters, 1969).

Godelier, Maurice, "The Origins of Male Domination," *New Left Review*, May–June 1981.

—————, *Perspectives in Marxist Anthropology* (New York: Cambridge University Press, 1977).

Gornick, Vivian, *Essays in Feminism* (New York: Harper & Row, 1978).

Gould, Carol C. and Marx W. Wartofsky, eds., *Women and Philosophy* (New York: G.P. Putnam, 1976).

Guettel, Charnie, *Marxism and Feminism* (Toronto: Canadian Women's Education Press, 1974).

Heitlinger, Alena, *Women and State Socialism: Sex Inequality in the Soviet Union and Czechoslovakia* (Montreal: McGill—Queens University Press, 1979).

Honeycutt, Karen, "Clara Zetkin: A Left-Wing Socialist and Feminist in Wilhelmian Germany," Doctoral Thesis submitted to Columbia University, 1975.

Huston, Peredita, *Third World Women Speak Out* (New York: Praeger Publishers, 1979).

Kristeva, Julia, "On the Women of China," *Signs*, Autumn 1975. A full issue of *Signs* was devoted to "The Women of China" in Autumn, 1976.

Lerner, Gerda, *The Majority Finds Its Past* (Oxford: Oxford University Press, 1979).

Mamonova, Tatyana, ed., *Woman and Russia*, a Russian Almanac published by dissident feminists in *samizdat* inside Russia in 1980–81.

Maupin, Joyce, *Working Women and Their Organizations* (Berkeley: Union WAGE, 1974).

Mernissa, Fatima, "Veiled Sisters," *New World Outlook*, April 1971.

Millett, Kate, *Sexual Politics* (New York: Doubleday, 1970).

Mitchell, Juliet, *Woman's Estate* (New York: Vintage Books, 1973).

Mitchell, Pam, ed., *Pink Triangles: Radical Perspectives on Gay Liberation* (Boston: Alyson Publications, 1980).

Moraga, Cherrie, Gloria Anzaldua, eds., *This Bridge Called My Back: Writings by Radical Women of Color* (Watertown, Mass.: Persephone Press, 1981).

Morgan, Robin, ed., *Sisterhood is Powerful* (New York: Vintage Books, 1970).

Notes on Women's Liberation: We Speak in Many Voices (Detroit: News & Letters, 1970). Includes Raya Dunayevskaya, "The Women's Liberation Movement as Reason and as Revolutionary Force."

Reiter, Rayna R., ed., *Toward an Anthropology of Women* (New York: Monthly Review Press, 1975).

Revolutionary Feminism (Detroit: Women's Liberation—News & Letters, 1978). Includes articles on International Women's Day, Rosa Luxemburg, and "The Paris Commune and Black Women's Liberation."

Rosaldo, Michelle Zimbalist, and Louise Lamphere, eds., *Woman, Culture and Society* (Stanford: Stanford University Press, 1974).

Rowbotham, Sheila, Lynn Segal, and Hilary Wainwright, *Beyond the Fragments* (London: Merlin Press, 1979).

Rowbotham, Sheila, *Hidden From History* (London: Pluto Press, 1973; New York: Pantheon, 1975).

——————, *Woman's Consciousness, Man's World* (Harmondsworth: Penguin, 1973).

——————, *Women, Resistance and Revolution* (London: Allen Lane, 1972; New York: Pantheon, 1972).

Russell, Diana E.H., and Nicole Van de Ven, eds., *Crimes Against Women: Proceedings of the International Tribunal* (Millbrae, Cal.: Les Femmes, 1976).

Saffioti, Heleieth I.B., *Women in Class Society* (New York: Monthly Review Press, 1978).

Salper, Roberta, ed., *Female Liberation: History and Current Politics* (New York: Alfred A. Knopf, 1972).

Sochen, June, *Movers and Shakers: American Women Thinkers and Activists, 1900–1970* (New York: Quadrangle, 1973).

Tabari, Azar, *No Revolution Without Women's Liberation* (London: Campaign for Solidarity with Iran, 1979).

Tax, Meredith, *The Rising of the Women: Feminist Solidarity and Class Conflict, 1880–1917* (New York: Monthly Review Press, 1980).

Terrano, Angela, Marie Dignan and Mary Holmes, *Working Women for Freedom* (Detroit: Women's Liberation—News & Letters, 1976). Includes as Appendix "Women as Thinkers and as Revolutionaries," by Raya Dunayevskaya.

PART THREE: KARL MARX—FROM CRITIC OF HEGEL TO AUTHOR OF CAPITAL AND THEORIST OF "REVOLUTION IN PERMANENCE"

Adorno, Theodor W., *Negative Dialectics* (New York: Seabury Press, 1973).

Althusser, Louis, *For Marx* (London: Penguin Press, 1969).

——————*Lenin and Philosophy and Other Essays* (London: New Left Books, 1971).

——————*Reading Capital*, (London: New Left Books, 1970).

Avineri, Shlomo, *The Social and Political Thought of Karl Marx* (London: Cambridge University Press, 1968).

Balazs, Étienne, *Chinese Civilization and Bureaucracy* (New Haven: Yale University Press, 1964).

Bloch, Maurice, ed., *Marxist Analyses and Social Anthropology* (London: Malaby Press, 1975).

Bukharin, N., *Economics of the Transition Period* (New York: Bergman, 1971).

——————, Paper given at "Second International Congress of the History of Science," *Archeion*, vol. 14, 1932, pp. 522-25.

Carver, Terrell, "Marx, Engels and Dialectics," *Political Studies*, vol. 28, no. 3, Sept. 1980.

Deutscher, Isaac, *The Prophet Armed; The Prophet Unarmed; The Prophet Outcast* (New York and London: Oxford University Press, 1954; 1959; 1963).

Draper, Hal, *Karl Marx's Theory of Revolution* (New York: Monthly Review Press, 1977).

Dunayevskaya, Raya, *Marxism and Freedom... from 1776 to Today* (New York: Bookman, 1958). Contains first English translation of Marx's early essays and of Lenin's *Abstract of Hegel's Science of Logic*; 2nd edition (New York: Twayne, 1964) contains new chapter, "The Challenge of Mao Tse-tung"; 3rd edition (London: Pluto Press, 1971) has new chapter, "Cultural Revolution or Maoist Reaction"; 5th edition (Humanities Press; Harvester Press, 1982) contains new Introduction by author. International editions: Italian (Florence: La Nuova Italia, 1962); Japanese (Tokyo: Modern Thought, 1964); French (Paris:

Champ Libre, 1971); Spanish (Mexico, D.F.: Juan Pablos, 1967).
_____*Marx's Capital and Today's Global Crisis* (Detroit: News &
Letters, 1978). Contains Introduction on "Today's Epigones Who Try to
Truncate Marx's *Capital*," and Appendix on "Tony Cliff Reduces
Lenin's Theory to 'Uncanny Intuition.' "
_____*Nationalism, Communism, Marxist-Humanism and the Afro-
Asian Revolutions* (London: Cambridge University Labor Club, Left
Group, 1961).
_____*New Essays* (Detroit: News & Letters, 1977). Includes "Post-
Mao China: What Now?"; "Dialectics of Liberation in Thought and in
Activity"; "Leon Trotsky as Man and as Theoretician."
_____*Philosophy and Revolution: from Hegel to Sartre and from
Marx to Mao* (New York: Dell, 1973); 2nd edition (Humanities Press;
Harvester Press, 1982) contains new Introduction by author. International
editions: Spanish (Mexico, D.F.: Siglo Veintiuno, 1977); Italian (Milan:
Feltrinelli, 1977); German (Vienna: Europa Verlag, 1981).
_____*The Political-Philosophic Letters of Raya Dunayevskaya*, 2
vols. (Detroit: News & Letters, 1977, vol. 1; 1980, vol. 2).
_____*The Raya Dunayevskaya Collection: Marxist-Humanism, Its
Origin and Development in the U.S., 1941 to Today* (Detroit: Wayne
State University Labor History Archives, 1981). Available on microfilm.
Dupré, Louis, *The Philosophical Foundations of Marxism* (New York:
Harcourt, Brace, 1966).
Fay, Margaret A., "Marx and Darwin, a Literary Detective Story," *Monthly
Review*, March 1980.
Gramsci, Antonio, *Letters from Prison* (New York: Harper & Row, 1973).
_____*Prison Notebooks* (New York: International Publishers, 1971).
_____*Selections from Political Writings, 1910–1920* (New York:
International Publishers, 1977).
Haithcox, John Patrick, *Communism and Nationalism in India* (Princeton:
Princeton University Press, 1971).
Herzen, Alexander, *Selected Philosophical Works* (Moscow: Foreign
Languages Publishing House, 1960).
Hyndman, H.M., *The Record of an Adventurous Life* (New York: Macmillan,
1911).
Hyppolite, Jean, *Studies on Marx and Hegel*, ed. and trans. by John
O'Neill (New York: Basic Books, 1969).
Joravsky, David, *Soviet Marxism and Natural Science, 1917–1932* (New
York: Columbia University Press, 1961).
Kamenka, Eugene, *The Ethical Foundations of Marxism* (New York:
Praeger, 1962).
Kelly, George Armstrong, *Hegel's Retreat from Eleusis* (Princeton: Princeton
University Press, 1978).
_____*Idealism, Politics and History: Sources of Hegelian Thought*

(Cambridge: Cambridge University Press, 1969).

Knei-Paz, Baruch, *The Social and Political Thought of Leon Trotsky* (Oxford: Clarendon Press, 1978).

Korsch, Karl, *Karl Marx* (New York: John Wiley, 1938).

—————————*Marxism and Philosophy* (London: New Left Books, 1970; New York: Monthly Review Press, 1970).

Latin America's Revolutions/Las Revoluciones de Latinoamérica (Detroit: News & Letters, 1981). Includes articles by Raya Dunayevskaya, Mike Connolly, Eugene Walker, Francisco Aquino.

Levine, Norman, *The Tragic Deception: Marx Contra Engels* (Santa Barbara: Clio Books, 1975).

Levenson, Joseph R., *Confucian China and Its Modern Face*, 3 vols. (Berkeley: University of California Press, 1965).

Lewin, Moshe, *Lenin's Last Struggle* (New York: Pantheon, 1968).

Lichtheim, George, "Marx and 'the Asiatic Mode of Production'," *St. Antony's Papers*, no. 14 (Carbondale, Ill.: Southern Illinois University Press, n.d.)

—————————, *Marxism: An Historical and Critical Study* (New York: Praeger, 1961).

Lifshitz, Mikhail, *The Philosophy of Art of Karl Marx* (London: Pluto Press, 1973).

Livergood, Norman D., *Activity in Marx's Philosophy* (The Hague: Martinus Nijhoff, 1967).

Lobkowicz, Nicholas, *Theory and Practice: History of a Concept from Aristotle to Marx* (Notre Dame: University of Notre Dame Press, 1967).

Lukacs, Georg, *History and Class Consciousness* (London: Merlin Press, 1971).

—————————*The Young Hegel* (London: Merlin Press, 1975).

Marcuse, Herbert, *Negations* (Boston: Beacon Press, 1960).

—————————*Reason and Revolution: Hegel and the Rise of Social Theory* (New York: Oxford University Press, 1941).

—————————*Studies in Critical Philosophy* (London: New Left Books, 1972).

Maurer, Reinhart Klemens, *Hegel und das Ende der Geschichte: Interpretationen zur Phänomenologie* (Stuttgart-Berlin-Cologne-Mainz, 1965).

McLellan, David, *Karl Marx: His Life and Thought* (New York: Harper & Row, 1973).

Meisner, Maurice, *Li Ta-chao and the Origins of Chinese Marxism* (Cambridge: Harvard University Press, 1967).

Mehring, Franz, *Karl Marx: the Story of His Life* (New York: Covici, Friede Publishers, 1935; Ann Arbor: University of Michigan Press, 1962).

Merleau-Ponty, Maurice, *In Praise of Philosophy* (Evanston, Ill.: Northwestern University Press, 1963).

Moon, Terry and Ron Brokmeyer, *On the 100th Anniversary of the First General Strike in the U.S.* (Detroit: News & Letters, 1977).

Mepham, John, and D-H. Ruben, eds. *Issues in Marxist Philosophy* (Atlantic Highlands, N.J.: Humanities Press, 1979; Brighton: Harvester Press, 1979).

Morgan, Lewis Henry, *Ancient Society* (Chicago: Charles H. Kerr, 1907); the reproduction of the original 1877 edition. Reprinted in 1964 (Cambridge, Mass.: Belknap Press of Harvard Univ.).

Padover, Saul K., *Karl Marx: An Intimate Biography* (New York: McGraw-Hill, 1978).

Rubel, Maximilien, and Margaret Manale, *Marx Without Myth* (New York: Harper & Row, 1976).

_____*Rubel on Karl Marx (Five Essays)*, ed. and trans. by Joseph O'Malley and Keith Algozin (Cambridge: Cambridge University Press, 1981).

Schwartz, Benjamin I., *Chinese Communism and the Rise of Mao* (New York: Harper & Row, 1967).

Shklar, Judith N., *Freedom and Independence* (London: Cambridge University Press, 1976).

Steinkraus, Warren E., and Kenneth L. Schmitz, eds. *Art and Logic in Hegel's Philosophy* (Atlantic Highlands, N.J.: Humanities Press, 1980; Sussex: Harvester Press, 1980).

Voden, A., *Reminiscences of Marx and Engels* (Moscow: Foreign Languages Publishing House, n.d.).

Wislanka, Urszula, ed. and trans., *Today's Polish Fight For Freedom*, (Detroit: News & Letters, 1980).

Index

I would like to thank Michael Flug for having created this rigorous index to reflect the philosophic categories of the book, which required also consulting the multilingual sources in Russian, Polish, German, and French.—R.D.

Biographical Note

To Raya Dunayevskaya, the most crucial kind of biography was the "biography of an idea," in this case, the development of the idea of Marxist-Humanism. Born in 1910 in the Ukraine and brought by her family to the United States as a child, she joined the revolutionary movement in Chicago at thirteen. Her activities in the twenties centered around the American Negro Labor Congress and its newspaper, the *Negro Champion*. Expelled from the Communist party's youth group in 1928, she joined the Trotskyists and remained active in the struggles of workers and blacks.

She became Leon Trotsky's Russian-language secretary in 1937 during his exile in Mexico, but broke with him in 1939 at the time of the Hitler-Stalin Pact. Her simultaneous study of the Russian economy and of Marx's early writings (later known as his 1844 Humanist Essays) led to her 1941–42 analysis that not only was Russia a state-capitalist society but that state-capitalism was a new world stage.

After more than a decade developing the theory of state-capitalism, Dunayevskaya made a philosophic breakthrough. In two letters written May 12 and 20, 1953, she deepened her study of the Hegelian dialectic and saw in Hegel's Absolutes a *dual* movement—a movement from practice that is itself a form of theory and a movement from theory reaching to philosophy. She considered these 1953 letters to be "the philosophic moment" from which the whole development of Marxist-Humanism flowed.

Three major works became what she called her "trilogy of revolution." The first of these, published in 1957, was *Marxism and Freedom: From 1776 until Today,* which aimed "to re-establish Marxism in its original form, which Marx called 'a thorough-going Naturalism, or Humanism.'" Dunayevskaya included as appendixes to this work her translations of Lenin's Philosophic Notebooks and Marx's Humanist Essays, the first ever published in English. Throughout the turbulent sixties she participated in freedom movements and exchanges of ideas internationally, traveling to Europe, Africa, and East Asia and writing for an international symposium on *Socialist Humanism,* edited by Erich Fromm. In the United States, Dunayevskaya was deeply involved in civil rights, labor, and anti-war struggles, authoring a 1963 study of the history of American freedom movements and ideas, *American Civilization on Trial.*

Her 1973 book, *Philosophy and Revolution: From Hegel to Sartre and from Marx to Mao,* developed her studies on both the Hegelian dialectic and the post–World War II world into a new view of "Absolute Negativity as New Beginning." From the vantage point of that concept, the three parts of this book examined the work of Hegel, Marx, and Lenin; of Trotsky, Mao, and Sartre; and developments in Africa, East Europe, and the United States. She considered this work "the turning point" in the development of the idea of Marxist-Humanism.

By 1982 she completed *Rosa Luxemburg, Women's Liberation, and Marx's Philosophy of Revolution,* which singled out Marx's philosophy of "revolution in permanence" and tested all who followed Marx against its totality. In this work she articulated the category of "post-Marx Marxism, beginning with Engels" not as chronology, but as a pejorative. She extended her discussion of this historic-philosophic category in a 1985 collection of essays, *Women's Liberation and the Dialectics of Revolution: Reaching for the Future.*

In the last year of her life she was at work on a new book, which she had tentatively titled "Dialectics of Organization and Philosophy: The 'Party' and Forms of Organization Born out of Spontaneity." It was left unfinished at her death in June 1987.